THE RETURN OF PROSERPINA

The Return of Proserpina

CULTURAL POETICS OF SICILY
FROM CICERO TO DANTE

SARAH SPENCE

PRINCETON UNIVERSITY PRESS
PRINCETON & OXFORD

Copyright © 2023 by Princeton University Press

Princeton University Press is committed to the protection of copyright and the intellectual property our authors entrust to us. Copyright promotes the progress and integrity of knowledge. Thank you for supporting free speech and the global exchange of ideas by purchasing an authorized edition of this book. If you wish to reproduce or distribute any part of it in any form, please obtain permission.

Requests for permission to reproduce material from this work should be sent to permissions@press.princeton.edu

Published by Princeton University Press
41 William Street, Princeton, New Jersey 08540
99 Banbury Road, Oxford OX2 6JX

press.princeton.edu

All Rights Reserved
ISBN 9780691227184
ISBN (pbk.) 9780691227177
ISBN (e-book) 9780691227160

British Library Cataloging-in-Publication Data is available

Editorial: Anne Savarese and James Collier
Production Editorial: Sara Lerner
Cover Design: Katie Osborne
Production: Lauren Reese
Publicity: Alyssa Sandford and Charlotte Coyne
Copyeditor: Robert Birdwell

Cover Credit: jozef sedmak / Alamy Stock Photo

This book has been composed in Arno

10 9 8 7 6 5 4 3 2 1

for Sandra Pierson Prior

friend, colleague, fellow traveler

and for Emma and Ned, whose journey begins on Sicily

CONTENTS

List of Illustrations   ix
Acknowledgments   xi

Introduction: Negotiating Empire … 1

1 The Straits of Messina: Geography and Empire … 10

2 Drepanum and the Limits of the *Aeneid* … 31

3 Venus's Other Son: Cupid and Ovid's Empire of Poetry … 54

4 Claudian, Etna, and the Loss of Proserpina … 76

5 The Redemption of Proserpina … 97

6 *Quando n'apparve una montagna*: Purgatory and the Voyage of Ulysses … 115

7 *Purgatorio*, Etna, and the Empire of Love … 136

Conclusion … 160

Notes   163
Bibliography   189
Index   211

ILLUSTRATIONS

Map of Sicily — xiii
1. Hereford *mappa mundi*, detail of Sicily, Hereford Cathedral — 88
2. Peter of Eboli, *Liber ad honorem Augusti*, lat. Bern, Burgerbibliothek, Cod. 120.II, f. 120r — 98
3. Cicero, *Verrine Orations*, Paris, BnF, lat. 7776, f. 132v (detail) — 101

ACKNOWLEDGMENTS

THIS BOOK has benefited greatly from the expert advice of many, including specialists on volcanoes (Gilles Allard) and sailing around Sicily (Paolo Ferrari), as well as research assistants (Melissa Strickland and Maria Roberts), students in numerous classes, and audiences of many lectures (though Clayton Schroer and Laura Ingallinella, who read more drafts and heard more talks than most, do deserve special mention). Three Elizabeths share my interest in Sicily and its role in literary and intellectual history: Elizabeth Wright, Elizabeth Kassler-Taub, and Elizabeth Heintges; they seemingly never tired of hearing my latest thoughts about Trinacria. Colleagues who read drafts meticulously, James Simpson, Courtney Wells, and the anonymous readers for Princeton University Press, are owed deep gratitude, as is acquisitions editor Anne Savarese. Michael Putnam deserves special mention for the meticulous care he lavished on multiple phases of different drafts; I remain, as always, in his debt. I also thank the Department of Classics at the University of Georgia for support throughout the project (with a special nod to my colleague there, Erika Hermanowicz, who encouraged this project over the years) and the Department of the Classics at Harvard University for access to Widener and Smyth Libraries. Henry Gruber compiled the bibliography with rare precision, a true searchlight casting for faults. Thanks as ever to my husband, James McGregor, who, in addition to his recurring role as sympathetic and informed listener, also drove willingly around Sicily, including up and down more mountains and valleys than one island should really be allowed to contain.

Earlier versions of sections of these chapters were published in the following journals. They are reprinted with permission:

"Reading against the Grain: Hypercorrection in a Medieval Cicero,"
  Bollettino del centro di studi filologici e linguistici siciliani 29 (2018):
  5–19. Reprinted by permission.

"The Geography of the Vernacular in Dante," *Tenso* 28 (2013): 33–45. Reprinted with permission of the Société Guilhem IX, publisher of *Tenso*.

"Meta-Textuality: The Boat-Race as Turning Point in *Aeneid* 5," *New England Classical Journal* 29 (2002): 69–81. Reprinted by permission.

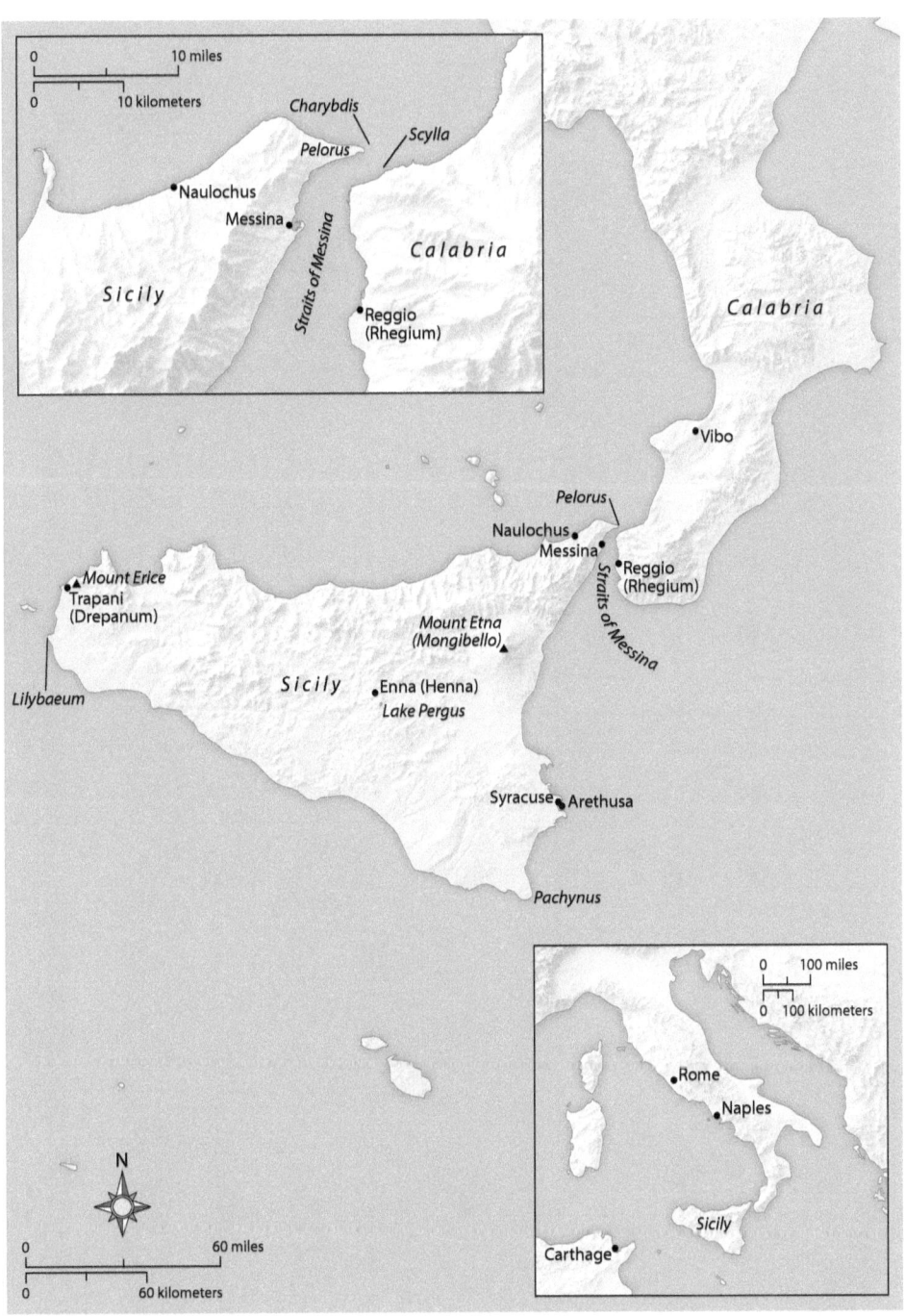

MAP. Sicily

Introduction

NEGOTIATING EMPIRE

To have seen Italy without having seen Sicily is not to have seen Italy at all, for Sicily is the clue to everything.

—JOHANN WOLFGANG VON GOETHE, *ITALIAN JOURNEY* <1786–1788>, TRANS. W. H. AUDEN AND ELIZABETH MAYER (NEW YORK: NORTH POINT PRESS, 1982), 240

SICILY, THE triangular island that all but touches its neighboring Italian peninsula, is a land rich in history and myth. Many of those accounts tell of invasion, yet there is one, the myth of Proserpina, that enables the island also to play a different role. In the Roman form of that myth, the goddess Ceres' daughter is abducted on Sicily by Hades, the god of the underworld, while she is picking flowers with her friends.[1] After she disappears, her mother travels throughout the world in search of her, learning only late in the process that her daughter has been taken to the underworld. In the most common ancient version of the myth, Ceres travels to Hades and negotiates her daughter's return, a negotiation necessitated by the fact that Proserpina ate a number of pomegranate seeds while there. Proserpina returns to Sicily for part of the year; the rest of the year she spends in the afterlife.[2]

From Roman antiquity through the Middle Ages, the history and culture of Sicily join with the myth of Proserpina to help poets shape a narrative of Western empire. Sicily's strategic location has been studied as key to many civilizations, from the Western development of the Greek world to the conflict of Muslim and Norman cultures in the Mediterranean, while the abduction and recovery of Proserpina has been used to explore a wide range of topics, including female maturation and the origin of the seasons.³ Her story has also been used to present empire as a form of rape. Yet from the moment in the orations against Verres (70 BC) when Cicero praises Sicily as both Rome's first overseas province and the mythic location for the tale of Proserpina, the island comes to offer poets a setting for forces resistant to empire and a location for displaying and even reclaiming what empire had subsumed. In the poetry we will investigate, Sicily enables a discussion of empire in terms of balance, loss, and negotiation by authors as separated in time and culture as Vergil, Claudian, and Dante. Analyzing why and how such an affiliation remains meaningful throughout a time of great cultural turbulence is the project of this book.

It is no coincidence that the literary representation of Sicily in the Latin literary tradition is rooted in the rhetoric of Cicero, since rhetoric as a genre explores the interdependence of language and culture. Nor is it surprising that Dante's concerns about the nature of Purgatory and the process of redemption are likewise situated, at least on some level, on Sicily. From the time Cicero identifies Sicily as both the first province and the location of the abduction of Proserpina, the notion of empire becomes linked inextricably with a dual negotiation: in texts that draw on Cicero, empire becomes perceived and described in terms of issues of loss and recovery, and these abstract concerns are thereby granted a specific location, a "local habitation and a name."

The texts studied here all explore this cluster of ideas: the poets draw on Cicero, either directly or indirectly, and all are engaged in the process of debating the nature of effective government, whether it be the Roman Empire rising during the time of Vergil and Ovid, the changing empire in the time of Claudian, or the new vision of *imperium* Dante proposes in the *Commedia*. In every case Sicily offers a setting for negotiating empire: it is as important that these texts take place on Sicily as it is that they bear only a passing resemblance to the Sicily of their day. At the same time, the myth of Proserpina not only remains identified with the island, but offers in its narrative a means for revising the very shape of empire. That tale, known perhaps most widely through the *Homeric Hymn to Demeter*, is often read as an agricultural or maturation myth and was situated originally in the eastern Mediterranean. Through the course of the texts studied here, though, it comes to be centered on Sicily and to offer a myth of Western empire, even while critiquing it.⁴ Take for instance, Vergil, who, as we shall see, argues in the first book of the *Georgics* (1.39) that if Octavian should conquer the underworld, Proserpina, wooed anew (*repetita*), might choose not to return to her mother, but opt instead to spend the year with Octavian in Hades. If this were to happen, the cycles of seasons, crops, and animals—everything that makes Italy Italy in the *Georgics*, and everything traditionally ascribed to the annual return of Proserpina—will no longer exist. Vergil encourages Octavian to expand his rule, but not to conquer the underworld and encounter Proserpina, which would meddle with the agricultural balance of Italy. Yet in the *Metamorphoses*, Ovid's lines counter Vergil's plea, as they show Venus and her other son, not Aeneas but Cupid, primed to do just that, to conquer the underworld in the context of the Proserpina tale.[5] Like Vergil, Ovid sees this form of imperialism as destructive of Italian culture. But by revisiting Venus's conquest of the underworld in the context of other imperial texts, Ovid launches his own understanding of empire, which is less about Italy and more about poetry. As we shall see, Ovid's interest in empire is split: in the political world he presents it as destructive; in the poetic world, he sees it as creative. For Ovid, conquering the underworld means, above all, gaining control of the future of poetry. In Ovid's hands, empire becomes a textual strategy.

Cicero, Vergil, and Ovid, then—or Cicero and Vergil through Ovid—use Sicily as the setting for questions relating to empire, and the myth of Proserpina as key to its understanding. Equally central to this debate, however, is the context Ovid establishes, one that sets the three writers in conversation about empire (and one that mimics the poetic competition where the tale is told). Stephen Hinds has noted the affinity between Sicily and poetic debate in particular, and landscape and intertextuality in general.[6] He also emphasizes the importance of the myth of Proserpina to the literary history of Sicily.[7] Here I will argue something slightly different: that for these writers, starting with Vergil and continuing through the Middle Ages to Dante, poetic treatment of Sicily, which often entails consideration of Proserpina and her abduction, is presented as both mimetic of the origins of empire and central to their critique. What this suggests is that for these writers empire offers a way of thinking that enables intertextual dialogue even as it refines and debates the political pros and cons of this form of power. Moreover, Ovid's move here is key, for as we shall see, the extension of empire into the future, and beyond this life, becomes central to considerations of empire during the Middle Ages. Throughout the tradition, that very debate is signaled by the presence of Sicily.

In short, Cicero's version of the Proserpina myth, which explicitly ties the story to both Sicily and empire, establishes parameters for the Latin literary discussion of empire that follows.[8] It is, of course, itself based on Greek events and Hellenic stories and myths of Sicily, yet these will not concern us here. Nor will we consider other imperial narratives of Sicily: the Athenian expedition, for instance, offers an antitype for the expansion the Romans accomplish later, particularly in their failed approach to Sicily as protocolony. But our story begins with Cicero. Cicero situates the myth in the Roman world, a move Ovid gladly follows. By the same token, Vergil will acknowledge the Greek past in an effort to provide the underpinnings for what he presents as the truly Roman future, but our focus here will remain on the Latin tradition following Cicero.⁹

In addition, Cicero uses the myth of Proserpina to establish key factors about empire. Underlying the Verrine orations rests a particular version of the myth of Ceres and Proserpina: the crucial speech suggests that if Verres returns the goods stolen from Ceres' shrine, Sicily will be restored to its pristine status and the promise of empire will be fulfilled. In this scenario empire offers the means for rediscovering the time before Proserpina was abducted, and the myth is presented as non-cyclical: that is, once righted, the empire will not break apart again. This version of the myth of Proserpina, in other words, is not about seasons and agricultural cycles. Rather, it is presented as a myth of a golden age, lost but capable of recovery and, once recovered, sustained. As such, Sicily serves as a reminder of the past that remains a resistant force in the present, since the basis of a good empire, even Cicero suggests, is a negotiated balance between past and future. This fact will become crucial in the deployment of the myth throughout the period we are investigating.

Because this Ciceronian, and imperial, version of the Proserpina myth differs from other variants, it is possible to track, and it provides a cogent starting point for this study. In the texts we will look at, the treatment of the Proserpina story plays a central role, and because of its dual message it works well as a foundation myth. The myth of Orpheus could, perhaps, have served to speak of loss; other stories speak loudly of expansion. Yet the tale of Proserpina, especially in Cicero's and Ovid's hands, is well suited to represent the complicated textual narrative of empire that speaks of expansion and displacement against a backdrop of wholeness. It is significant that Vergil omits the story of her abduction and recovery, while including many other Sicilian myths—stories of Polyphemus, Arethusa, Scylla and Charybdis, for instance—as well as, suggestively, other variants that could well be alluding to aspects of the Proserpina story. And yet he focuses on Sicily and he does so in an imperial context. The island is in the center of the action of the *Aeneid*—literally—between Carthage on the west and Rome to the north, and it is where the action of the poem starts, *vix e conspectu Siculae telluris* ("barely out of sight of the Sicilian land," *Aen*.1.34). But rather than talking about it as a land of the golden age, Vergil inverts Cicero's myth of imperialism and asserts one that is rooted in the crux between the promise of Augustan propaganda and the cost that promise might entail. The myth of Proserpina is relegated to the background by Vergil, yet hovers at the edges, guiding his choices of narrative, especially in *Aeneid* 5. As we shall see, Vergil stages his myth of empire in the time between her loss and recovery.

Ovid, by contrast, explicitly echoing Cicero's *Verrines* and Vergil's *Georgics* and *Aeneid* in his Ceres tale in book 5 of the *Metamorphoses*, frames the Proserpina tale as a myth of Western empire. Ovid's evocation of Cicero's *Verrines* here affirms the imperial role Sicily plays in the *Metamorphoses*, even as it critiques the version Vergil presents. The fact that that narrative in particular echoes the start of the *Aeneid* suggests that Ovid is remarking on Vergil's choice not to foreground Proserpina in his poem of empire. In Ovid's treatment, her recovery and expansion, far from absent, are relegated to the realm of poetry. Always the keen rhetorician, Ovid distinguishes between good and bad empire precisely in terms of good and bad rhetoric, which he, in turn, identifies with his own understanding of empire and that of Vergil. The basis of imperial culture Ovid presents as rhetorical—language creates empire through a seductive use of words—which is useful for the poets and disastrous for mankind. Ovid suggests, I will propose, that the very mechanism that creates empire, which he identifies as the aggressive approach to time and space, is the very one that nonetheless enables poetic interaction and growth. Intertextuality in his hands is modeled on a form of imperialism. While Ovid criticizes Augustus for his imperialism, he also celebrates the poetic possibilities of such an approach; he applauds the one and condemns the other.

In Ovid's wake, Sicily remains a locus for poetic debate, most notably for Seneca, but also in authors, pagan and Christian, who turn to the Roman past for poetic inspiration, such as Claudian. Yet, strikingly, Sicily itself is redefined, since the debate moves from Enna, where Cicero and Ovid focus, and Drepanum, where Vergil's interest lies, to Mt. Etna and the straits of Messina. The tale of Proserpina is still key, though the abduction, too, moves from Enna to Etna, and in the late antique and medieval texts about Sicily that touch on the ancients and empire, it is Etna that increasingly gains prominence. Etna's role in the conception of empire is determined by a series of factors. Above all, the fact that it is volcanic and erupts periodically enables it to offer the Christian world an image of the underworld and a passage to it, a means, in other words, for everyman to explore the expanded empire Venus proposes in the *Metamorphoses*. Yet as it becomes merged with Enna, the site of Proserpina's abduction, it acquires some of the beauty of that site and, as such, comes to offer a location where wonder and horror coexist. First a locus of poetic debate,

Etna rapidly becomes a site for testing the soul; as the idea of an intermediary space between Hell and Heaven that will become Purgatory gains traction, and the empire of the soul and the expansion of the empire into the afterlife gain prominence, Mt. Etna comes to serve a key role.[10]

Moreover, the best-known version of the Proserpina tale during this time, that of Claudian, offers its own set of variants. As transmitted, the narrative, indeed, sets the story on Etna, but concludes before Proserpina is found by her mother Ceres in the underworld. This text was sufficiently canonical that well into the thirteenth century Claudian became one of the *sex auctores* featured in medieval classrooms, arguably to teach students aspects of *Romanitas*. When this tale was coupled with other well-circulated texts about Etna, such as the *Dialogues* of Gregory the Great that link the volcano with Gehenna-like punishment, it came to serve a different purpose from that of the tale in Cicero, Vergil, or Ovid. Instead, it offers a narrative that speaks of departure and loss.

Sicily in the Middle Ages is increasingly studied as a location of encounter between a vast array of cultures, producing extraordinarily complex results in settings such as the court of Frederick II.[11] However, the Latin thread is not entirely lost, and the version of the myth acquired via Claudian does not remain unchallenged. Following the ancient version of the Proserpina myth through the Middle Ages leads us through a series of texts, all of which touch on Sicily and the new Christian empire expanded and defined by the Crusades, while also introducing elements of purgatorial redemption into the story. Cicero's Verrine orations re-enter the mainstream at a key moment, shortly before the first Crusade, and in the Christianized texts the return of Proserpina provides an opportunity for discussion of purgation and redemption in the context of a new form of empire, where language is shown to be an instrument of redemption, and the empire created and brought about through language is one that extends into the afterlife through the redemptive Word.

But the Proserpina myth is also significant in its medieval use because of its reliance on the Western Latin tradition. While the myth originated in the Greek East, one of the effects of the *Verrines* in locating the myth on Sicily is to insist that that story, and the imperial tales that develop from it, are rooted in the western Mediterranean. Though Sicily is indeed a crossroads of many kinds—north and south, east and west, Arabic and Christian—those authors that chose the version of the Proserpina myth found in the Verrine orations also chose to highlight a classical, Latin-based, Western version of the narrative of empire. To put this another way: the tales we are following here are ones that deliberately return to the myth of empire as spelled out during Roman imperial times because that myth offers a network of arguments about loss, balance, and negotiation.

The approach to empire that fascinates these medieval authors, then, is the one developed by Cicero and expanded by Vergil and Ovid. Choosing to foreground the version of the Proserpina myth found in the *Verrines* is a political choice made by the poets. It may be read allegorically, but it remains set on Sicily, and while it comes to include elements of purgation and redemption not found in the original, it also does not reflect the reality of contemporary Sicilian life, such as events at the court of Frederick II. What it does reflect, however, is a humanistic trend begun most likely in Rheims in the years leading up to the first Crusade, a trend that downplays the political realities, opting instead to suggest that the Proserpina myth offers a model for present-day imperial growth. Having chosen to locate the Proserpina myth on Sicily and assert that it is a myth of the Romans, not the Greeks, Cicero offers later writers a vehicle for arguing whether there exists a Western strength and Latin continuity that can be rediscovered. The blatant denial of the power of the East in Sicily is a political statement asserting the strength of the Roman West, in the Crusades and in imperial history in general, but it is one founded on a return to origins.[12]

This association of purgation and redemption with the Proserpina myth and Sicily is adopted by Dante in the *Commedia*, where it is affiliated with a new sense of empire, one focused on the future, while drawing on the need for an on-going negotiation with the past that Cicero's text introduced. Empire, according to Dante, is as much about the community of poets as it is about government. *Imperium*—good empire, the best kind of government—in the *Commedia* then, is a community of man sustained and defined by the vision of the poets; since language is now potentially redemptive, the role they play is crucial. In particular, the figure of Ulysses, and his associations with Sicily in a variety of texts, set the scene for what Dante will argue in *Purgatorio* about the necessities for good government and the possibilities for empire. Far from serving a negative function in the *Commedia*, the literary portrayal of Ulysses is a key source for the typological persona Dante will assume in *Purgatorio*, even as the poetic competition between Ovid and Vergil is highlighted through the textual references to Sicily. From the end of *Inferno*, where the Ulysses canto occurs, to the last cantos of *Purgatorio*, Dante moves us through the depictions of Sicily and Proserpina from Cicero, Vergil, Ovid, and others to introduce two key elements essential to his understanding of empire which is bolstered by poetic vision and redemption through poetic community.

What links Vergil to Dante further is a belief that at its heart the business of empire is best mapped out by the poets. Vergil's case is, on the surface, more obvious, though the reality of it may be slightly more complex. The *Aeneid*, written in part to establish a link between Augustus and the gods and justify the enormous imperial expansion Augustus was undertaking, is indeed a story of empire. Yet the epic tells that story in a complex way, laying the groundwork for what was taking place, pointing out the pitfalls encountered along the way and, perhaps most importantly, using the medium of poetry to articulate what the potential for empire might be. Alessandro Barchiesi employs the term "geopoetics" in his discussion of a similar, complex interplay between poetry and politics in the *Aeneid*, a term he defines as "the dynamics formed by the representation of the world, in particular its geopolitics, when it encounters the active participation of the poetic text in the making, aetiology and transformation of this world."[13]

Dante's situation is in some ways richer than that of Vergil, for in the *Commedia* the role of poetry, and of his epic, in the matter of empire is paramount. *Inferno* presents an empire that is devoid of the illumination of poetry, but *Purgatorio*, that space that so mimics our world even as it shows us its potential, is the place in the *Commedia* where poetry and politics go hand in hand. The ascent up the mountain of Purgatory is a climb of self-discovery for Dante, yet it is also a journey towards and, in a sense, into poetry, even as the communities of penitents he encounters along the way become increasingly models of humane governance. As such, it is *Purgatorio* that plays out the ways in which poetry and civil community work together, and those, in Dante's hands, are the fundamental elements of true empire.

For Vergil and Dante, then, empire is guided, at some stage, by the poets. Both the *Aeneid* and *Purgatorio* evince this bias, and this assertion is made all the clearer by the fact that both take such advantage of Sicily. The island of Sicily, with its story of Proserpina, offers to each of these poets a setting for framing imperial vision. Although Dante's vision of empire includes the beyond, Sicily remains the *point de départ*, even as the scope of that vision moves from this world to the next, and the capacity of poetry to affect empire shifts from powerful story-telling to actual redemption.

The story of Sicily that follows in Cicero's wake, then, is a story of two seemingly unrelated things: poetic competition and the strategies of—and resistances to—Western empire. How these two factors are treated, how they interact and how they are valued, shift with each poet, yet they are both always present. In what follows I will lean heavily on arguments made by Stephen Hinds and David Quint, Hinds for his assertions about the importance of poetic rivalry in treatments of Sicily, Quint for his foundational observations about the relationship of epic to empire.[14] Yet my purpose here is rather to trace how the myth of Proserpina guides the relationship of poetry, poetic competition, and definitions of empire in the changing political worlds from Vergil to Dante and how the negotiation related to her return maps onto prevailing notions of empire. The balance her story proclaims between power and subjugation, and past and future, offers each of these poets a narrative for the critique of empire, and that discussion centers on the island of Sicily. The nature of empire changes radically from Cicero's republican notions to Dante's eschatological ones—and from rhetorical to redemptive powers of language—yet literary treatments of Sicily continue to offer an arena for that discussion. My project overall, then, is dual: on the one hand, I examine texts associated with Proserpina, Sicily, and empire from Cicero to Dante; on the other, I use the conversation of the poets about Sicily as a test case for the ways in which literature can and does serve a unique role in offering a space for negotiation. As Susan Wolfson has argued, "there is a loss in discounting literary agency in the world, and a loss, moreover, in neglecting literature itself as a context in which the ways of the world are refracted by oppositional pressure, critical thinking."[15] Put more generally, the thrust of my argument is about literature and the kinds of space a literary text creates and inhabits that in some real way helps to formulate a political vision that acknowledges complexity.

Different as they may be, however, each of the poets asserts a fundamental connection among these elements, arguing for the importance of poetic negotiation in the framing of political visions. Empire rises from many things, but in the hands of these poets in this tradition, poetry offers a space for political deliberation, a space reified by the island of Sicily and mythologized by the tale of Proserpina. While the Roman tales focus on the abduction and rely on that as a means for discussing the problems of imperial expansion, both in the political and poetic realms, the high medieval versions of the story train their gaze first on her loss, then on her return and the necessity for negotiation that entails. As a result, the tale of Proserpina, as told by Cicero and adopted by a long series of authors, offers an index to the changing needs and understanding of empire, from Augustan territorial expansion to Christian spiritual redemption, and the return of Proserpina comes to serve, at least in part, as an allegory of the Christianization of the classical tradition. The empire of poetry, along with its political counterpart, is also redefined, as the ability to conquer the afterlife through the language of love becomes itself a way to negotiate a relationship with the past.

1

The Straits of Messina

GEOGRAPHY AND EMPIRE

The Geography of Rhetoric

The interconnection of Sicily, Proserpina, and the Roman Empire shows up prominently in rhetorical works of Cicero. In this chapter we will focus solely on the importance of Sicily to the beginnings of the Roman Empire; in the next two we will turn to the myth of Proserpina in the Roman poetry of Vergil and Ovid. To do this we will let the texts speak for themselves: by analyzing geographic and geological treatments of Sicily in the Latin writings of rhetoricians, poets, and historians, this chapter will interrogate the physical presence of Sicily in the textual formation of the Roman Empire, a formulation that becomes crucial to the literary tradition that follows.

Speeches and rhetorical treatises offer a blueprint for ancient Roman culture, as the nature of rhetorical argument—its logic, language, and method—is tied specifically to the defining characteristics of Roman culture.[1] Moreover, as this affiliation between *Romanitas* and oratory grew, it helped define even as it reflected the specific nature of the empire. With Cicero, working in the waning days of the Republic, the orator, in his capacity as the individual who best defines the common good, captures the essence of Roman man; with Quintilian, writing after the empire is in full swing, oratory has come to be identified with empire, and the understanding of the nature of a speech or argument reflects, often in surprisingly literal terms, the reach and limits of the Roman world.

Sicily's importance to Rome is clear from its history. Until the end of the Republic, Sicily had been perceived as a foreign nation: its language was Greek, as was its calendar. There was no Roman army there, no police force except for the slaves that belonged to the temple of Venus at Erice. Cicero points out that Sicily employed a different system of land taxation.[2] There was little Italian architecture, no Latin inscriptions, little integration of Romans with Sicilians. Moreover, there was a reluctance to extend civil rights there. This is not to suggest that Sicily was not important to Rome. On the contrary, as Italy's granary,[3] as the prize in the First Punic War, it clearly served an important function. As Ennius reminds us,[4] during the Second Punic War Juno is placated; Karl Galinsky points out that the antipathy of Rome and Carthage became important for the Aeneas legend, while Sicily and the appeasement of Juno (key, of course to the plot of the *Aeneid*) are linked in a Roman reader's mind.[5] Mythologically, it was viewed as the retreat of goddesses;[6] it was the traditional location for the landing of Daedalus,[7] and it is where Arethusa resurfaces.[8] It is where Polyphemus lives, as Vergil tells us, and, as Callimachus spells out, the land of numerous other myths as well.[9] Diodorus, for example, places Hercules in Sicily shortly after his trips to Italy.[10] Despite the differences, however, Sicily was often represented in terms of its familiarity. Though a boat ride away, that ride was short, and once one arrived it looked a lot like home.[11]

Perhaps most crucially, Sicily was the first overseas *provincia*. As Ernst Badian has shown, the word *provincia*, used first of Rome itself, comes to have our sense of province only after the incorporation of Sicily, the second *provincia*, but the first away from the center.[12] The tension, or balance, created between these two *provinciae* is what became, quite simply, the defining model for the developing Roman Empire. Even after the empire expanded east, and the incorporated societies were no longer labeled explicitly as provinces, the essential relationship between the outlying culture and the Roman center remained that first developed by Rome and Sicily. To put this another way, Roman empire can be defined in terms of the relationship between its center and its edges, a relationship first created by the identification of Sicily as *provincia*.

This abstract formula for empire is clearly laid out in Cicero's lengthy attack on Verres, governor of Sicily from 73 to 71 BC, in the *Verrines*. In these speeches, Cicero capitalizes on an opportunity offered him by history to make his name as an orator and, beyond that, takes advantage of these speeches to contrast the values of bygone republican Rome with the corruption of his day. The result of this argument against the Sicilian governor can be summed up briefly: Sicily serves as a repository of ancient values; its people are the hardworking types of the past; the strength of the people is what led Cicero to undertake this attack, an attack that is as much against the plutocracy of his day as it is against the extortion and robbery of the Sicilian people by their governor. In the end Cicero can be seen to have asserted that what makes Sicily valuable is that it retains values lost to Rome: it is more Roman than Rome itself.[13]

Underlying Cicero's argument is the notion that Sicily represents a unique location from Rome's perspective: it maintains the capacity to retain values lost elsewhere even as Cicero can defend its rights in Roman law courts. Much of this stems from the fact that Sicily is a province of Rome, but what Cicero makes clear in the course of the Verrine orations is that Sicily is viewed not just as a province but, rather, as the original province:

> prima omnium, id quod ornamentum imperi est, provincia est appellata; prima docuit maiores nostros quam praeclarum esset exteris gentibus imperare. (*Verr.* 2.2.1.2)[14]

> (She was the first of all to be called province, that embellishment of empire. She was the first who taught our forefathers how splendid it is to govern foreign peoples.)

Sicily's relationship to the imperial center remains important because, as Cicero notes at the start of the second *Verrine*, it offers things unavailable in Rome (food, harbors) while also not being far removed geographically from them. Cicero argues that it is this delicate balance of similarity and difference that marks Sicily as the prototype of all Roman provinces; it is the destruction of this balance that he upbraids Verres for, claiming he has robbed, pillaged, and, as we will see, raped this nearby land.

Through this passage in Cicero, Sicily enters Roman literature as the first overseas province, the start of Rome's empire. Beyond that, this argument asserts a connection between the moral citizen, native to Sicily, and Cicero himself, who, as orator, embodies comparable moral qualities. As in his early treatise on persuasion, *De inventione*, Cicero makes clear here how morality and language are, for the Romans, intertwined and, further, that evidence of that juncture is found both in the people of the uncorrupted province of Sicily and in his own skill as a speaker. Both, in short, represent what is valuable and defining about Rome. Through this speech, Cicero characterizes Rome by means of Sicily and the empire in terms of the province, focused throughout on the consistency of the true Roman nature.

When Quintilian, decades later, writes his rhetorical treatise *Institutio oratoria* (c. AD 95), it is for a very different world and purpose. The role of oratory, while still important in the political sphere, has expanded to include education.

Quintilian is as committed to identifying Roman qualities as Cicero was, yet he does something else as well. With the expansion to the classroom, and the identification of the logic of speech as the basis of the liberal arts, Quintilian assumes, throughout his treatise, a spatial, at times geographical approach to rhetoric. That is, while he, like Cicero, asserts a continuity between man and his use of language—rhetoric is defined as the art of speaking well, where the "well" refers to both the aptness of the speech and the moral stance of the speaker—Quintilian projects that morality and Roman characterization onto the landscape of the speech itself. For Quintilian, every good speech reflects the geography, with its strictures and values, of the empire itself.

Part of this geographic identification between speech and empire can be seen in Quintilian's treatment of digression. In the fourth and eleventh books of the *Institutio oratoria*, Quintilian criticizes the common practice of using digression as merely a weak form of transition that follows a statement of facts, and seems at first to suggest that digression is only a sign of laziness. If practiced *sine discrimine*—by which he means without proper attention to the details of the particular case—digression (*digressio*) serves as a diversion, distracting a crowd as it enables a speech to move from the dry statement of facts into the more combative proof. The problem with this use of digression, Quintilian says, is that it is often inserted without consideration of context, *tamquam semper expediat aut etiam necesse sit* ("as if it were always advantageous and even necessary," 4.3.3). Speakers, he continues, *eoque sumptas ex iis partibus quarum alius erat locus sententias in hanc congerunt* ("remove select thoughts from those parts of the speech where they properly belong and gather them here," 4.3.3).[15]

There is, however, a second use of digression that Quintilian feels more sympathetic toward, which is *egressio*:

> Ego autem confiteor hoc exspatiandi genus non modo narrationi sed etiam quaestionibus vel universis vel interim singulis oportune posse subiungi cum res postulat aut certe permittit, atque eo vel maxime inlustrari ornarique orationem, sed si cohaeret et sequitur, non si per vim cuneatur et quae natura iuncta erant distrahit. (*Inst. orat.* 4.3.4–5)

> (I admit, however, that this form of expansion can be opportunely attached not only to the narrative but also to the questions (taken either as a whole or, from time to time, individually) when the situation demands or at any rate allows it, indeed also this is a very important means of polishing and embellishing the speech, but only if it coheres and follows, not if it is driven in forcibly like a wedge and splits apart what nature had joined.)

Andreas Härter distinguishes between Quintilian's two forms of digression in terms of aptness.[16] According to Härter, *egressio* entails the introduction of a passage that is suitably connected to the speech and its order overall, while *digressio* introduces a concept of conflict. *Egressio*, Quintilian argues, need not be limited to one place in a speech—as others, including Cicero have argued— but can be used for varying reasons throughout:

> Sed hae sunt plures... quae per totam causam varios habent excursus, ut laus hominum locorumque, ut descriptio regionum, expositio quarundam rerum gestarum vel etiam fabulosarum. Quo ex genere est in orationibus contra Verrem compositis Siciliae laus, Proserpinae raptus, pro C. Cornelio popularis illa virtutum Cn. Pompei commemoratio: in quam ille divinus orator, velut nomine ipso ducis cursus dicendi teneretur, abrupto quem inchoaverat sermone devertit actutum. (*Inst. orat.* 4.3.12–14)

> (There are however... several types which allow excursuses throughout the cause: such as praise of persons or places, descriptions of areas, exposition of certain historical or even legendary events. Examples of this include the praise of Sicily and the Rape of Proserpina in the orations against Verres, or that populist memorial of the virtues of Gnaeus Pompeius in the *Pro Cornelio*, where that divine orator, as if the flow of speaking was held up by the very name of the general, once the initial topic broke off, instantly diverted the speech.)

The difference noted between *digressio* and *egressio* is borne out, in a telling way, by the metaphoric language and examples Quintilian selects to talk about the two types of digression. Not only is *digressio* presented as oppositional and *egressio* transitional, but *digressio* is explained in terms of metaphors of aggression, while *egressio* is affiliated with "gentleness, calm and placidity, as for example, in Cicero's description of the Rape of Proserpina, his picture of Sicily, or his panegyric of Pompey" (*Egressiones fere lenes et dulces et remissae, raptus Proserpinae, Siciliae descriptio, Cn. Pompei laus*, 11.3.164–65). What is striking here is that the examples of *egressio* all relate explicitly, if surprisingly, to the island of Sicily and, in particular, to Cicero's treatment of Sicily in the Verrine orations.[17]

Through reference to Cicero's treatment of Sicily, Quintilian alludes to an existing connection not only between Sicily and a form of digression that bolsters a speech but, more crucially, between Sicily and empire.[18] It is worth pointing out that, in addition to the references to the island, Quintilian also uses a form of Cicero's tag for Sicily: Sicily, for Cicero is the *ornamentum imperi*, or embellishment of empire, while, for Quintilian, the right form of digression can *ornarique orationem*, or embellish the speech. This suggestion is supported by the text's alignment of Sicily with *egressio*, which can be joined (*posse subiungi*) to a topic to which it coheres or follows logically and contrasts it with *digressio*, which proceeds *sine discrimine*. *Subiungere* is a verb often associated with the mechanics of empire: Velleius, for example, refers to Tiberius, Augustus's stepson, as the one who *novas imperio nostro subiunxit provincias*, ("attached new provinces to our empire" [2.39.3]).

Quintilian's reference to the association Cicero makes between Sicily and empire here seems quite clear. However, his references to Sicily point in another direction as well. Having specified that the difference between the two types lies in the suitability of the example, Quintilian then states that bad *egressio* is a digression that *per vim cuneatur et quae natura iuncta erant distrahit* ("is driven in forcibly like a wedge and splits apart what nature had joined"). By including it here, as a counterexample, in effect, of *egressio*, Quintilian alludes to the second, complementary aspect of Sicily in Roman literature: connected to Rome, in many ways Sicily is nonetheless separate from it. What Cicero refers to repeatedly in the *Verrines* is that it is Sicily's status—as similar to yet separate from Rome—that makes it desirable. In fact, the language Quintilian employs here echoes strongly the geographic relationship believed to have existed between the island and the mainland, where Sicily, once attached to the peninsula, marks its separation through the rivers that pour from the mountains into the straits of Messina, much as Quintilian argues that the *cursus dicendi* of Cicero in the *pro Cornelio* is broken off by the mere thought of Pompey's deeds, thus echoing the ancient belief that Sicily originated from the force of the waters breaking through the narrow neck, dividing what nature had originally joined:[19]

> The ancient mythographers, that is, say that Sicily was originally a peninsula, and that afterward it became an island, the cause being somewhat as follows. The isthmus at its narrowest point was subjected to the dash of the waves of the sea on its two sides and so a gap ... was made.... Some men say, however, that mighty earthquakes took place and the neck of what was the mainland was broken through, and in this way the Strait was formed, since the sea now separated the mainland from the island. (Diod. Sic. 4.85.3–4)[20]

Pliny reiterates this sentiment: *Namque et hoc modo insulas rerum natura fecit: avellit Siciliam Italiae* ("For nature has created islands in another way as well: she tore Sicily away from Italy," Pliny, *Nat. Hist.* 2.90.204); so does Ovid: *Zancle quoque iuncta fuisse/dicitur Italiae, donec confinia pontus / abstulit et media tellurem reppulit unda.* ("Zancle [Messina] also is said to have been joined to Italy, until the sea washed away their common boundary and thrust back the land by the intervening water," Ovid, *Met.* 15.290–92). Quintilian sums up his discussion of the strength of *egressio* by describing it as a passage that has some bearing on the case, even if it runs away from (*excurrens*) the logic of the speech; there are, he concludes, "so many different ways a speech may diverge from the straight path" (*tot modis a recto itinere declinet oratio*, *Inst. orat.* 4.3.14). The word choice echoes the canonical description of Sicily's relation to the mainland.

The coexistence of continuity and difference is clearly central to the proper functioning of good digression, as is borne out by the final line of Quintilian's description, where the assertion about the need to avoid violent disruption is, itself, rent apart by that very statement: *in quam ille divinus orator, velut nomine ipso ducis cursus dicendi teneretur, abrupto quem inchoaverat sermone devertit actutum* ("where that divine orator, as if the flow of speaking was held up by the very name of the general, once the initial topic broke off, instantly diverted the speech"). It is also, as we shall see, key to the relationship of province to imperial center, particularly as exemplified, from Cicero's time, by Sicily.

Between the time of Cicero and that of Quintilian, empire had grown from an abstract ideal to an often-grim reality. Yet Cicero's notion of empire's potential—captured in his glowing description of Sicily in the Verrine orations—remains a locus classicus for the possibilities empire continued to hold out. Because of Sicily's role as first overseas province, and Cicero's designation of it as such, the island of Sicily serves throughout the literature as the locus for discussions of the potential of empire.[21] What we see in Quintilian's discussion of *egressio*—and its focus on Cicero's Sicily—is an attempt to offer at the very least an analogy, at best an allegory, for the purpose and structure of early empire. If we reverse the poles of the rhetorical text, and see it not as prescriptive but descriptive, taking the examples as the argument and the argument as exemplary, Quintilian's writing on *egressio* becomes an essential guide to treatments of empire that put Sicily at the core.

Modern texts that have examined links between rhetoric and empire, such as those by Tzvetan Todorov and Eric Cheyfitz, tend to cast imperialism as a form of translation and, at least in the case of Cheyfitz, place metaphor, or *translatio*, at the center: "The *translatio*, then, is inseparably connected with a 'civilizing' mission, the bearing of ... Western letters to ... those who do not speak the language of the empire. From its beginnings the imperialist mission is, in short, one of translation: the translation of the 'other' into the terms of the empire, which . . . also alienates the other from the empire."[22] Given this argument, it is particularly striking to find that Quintilian does not associate empire with metaphor, but rather chooses to align *egressio* with the imperial cause, through both his use of Sicily as exemplum and his references to Cicero's discussion of Sicily in the Verrine orations. Rather than presenting empire as something that occurs in the interstices, in the space of "metaphor that figures the possibility of authentic intercultural communication,"[23] Quintilian presents empire in terms of continuities, and suggests that even as digression, appropriately done, confirms the power of the main speech, so colonization strengthens the imperial center. These "colonies" have a complex relationship with the main part of the speech, much as first Sicily, then other provinces, did to Rome.

The Politics of Geography

Given this context, it is perhaps not surprising that the two halves of Vergil's imperial epic *Aeneid* each open focused on Sicily.[24] While the opening lines offer an overview of the journey of Aeneas from Troy to Rome and the concerns of the Trojans' antagonist Juno—her love of Carthage and hatred of the Trojans—the action per se of the poem begins with the line *vix e conspectu Siculae telluris* ("barely out of sight of the Sicilian land," *Aen.* 1.34). At the parallel spot at the start of the second half of the poem, Juno is shown surveying the Trojans who have landed in Latium from a location over the Sicilian cape of Pachynus: *et laetum Aenean classemque ex aethere longe / Dardaniam Siculo prospexit ab usque Pachyno* ("and all the way from Pachynus from high up in the skies she spied joyful Aeneas and his Trojan fleet," *Aen.* 7.288–89). What does Sicily have to do with the message and structure of the *Aeneid*, and how does Vergil's treatment of Sicily relate to and expand our understanding of the ancient Roman view of the island?[25]

As we shall see in the next chapter, Sicily is described in detail in *Aeneid* 5 as the location where the anniversary games for Anchises' death are held. Yet in *Aeneid* 3, Sicily, like many of the locations where Aeneas and his men land, is a land of terror: through the story of Achaemenides they hear the tale of the Cyclopes, and, at the very end of the book, Aeneas witnesses the death of his father.[26] Nevertheless, in *Aeneid* 3, Sicily is also the land associated with Trojan *pietas*: Anchises' embrace of Achaemenides at the end of the book reminds the reader of the disastrously naïve acceptance of the comparable figure of

Sinon in *Aeneid* 2, even as it insists on the unchanging and positive quality of the Trojan character.

When Sicily is dwelt on in the *Aeneid*—and in the critical literature—it is the location of the games at Drepanum that is most often discussed. The western corner of the island is where Aeneas lands before being blown off course to Carthage. It is where the poem begins and where Aeneas's father dies; also, the anniversary games for Anchises are held on Sicily after Aeneas leaves Carthage and Dido. But I would argue that Drepanum is not the first important location on Sicily for Aeneas. Rather, it is the straits of Messina that figure first both in Vergil's imagination and in the poem at large. Drepanum, in fact, is important in part because it plays out, as a veritable *mise en abîme*, the issues raised by the history—geographical, literary, and political—introduced first by the straits.

It should not surprise us, then, to see in the *Aeneid* yet another iteration of the story of Sicily's geological origins joining the examples discussed above. When Helenus first describes Sicily to Aeneas and his men in *Aeneid* 3, he states:

> haec loca vi quondam et vasta convulsa ruina
> (tantum aevi longinqua valet mutare vetustas)   415
> dissiluisse ferunt; cum protinus utraque tellus
> una foret, venit medio vi pontus et undis
> Hesperium Siculo latus abscidit, arvaque et urbes
> litore diductas angusto interluit aestu (*Aen.* 3.414–19)

> (These lands, they say, once wrenched by force and great catastrophe (long stretches of time can make such changes), tore apart; when before both lands were one, the sea came between with force and with its waters cut the Hesperian side from the Sicilian, and washed between fields and towns divided from its shore by a narrow tide.)

While complementing the descriptions cited earlier in this chapter that emphasize the separation of Sicily from Italy, these passages highlight the original connection between the two landmasses.[27]

Vergil's reasons for emphasizing Sicily's geography point toward the complex treatment of Sicily in the poem overall and urge us to consider further reasons for Sicily's importance to the origins of Roman Empire. For not only do we hear, yet again, that Sicily, now separated, was once joined to the mainland but, as Dido (and the reader) hear not once but twice, Aeneas avoids the divide, the strait where the lands were once joined, and goes instead all the way around the island, thus reconnecting, at least conceptually, the two lands:

praestat Trinacrii metas lustrare Pachyni
cessantem, longos et circumflectere cursus,   430
quam semel informem vasto vidisse sub antro
Scyllam et caeruleis canibus resonantia saxa. (*Aen.* 3.429–32)

(Better to round the turning point of Trinacrian Pachynus, delaying, and take the long route round, than once to have seen hideous Scylla in her vast cave and rocks echoing with seagreen dogs.)[28]

This act clearly separates Aeneas from Jason: as the Argonauts reach the straits, "And as long as the portion of a spring day is lengthened, for that long a time they toiled, heaving the ship out through the resounding rocks. Then the heroes, benefiting once again from the wind, sped onward and soon passed the meadow of Thrinacia, where Helius' cattle graze" (*Argonautica* 4.960–65; see also the wider context, 4.921–81),[29] much like Odysseus who first "sailed up the narrow strait lamenting" (*Odyssey* 12.234, trans. Lattimore) and then, more memorably, alone, hangs on the fig tree and waits as long as a long day in court for his mast and keel to return (12.426–46.). This divide is smudged in the *Aeneid* as Aeneas, in identifying those mythological straits with the straits of Messina, avoids them at the last minute, and distinguishes himself from the earlier heroes by going around Sicily, both marking and erasing the divide.[30] Where other heroes and authors find and emphasize division at and through these straits, Vergil and Aeneas assert a more complex relationship as a new, tentative unity emerges from the divided land.

The line that Aeneas draws around the island, embracing it, drawing it back toward the mainland without fully connecting it, offers a model for future empire and for province. Sicily is one of us: like us, but different; still separate, still divided, but one of ours. So Strabo: "The island is a part of Italy, as it were, and ready and without great labor supplies Rome with everything it has, as though from the fields of Italy" (6.2.7–8; see also 6.1.5). Polybius, echoing Thucydides, provides ancient evidence for this by asserting in *Histories* 1.5 that the first crossing of the Romans outside of Italy was to Sicily and so, in a sense, makes Sicily the prototype of the first province, ταύτῃ γὰρ τῇ γῇ πρῶτον ἐπέβησαν τῶν ἐκτὸς τόπων τῆς 'Ιταλίας ("for in that land they went first outside of the places of Italy"). Vergil echoes this in his treatment offered the Trojans who wish to stay behind on Sicily at the end of book 5: unlike the other stops along the way to Rome, here the Trojans will create a settlement that bears all the marks of a province, both in geographic layout and in governance. Polybius is the first author to place Scylla and Charybdis at the straits of Messina.

Recent writing on the *Aeneid* has emphasized how Vergil's narrative choices and strategies are often made with an eye toward the future: the journey Aeneas takes from Troy to Rome circumscribes and lays claim to the lands Augustus later conquers in the name of empire.[31] This aspect of empire can be pushed even further. As we learn, again in *Aeneid* 3, the purpose of Aeneas's journey is not as much to discover a new Troy as to uncover the old Rome. That is, what the correct interpretation of the earlier prophecy by Apollo on Delos makes clear—*antiquam exquirite matrem* ("seek out the ancient mother," *Aen.* 3.96)—is that it is not the Olympian roots of the Dardanians that are being sought out but rather their pre-Trojan ones, and the purpose of Aeneas's journey is to reveal their rights to the land of their forebears, which is Italy:

> est locus, Hesperiam Grai cognomine dicunt,
> terra antiqua, potens armis atque ubere glaebae;
> Oenotri coluere viri; nunc fama minores   165
> Italiam dixisse ducis de nomine gentem.
> hae nobis propriae sedes, hinc Dardanus ortus
> Iasiusque pater, genus a quo principe nostrum (*Aen.* 3.163–68)

(There is a place called Hesperia by the Greeks, an ancient land, powerful in arms and in the richness of its soil. Oenotrian men lived there; now the story has it that a younger race has named it Italy after their leader. This is our true home; from here Dardanus and father Iasius arose, who initiated our race.)

By traveling to Hesperia, Aeneas will return to his origins and cause Troy to recede into the distance: Troy, in fact, becomes increasingly unimportant as his journey progresses. What matters more and more is the fact that the Dardanians came from Italy, that before Troy was even a glimmer in Helen's eye the Dardanians had laid claim to Italy. Not only does Vergil mention this here, but the first four lines of this passage are a direct quotation from Ilioneus's speech to Dido in *Aeneid* 1.530–33. (And, as we have noted, Italy was named for Italus, believed to have come from Sicily.)

This narrative strategy works to create a poetic space for Vergil in literary history. It also offers Vergil's patron, Augustus, a particular approach to empire: he, too, will claim rights going back through Aeneas to any land scouted out during Aeneas's journey. His imperial claims, in short, are "merely" a process of uncovering what is rightfully his. Like the geography of Sicily, the fact that these lands are presently separated from him is just a fluke of nature and time; originally these lands were united and, following Aeneas's model, they will be returned to their original state once again. So too with the Greek settlements identified by Achaemenides as the Trojans sail along the southern coast of Sicily: Vergil draws the names from Callimachus, and so points forward to the time of Greek settlement, while apparently affirming Aeneas's, and Augustus's, originary rights to that land.[32]

The ramifications of this are immense. On the one hand, Aeneas's journey maps out the scope of Augustus's empire. On the other, the very fact that Aeneas's efforts are aimed at returning to the origin of his people offers Augustus a model for empire. By the end of Aeneas's journey, Augustus can lay claim to an empire that extends as far back in time as it does out in space, and the source of that empire is rooted in Vergil's presentation of Sicily and its relationship to the mainland.

But Aeneas's journey around Sicily may well have its roots in a particular proto-imperial move by the future Augustus, or Octavian, which adds further nuance to Vergil's depiction of Sicily and Sicily's place in the early empire.[33] The struggles that culminated in the battle of Actium and the victory of Octavian over Antony—a victory that led to Octavian assuming sole power and a change of name to Augustus—included a series of confrontations not just between Octavian and Antony but also, and critically, between Octavian and Sextus Pompey, the son of Pompey the Great. The endgame that resulted in the beginning of the empire is arguably a power struggle among these three figures—Octavian, Antony, and Sextus—and the political maneuvering that led to Augustus's rule involves Sicily in a way that curiously reflects Cicero's succinct assertion of the island's importance to empire.

Nowhere is the internal aspect of his fight against Sextus more clearly marked than in Octavian's first real loss at Sextus's hands. In 42, having been bested by Sextus at Rhegium, on the Italian coast south of the straits of Messina, Octavian orders his fleet to sail to Brundisium to meet up with Antony, as Appian tells us in *Civil Wars* 4.86, ἐν ἀριστερᾷ ἔχων Σικελίαν καὶ Πομπήιον ("keeping Sicily and Pompeius on his left hand"). Moses Hadas explains the event this way:

> Antony was urging his colleague to hasten to join him in the campaign against the Liberators in Macedonia, but it was essential for Octavian to secure the good will of the cities of Vibo and Rhegium before leaving Italy; this he did by giving solemn promises that he would never distribute their fields and houses to the soldiers. Then he left to join Antony, sailing "with

Sicily on his left," according to Appian, that is, he was forced by Sextus to circumnavigate Sicily in order to reach Brundisium.[34]

Yet the strangeness of the move is little dwelt on, by Hadas or anyone else. If Octavian was in fact at Vibo or Rhegium, there was no—or certainly little—justification for sailing around Sicily in order to get to Brundisium.[35] The reason for taking this route probably lies with Sextus, who, having won, could force Octavian away from the straits, an extremely difficult passage.[36] But sailing, and especially sailing around Sicily, are actions associated more with Sextus than with Octavian himself. His defeat may, ironically, have opened the door for him to identify more strongly, more absolutely, with Sextus. Appian's description provides a glimpse of the creation of the Octavian we are later officially presented with, and that Octavian is constructed of an almost pathological identification with a variety of other people who represented his ideals, including Sextus. By sailing around Sicily, Octavian can both deny his defeat and look forward to the day when the sea and Sicily will be his, when, as he says in the *Res Gestae*, he has freed the sea from pirates. From his defeat at Sextus's hands, Octavian rises triumphant.

With this in mind, the beginning of Helenus's advice to Aeneas takes on particular importance:

> ast ubi digressum Siculae te admoverit orae   410
> ventus, et angusti rarescent claustra Pelori,
> laeva tibi tellus et longo laeva petantur
> aequora circuitu; dextrum fuge litus et undas. (*Aen.* 3.410–13)

(But when, as you leave, the wind has taken you to the Sicilian coast, and the gates of narrow Pelorus grow apart, let the lands on the left and the seas on the left be sought by a long route; flee the righthand shore and waters.)

Notice that in Vergil, as in Appian, the men are told to keep Sicily on their left, which Aeneas does, by avoiding the straits.[37] Instead, he sails on the "long route" around the coast of Sicily, stopping briefly near Etna, but then sailing, with Achaemenides on board, to Drepanum. This move ensures that Aeneas's route around Sicily marks the exact path later taken in reverse by Octavian while, at the same time, asserting, proleptically, Octavian's preemptive rights to Sextus's land of Sicily. It seems plausible to suggest that Aeneas's own atypical journey around the island of Sicily, rather than through the straits of Messina, is an attempt on Vergil's part to pre-enact Octavian's reverse trip in 42.

The Geography of Empire

It is clear that Sicily plays a particular role in the final skirmishes preceding the establishment of Augustan rule.[38] Here again it is the geography that surfaces, and here again it is the straits of Messina that play a critical role. Yet even more crucial is the relationship between the people who all but personify the lands involved. Sextus's father, Pompey the Great, had laid claim to power through his rule over the Mediterranean Sea; Sicily, as a result, was his headquarters. When his son rose to power it was first as ally with Octavian, then in opposition to him, and Sicily, and its geography, remain critical to the evolution of empire. Following arguments made, for instance, in *Sextus Pompeius*,[39] I would propose that the final civil battles that preceded the rule of Augustus be considered in the context not just of Actium but also of Sicily, and that Octavian's two major antagonists, Sextus Pompey and Antony, be approached in very different terms, as indeed they were in the literature.[40]

In addition to the defeat by Sextus discussed above, Sicily is the site of one of Augustus's most important victories, that over Sextus in 36 (*mare pacavi a praedonibus*).[41] That this victory preceded the final defeat of Antony at Actium is important to explore. With the death of Julius Caesar, Pompey's son Sextus organized an army and fleet in Spain. Having been placed on the proscription list of the first triumvirate, Sextus Pompey went on the offensive and tried to become a major force in the power struggle between the triumvirs and Brutus and Cassius. Most notable among the ancient sources here is Velleius 2.73.2:

> quem senatus paene totus adhuc e Pompeianis constans partibus post Antonii a Mutina fugam, eodem illo tempore quo Bruto Cassioque transmarinas provincias decreverat, revocatum ex Hispania... in paterna bona restituerat et orae maritimae praefecerat. is tum... occupata Sicilia servitia fugitivosque in numerum exercitus sui recipiens magnum modum legionum effecerat;... latrociniis ac praedationibus infestato mari... cum eum non depuderet vindicatum armis ac ductu patris sui mare infestare piraticis sceleribus.[42]

(The senate, which still consisted almost entirely of Pompeians, in the period that followed the flight of Antony from Mutina, and at the very time when it had assigned to Brutus and Cassius the provinces across the sea, had recalled Sextus from Spain... restored him to his father's property and had entrusted to him the guarding of the coast. Seizing Sicily... and admitting into his army slaves and runaways, he had raised his legions to their full complement.... [H]e infested the seas by predatory and piratical expeditions; nor was he ashamed thus to infest with piracy and its atrocities the sea which had been freed from it by his father's arms and leadership.)

Because Octavian was preoccupied with Antony in Italy and Brutus and Cassius in the east, he had little time, at first, to deal with Sextus Pompey. In 39 BC near Misenum, the second triumvirate granted Sextus Pompey authority in Sicily, Sardinia, and Corsica, an agreement that was soon disputed. After the defeat at Naulochus in 36, Sextus Pompey was forced to flee to the east, where he was soon killed; Octavian took control of the island and imposed a new administrative superstructure. Caesar had given "Latin rights" and near-full Roman citizenship for any man who held an annual municipal office; Octavian, however, returned only three towns to full "Latin status" and made six of the cities into *coloniae*. They were filled with Roman veterans. At least two others were made *municipia*.[43]

Anton Powell has argued that "Sextus' Roman virtues obstructed the picture; Antony with his eastern base and foreign queen lent himself far better to the claim of 'unRoman vices,' and thus made a better foil than Sextus for the image of Augustus as true Roman. It was because Antony became the explicit antitype that Sextus had to become a ghost, a figure to be exorcised."[44] Perhaps because he was the last opponent, the one that stood between Octavian and single rule, perhaps because of his familial connections to Octavian, Antony has received by far the greater press of the two, while Sextus's role has been relegated to brief mentions, a mere prelude to the major opus that is Antony and Octavian at Actium. Let me reverse this trend, and speak first, briefly, of Antony as prelude to the neglected discussion of Sextus.

Throughout the literature Antony is presented in terms that oppose him diametrically to Octavian. In both Velleius's account and that of Dio, the opposition of matched forces is indicated by grammatical structure and lexical choice, even as Octavian's victory is assured through careful selection of word and phrase. In Velleius's version, Octavian ("Caesar") is at once matched by and elevated above Antony.[45] The description of the showdown at Actium begins:

vigebat in hac parte miles atque imperator, <in> illa marcebant omnia; hinc re<mi>ges firmissimi, illinc inopia adfectissimi; navium haec magnitudo modica nec celeritati adversa, illa specie [et] terribilior; hinc ad Antonium nemo, illinc ad Caesarem cotidie aliquis transfugiebat... Advenit deinde maximi discriminis dies, quo Caesar Antoniusque productis classibus pro salute alter, in ruinam alter terrarum orbis dimicavere. (2.84–5)

(On the one side, commander and soldiers alike were thriving, on the other all were withering: on the one side the rowers were strong, on the other, they were weakened by privations; on the one side, ships of moderate size, not too large for speed, on the other, more terrifying in appearance only; on the one side, no one was deserting to Antony, on the other, someone was deserting to Caesar daily.... At last came the day of the greatest conflict, on which Caesar and Antony led out their fleets and fought, the one for the safety, the other for the ruin, of the lands of the world.)[46]

The day of the greatest conflict (*maximi discriminis dies*) is one that sets Caesar against Antony, linked by the enclitic-*que*, even as they are opposed through the *hinc... illinc* and *alter... alter* constructions. When the battle actually begins, "on the one side was everything—commanders, rowers, soldiers; on the other, soldiers alone": the *alter... alter* construction serves again to highlight the matched quality of the two men as well as to highlight the differences in their strengths.

Antony is labeled as an enemy of the state by both Velleius and Suetonius (*hoste iudicato* [Velleius, *Historiae* 2.63] / *hosti iudicato*, [Suet. *Aug.* 17.2]), a designation expanded upon by Dio. In Dio's account, the two are paired through opposing speeches, and within Octavian's speech, the opposition between the two is made clear through rhetorical structure above all. Dio initially opposes Antony to Cleopatra (he, citizen; she, foreign) and then moves to argue that Antony assimilates to her in all ways and so stands in direct opposition to Octavian. In 50.27 comes the famous hortatory pronouncement:

μήτ' οὖν ‘Ρωμαῖον εἶναί τις αὐτὸν νομιζέτω, ἀλλά τινα Αἰγύπτιον, μήτ' Ἀντώνιον ὀνομαζέτω, ἀλλά τινα Σαραπίωνα· μὴ ὕπατον, μὴ αὐτοκράτορα γεγονέναι ποτὲ ἡγείσθω, ἀλλὰ γυμνασίαρχον.... ἀδύνατον γάρ ἐστι βασιλικῶς τέ τινα τρυφῶντα καὶ γυναικείως θρυπτόμενον ἀνδρῶδές τι φρονῆσαι καὶ πρᾶξαι, ... τὴν ἀκμὴν τοῦ σώματος; ἀλλὰ παρήβηκε καὶ ἐκτεθήλυνται. τὴν ῥώμην τῆς γνώμης; ἀλλὰ γυναικίζει καὶ ἐκκεκιναίδισται. τὴν εὐσέβειαν τὴν πρὸς τοὺς θεοὺς ἡμῶν; ἀλλὰ πολεμεῖ καὶ ἐκείνοις καὶ τῇ πατρίδι. τὴν πιστότητα τὴν πρὸς τοὺς συμμάχους; καὶ τίς οὐκ οἶδεν ὅπως τὸν Ἀρμένιον ἐξαπατήσας ἔδησε; τὴν [δὲ] ἐπιείκειαν τὴν πρὸς τοὺς φίλους; καὶ τίς οὐχ ἑόρακε τοὺς ὑπ' αὐτοῦ κακῶς ἀπολωλότας; τὴν εὐδοξίαν τὴν παρὰ τοῖς στρατιώταις; καὶ τίς οὐχὶ καὶ ἐκείνων αὐτοῦ κατέγνωκε. (50.27.1; 4–5; 7)

(Therefore let no one count him a Roman, but rather an Egyptian, nor call him Antony but rather Serapion; let no one think he was ever consul or *imperator*, but only gymnasiarch. . . . For it is impossible for one who leads a life of royal luxury, and coddles himself like a woman, to have a manly thought or do a manly deed. . . . His physical fitness? But he has passed his prime and become effeminate. His strength of mind? But he plays the woman and has worn himself out with unnatural lust. His piety toward our gods? But he is at war with them as well as with his country. His faithfulness to his allies? But who does not know how he deceived and imprisoned the Armenian? His kindness to his friends? But who has not seen the men who have miserably perished at his hands? His reputation with the soldiers? But who even of them has not condemned him?)[47]

The question-and-answer structure sets up the opposition Dio wishes to establish. Rather than *alter . . . alter* we here have a series of interrogations, each of which serves to underscore what is positive about Octavian by reiterating what is negative about Antony. Antony's traits—his uxuriousness, lack of piety, faithlessness, meanness, and miserable reputation with his soldiers all define his weakness in terms drawn from Octavian's strengths: indeed, they are derived from what will become the foundation of Augustus's moral program: masculinity, piety, faithfulness, clemency, *iustitia*. Antony, in Dio's depiction, creates Octavian's moral profile through negation.

David Quint has shown how one of the earliest treatments of Actium, that of Vergil in *Aeneid* 8, raises this opposition to a battle of cosmic proportions.[48] Yasmin Syed has succinctly discussed this confrontation as "a founding text for the Western discourse of orientalism."[49] In this context, it is important to recognize that two recurring motifs surface again and again in discussions of Antony's opposition to Octavian: Cleopatra and Egypt. As Quint has argued, these two come together in the battle of Actium, at which the personification of the East, Cleopatra, and the land she represents are both played out and defeated. In Dio, not only is Antony assimilated to Cleopatra, as we have seen, but Actium becomes identified with Egypt, poised on the eastern edge, or what passes for the eastern edge, of the empire. Octavian's victory at Actium is a cowboy-and-Indian showdown of the best spaghetti western sort. In a sense this view of the battle of Actium represents a replay of issues at stake in the Trojan War where, as Denis Feeney has argued, we find the clash of Asia and the West, represented in the literature as a battle of opposites: masculine versus feminine and West versus East. So, too, at Actium Octavian not only wins, but becomes the embodiment of the masculine West.[50]

But this view of the time does not include Sextus. Precisely because Sextus and Antony are both engaged in civil wars with Octavian, their differing relationships are, in the end, connected. The Temple of Apollo on the Palatine stands as a monument to this fact, since it was vowed at the victory over Sextus at Naulochus, then dedicated after the victory over Antony at Actium.[51] The fact that we associate it only or at least largely with Actium is a result of Augustan propaganda, a factor of what Powell identifies as Sextus's ghost-like qualities.[52] In the years that follow Actium, repeated efforts are made to inscribe the importance of Antony on the popular imagination as the antitype first of Octavian and then of Augustus. The opposition between the two that we see at play in the historians, and that we associate with the very nature of civil war, is emphasized, monumentalized even, in the temple and in its art: both the sculptures of the Danaids and the reliefs within it speak, it has been convincingly argued, to Octavian's defeat of Antony.[53]

However, Octavian's struggles with Sextus Pompey are of a different sort. There is no cataclysmic encounter of the type Actium represents, yet the defeat of Sextus is clearly central to Octavian's creation of an imperial self-image. The background to this is complex. In the thirteenth Philippic (13.21.50), Cicero argues strenuously for reintegrating Sextus into the Roman state, "stressing his role as the servant of the Senate in all things and reformatting him as a shining contrast to Antony."[54] Antony clearly served an admirable purpose in offering up the antitype to Octavian's delineation of Romanness. Sextus appears in different terms: he enters the discussion from the wings, as it were, in the wake of his father's triumphs and failures. In this, though, he establishes what will become a recurring theme in discussions of his relationship with Octavian: unlike Antony, who opposes Octavian as night does day, Sextus mirrors Octavian, offering often an *unheimlich* echo of his career. In rising to power by virtue of his father, Sextus recalls Octavian's own rise in the wake of his adoptive parent, Julius Caesar. As Sextus's goal seems at times to avenge the death of his father, by appropriating and attacking his father's enemies, so Octavian's vengeance against Caesar's enemies propels the civil wars forward, culminating in the assertion of the *Res Gestae*: *qui parentem meum trucidaverunt, eos in exilium expuli iudiciis legitimis ultus eorum facinus* ("I drove into exile those who had killed my father, avenging their crime through legal tribunals").[55]

Octavian's identification with Sextus is confirmed by iconographic evidence. Most strikingly, Pompey the Great's identification with Neptune is borrowed first by his son Sextus, who proclaims himself "son of Neptune,"[56] and then by Augustus, who later appropriates this very iconography and so identifies eerily with his earlier opponent, Sextus.[57] Moreover, Octavian appropriates two other images Sextus had taken as his own as well. According to Paul Zanker, coins from the era between the victories of Naulochus and Actium

(36–31) show further evidence of this usurpation of Sextus's iconography. An earlier denarius, from 42–40 BC, shows Sextus or his father with his foot on a rostrum, indicating his defeat of Octavian's fleet. He is accompanied by the brothers from Catania rescuing their parents, a story well known from earlier coins as an instance of *pietas*. Sextus uses it to justify the epithet of *pius* that he had added to his own name to characterize his relationship to his father. But a denarius of Octavian, dated before 31 BC, shows him in the same pose as Pompey, with his foot on a rostrum, while the story of the Catanian brothers, who escaped from burning Etna with their father on their backs is clearly appropriated by Augustus, both on coins and in the story Vergil tells of Aeneas departing from Troy carrying his father Anchises. This image of *pietas*, so closely associated with Augustus through Vergil, originates as an image identified with Sextus, just like the pose he is shown taking on this coin and his subsequent identification with Neptune.[58]

Kathryn Welch argues that Sextus is known in the literature for his Roman virtues. He is, in essence, more Roman than Octavian, certainly opposed to Antony in this regard. As such he encroaches on Octavian's turf not just in iconographic and propagandistic terms, but also, for the popular imagination, in terms of what constitutes a leader. It is a difficult task Octavian assumes in trying to counter his double, especially when that double appears to be more what he wants to be than he is himself. He must both become Sextus and destroy him at the same time, without destroying his image in the process.[59] Unlike Antony, whose very existence defines Octavian, Sextus threatens Octavian at every turn. Sextus must be appropriated and erased in order for Octavian to dominate, but—and here is the critical move—the distinction between the two must remain as strongly marked as the identification.

Sextus offers history no Cleopatra. He does, however, become identified with Sicily in a way that parallels Antony's identification with Alexandria. His insistence on Sicily as a base for his naval operations is clearly inherited from strategies he saw succeed for his father, in terms of control of the sea, the supervision of the grain supply, and the fact that this island serves as a "strong point and refuge." Unlike the East and its avatars—Alexandria, Carthage, even Actium—Sicily sits solidly in the center of the Roman world, echoing more than opposing Rome. Sextus, likewise, mirrors rather than opposes Octavian. Even as Cleopatra and Alexandria become joined as the defining other in the Antony of Actium, so the good son and Sicily offer up a defining cluster to Octavian that he will use in creating his imperial self-definition. Where Antony provides the outer limits to this definition, Sextus, like Sicily, offers up something quite different. Throughout the literature, Octavian's encounters with Sextus are marked not by the defining and combative opposition we find in the discussions of Antony but, rather, by a series of similarities and encroachments. Sextus, in other words, offers to Octavian a basis on which to build his imperial image even as Sicily is represented by Cicero and by Vergil as the founding land of empire. Octavian no more wants to become Sextus than he does Antony, but his rhetoric must differ: he cannot kill Sextus off; he must absorb his power and move on.[60]

In moving from civil war to empire, then, two things happen that are played out through the stories told of Antony and Sextus. On the one hand, difference is externalized through Antony. By demonizing him, Octavian reinforces his own image. Every story told of Antony is, as we have seen, a story told of Octavian. On the other hand, the rift created by civil war is internalized through Sextus. There the differences are incorporated into a larger story—Sextus is made to disappear by virtue of an almost metamorphic process: as Octavian becomes Augustus, he absorbs the history and legend of Sextus and his island.[61] The difference remains, but it is the difference of growth, of gestation. Sextus and Sicily provide what amounts to the backstory for Augustus and his empire.[62]

A Narrative of Empire

Sicily, in its peculiar relationship to the mainland, in its literary portrayal, in its history as a site of civil war and as reputed first province, stands as an emblem of empire. It also offers a hermeneutic model to the reader that helps explain the blurring of significant divisions within the *Aeneid* even as it helps chart the development of the epic overall from discord to compromise, from division to common ground, all by way of the island that is and is not separate from the mainland. Let me offer a distant, but useful, analogy: in "Bryn Glas," Terence Hawkes offers a powerful reading of Shakespeare's *Henry V* through an interpretation of the roles played by Wales, France, and England. In this "construction of a new entity called Britain," Hawkes argues, France and Wales serve two distinct purposes.[63] On the one hand, France is a place that has become "sufficiently referential to be joked at.... We are what we oppose," he says. "That, to speak broadly, is what the French are traditionally for."[64]

The Welsh, according to Hawkes, serve a different function. Like the Irish and the Scots, they are not foreign but, rather, evidence of a culture that is "native and true." Hawkes argues that Shakespeare's play chronicles not so much the imposition "of a culture on a society that pre-exists it ... as [a] discovery and lay[ing] bare [of] a substratum that" has been obscured, with Wales providing the "underpinning for the new [British] identity."[65] Both France and Wales serve to define Britain, though in different ways: France by opposition, Wales by dependence. In Augustan literature, Sicily serves a role comparable to that of Wales. Like Wales in Hawkes's reading of *Henry V*, Sicily offers a striking instance of a location that, by virtue of its unique, dependent relationship to Italy, provides the "underpinning for the new national identity." The reunification suggested by Aeneas's journey around the island, which prefigures the inclusion of Juno in the compromise at the end of the poem, maintains within it the possibility of an imperial relationship that acknowledges difference. It also, though, offers the specter of a ground that grows too common, of a line that becomes too smudged, of an annihilation of difference in the interests of power.

Cicero's assertion of Sicily's potential remains a *locus classicus* for the outlines of empire. Because of Cicero's identification of Sicily as the first province, the island comes to offer a space for discussions of empire throughout Roman literature. But Sicily's importance to empire extends beyond Cicero. What Quintilian makes clear is that the physical relationship of Sicily to the mainland, its former unity, also plays a part in its importance. Vergil makes this point too, while also alluding to the centrality of both Sicily and Sextus to the origins of Augustus's empire. Sicily's placement at the start of the action of the *Aeneid* makes sense in this context: the poem of the empire is a story that starts with Sicily. What we have seen in the Latin texts ranging from Cicero to Quintilian is an increasing reliance on Sicily in descriptions and formulations of empire.

Yet Cicero's argument in the Verrine orations that includes this identification of Sicily as the origin of empire also frames the discussion with the tale of Proserpina's abduction. For Cicero, returning goods stolen from Sicily will enable the island to return to its productive status as province of Rome, even as returning Proserpina to her mother will restore the golden age. Vergil, as we have seen, also harks back to an earlier time, as current imperial moves are shown to have ancient roots. The geographic treatment of Sicily is for Vergil, as for these authors who preceded him, supplemented by a dynamic and mythic treatment of the island. As we will see in the next chapter, a dream of empire rooted in Cicero's view of Sicily and expanded upon through historic events cannot avoid a reading of the Proserpina myth.[66]

2

Drepanum and the Limits of the *Aeneid*

O socii (neque enim ignari sumus ante malorum)
o passi graviora, dabit deus his quoque finem.

—AEN. 1.198–99

AT THE start of *Aeneid* 5, the Trojans land for the third time on Sicily.[1] Here they discover that a full year has passed since the death of Anchises at Drepanum, and Aeneas proposes that they celebrate the anniversary with a series of funeral games in honor of his father. The commemoration works on several levels, all reinforced by Sicily's geography as an island. By the end of *Aeneid* 5, we have Anchises (and, indirectly, Dido)[2] laid to rest; we have the older Trojans left on Sicily; we even have Palinurus, helmsman from the beginning, replaced by Aeneas. Things associated with the past are seemingly contained on the island of Sicily, left behind as the Trojans embark on the final leg of their journey to the mainland of Italy and the process of becoming Roman.

When, then, we start seeing a number of these reminders of the past reappear—including the Trojan Caieta, who does not remain on Sicily but is buried on the mainland of Italy; Anchises, who appears prominently in the underworld; and characters including Nisus and Euryalus who compete in a footrace in *Aeneid* 5 and then recall that event in battle in *Aeneid* 9—when, in other words, the effort to segregate things of the past on Sicily seems to fail, we are left wondering anew about the purpose of *Aeneid* 5 and Sicily. Sicily may be introduced as the burial ground of the first third of the epic, but when virtually everything buried there resurfaces on Italy, we are asked to rethink the dynamics of the plan sketched out in *Aeneid* 3.

Recall Helenus's description of the island's origin there:

> haec loca vi quondam et vasta convulsa ruina
> (tantum aevi longinqua valet mutare vetustas) 415
> dissiluisse ferunt, cum protinus utraque tellus
> una foret: venit medio vi pontus et undis
> Hesperium Siculo latus abscidit, arvaque et urbes
> litore diductas angusto interluit aestu. (*Aen.* 3.414–19)

(These lands, they say, once wrenched by force and great catastrophe (long stretches of time can make such changes), tore apart; when before both lands were one, the sea came between with force and with its waters cut the Hesperian side from the Sicilian, and washed between fields and towns divided from the shore by its narrow tide.)

Recall also how this description fits in *Aeneid* 3 with the definition of empire in the journey post-Troy: lands that once belonged to Aeneas and his men provide a source of continuity that empire is trying to recapture while also maintaining the identity of each incorporated culture. The recurrence of these Sicilian elements later in the *Aeneid*, however, suggests that the vision of empire that Vergil first presented may not be as simple as it seemed.

In the *Aeneid* as a whole, Sicily, with its peculiar relationship to the mainland, its mythic characterization, and its history as a site of the last skirmishes of civil war and reputed first province, stands as an emblem of empire. While we are inclined to approach the *Aeneid* as a poem of opposites—*furor* versus *pietas*; Juno versus Jupiter; Troy (or Carthage) versus Rome—the prominence of Sicily suggests that the poem resists such an approach, and to the extent that Sextus Pompey surfaces as significant in Augustan history, so Sicily offers Vergil a narrative model based as much on accommodation as on opposition.

Yet accommodation is a two-edged sword. If Sicily were present in the poem only to enable discussion of the push and pull of imperial rule, the political agenda outlined in the first chapter would be sufficient to capture Vergil's argument about the island. But the fifth book of the *Aeneid*, which takes place almost entirely on Sicily, offers a very different view of the island. Through this we are forced to revise our understanding of the relationship between the island and empire in Vergil. For while the political and geographic view of Sicily we are offered in *Aeneid* 3 presents a dream of future empire as accommodating and inclusive, the literary and mythic approach that accompanies it in *Aeneid* 5 demonstrates the pragmatic difficulties of such a scheme and the problems of such an imperial plan: the literary, in short, offers a commentary on, if not revision of, the political. To put this another way, while the geographic descriptions of Sicily we examined in the last chapter look forward to the imperial project of Vergil's day, with Aeneas presented as laying the groundwork for decisions Augustus later makes, the literary presentation developed in *Aeneid* 5 looks back to mythic origins, including the abduction of Proserpina, that predate Aeneas to expose rifts in the deep substrata of empire.

Absence of Proserpina

At the end of *Aeneid* 3, as Aeneas is rounding Sicily with the Greek Achaemenides on board, Vergil lists the names of Sicilian towns and their eponymous myths, including Ortygia, Alpheus, Arethusa, Helorus, Pachynus, Camerina, Gela, Acragas, Selinus, and Lilybaeum (*Aen.* 3.692–706). Vergil pointedly does not mention Proserpina herself, even though Alpheus and Arethusa are key players in her tale. That myth, in fact, is not mentioned at all, either in *Aeneid* 3 or when the Trojans return to the island in *Aeneid* 5.

Yet Vergil is not unaware of the myth of Proserpina or its imperial resonance. In the proem to *Georgics* 1, Vergil addresses Octavian, expounding on the unknown reach of his future empire and enthusiastically encouraging him, at first, to extend his empire on land and sea (and eventually even inhabit the sky):

> tuque adeo, quem mox quae sint habitura deorum
> concilia incertum est, urbisne invisere, Caesar,   25
> terrarumque velis curam, et te maximus orbis
> auctorem frugum tempestatumque potentem
> accipiat cingens materna tempora myrto;
> an deus immensi venias maris ac tua nautae
> numina sola colant, tibi serviat ultima Thule,   30
> teque sibi generum Tethys emat omnibus undis;
> anne novum tardis sidus te mensibus addas,
> qua locus Erigonen inter Chelasque sequentis.
> panditur (ipse tibi iam bracchia contrahit ardens
> Scorpius et caeli iusta plus parte reliquit) (*Geo.* 1.24–35)

(And you, indeed, Caesar, although it remains unclear what your place will soon be among the councils of the gods, whether you wish to watch over our cities and have care of the lands, so that the great expanse of the world, binding your temples with maternal myrtle, will receive you as creator of the crops and ruler of our seasons; or whether you will come as god of the enormous sea, your godhead alone sailors will worship, while ultimate Thule serves you, and Tethys offers all her waves as dowry for you as son-in-law; or whether you will add yourself as a new star to the late months, where between Virgo and the subsequent Claws a space opens up (burning Scorpio himself now draws in his arms to make more than adequate room for you in the sky).[3]

But Vergil balks at the notion of Octavian conquering the Underworld:

... nam te nec sperant Tartara regem,
nec tibi regnandi veniat tam dira cupido,
quamvis Elysios miretur Graecia campos,
nec repetita sequi curet Proserpina matrem) (*Geo.* 1.36–39)

(For Hell does not hope for you as king: do not let so dread a desire of ruling touch you, although Greece may admire the Elysian Fields, and Proserpina, sought again, may not care to follow her mother.)[4]

Octavian is advised to avoid extending his empire into the underworld since, if his reach extends there, Proserpina may refuse to return. In the *Georgics* this is expressed in agricultural terms: what is at stake is the very nature of Italy as a land rooted in agricultural fertility that would be destroyed if Proserpina did not return.[5] All versions of the myth provide a glimpse of this imbalance when Proserpina's temporary absence is allied with Ceres' wrath, and drought and infertility mark the landscape. To suggest that such a state could be permanent should Proserpina never return is to suggest a dire agricultural situation indeed. With this in mind, it seems disturbing that Proserpina is not mentioned in the list of Sicilian myths in *Aeneid* 3: is she in fact (still) missing? And, if she is missing, how does this play out in the epic, as opposed to the georgic, landscape? When we add to this the fact that Vergil does mention both Proserpina and her mother Ceres elsewhere in the epic, this omission seems telling indeed.

The first place Ceres is mentioned is perhaps the most critical. When Aeneas and his men prepare to leave Troy on its last night, Aeneas instructs his men to meet at the temple of Ceres outside the city:

est urbe egressis tumulus templumque vetustum
desertae Cereris, iuxtaque antiqua cupressus

religione patrum multos servata per annos;   715
hanc ex diverso sedem veniemus in unam. (*Aen.* 2.713–16)

(As one leaves the city, there is a mound and ancient temple of abandoned Ceres, and an ancient cypress nearby preserved for a long time by the beliefs of our fathers. We will meet at this one spot from many directions.)

It is Servius who suggests a telling reading of this passage, arguing that Ceres in *Aeneid* 2 is *deserta* because Proserpina has been abducted.[6] If this is so, the Trojans' journey would be set in the time between Proserpina's abduction and recovery, during the time, that is, when all limits are erased and Ceres blights the landscape. This reading is supported by her next mention where Ceres' loss of Proserpina is linked with Aeneas's own loss of Creusa:

nec prius amissam respexi animumve reflexi
quam tumulum antiquae Cereris sedemque sacratam
venimus: hic demum collectis omnibus una
defuit... (*Aen.* 2.741–44)

(I did not look back for her, missing, or cast my mind back before we reached the mound and sacred site of ancient Ceres: here, with everyone gathered at last, she alone was missing...)

It is at the tomb of Ceres that Aeneas realizes that he has lost sight of his wife Creusa somewhere in the chaos of leaving Troy: Ceres' loss is replayed in Aeneas's own as the ambiguity of *una defuit*—is it Creusa or Proserpina?—rings in our ears.[7]

At the end of *Aeneid* 4, after Dido has committed suicide, Iris releases Dido's spirit to the afterlife by cutting a symbolic lock of hair as an offering to Proserpina (*nondum illi flavum Proserpina vertice crinem / abstulerat... ergo Iris... "hunc ego Diti / sacrum iussa fero teque isto corpore solvo": / sic ait et dextra crinem secat*, *Aen.* 4. 698–700, 702–4 [not yet had Proserpina borne away the golden lock from her head... so Iris...: "I take this offering to Dis as ordered and free you from that body of yours"; thus she speaks and cuts the strand with her right hand]), which reinforces both Vergil's awareness of the myth of Proserpina and Aeneas's place on the mythic timeline.[8] At the time of Aeneas's visit to Carthage, Proserpina is queen of the underworld, ruling the spirits there and judging their fitness for the afterlife. No mention is made of her return to earth; the suggestion is, rather, that she resides in the underworld and that she is therefore still absent.[9]

These references to Proserpina suggest that the chronology of the *Aeneid* overall is located after her abduction by Hades but before a regular cycle of return has been established. Nowhere does Vergil suggest that Proserpina ever comes to earth, that her mother and her temple are associated with anything other than loss.[10] We seem to be locked in the moment after Ceres loses Proserpina, but before any compromise is struck with Hades that would allow for even temporary or cyclical resolution. What I am suggesting is that the *Aeneid* overall, the journey from Troy to Rome, takes place in the time between Proserpina's abduction and Ceres' compromise.

The next time Iris appears, again at the request of Juno, it is on Sicily, towards the end of *Aeneid* 5 as the Trojan women are weeping over the loss of Anchises and the retreating goal of Italy (*Aen.* 5.613–40). Again, the theme is one of loss, and mothers weeping over loss. Since, at least from Cicero on, the site of Ceres' loss and her journey were identified with Sicily, the vignette of maternal figures weeping on Sicily brings the Proserpina myth to mind, a suggestion reinforced by the fact that Iris's previous act in the poem was to visit Proserpina in the underworld. Both Troy and Italy stand in for Proserpina here as the women speak of loss, past and future: of Anchises, Troy, and *Italiam fugientem*. Iris inspires the women to set fire to the boats; because of the destruction of four ships, the old women and some old men are left on the island. Sicily is a place that becomes identified with familial loss.[11]

As we have seen, the myth of Proserpina is deployed in the Verrine orations to speak about the nature of empire. For Cicero, the past is presented as golden, and the myth of Proserpina is written as a myth of return: once extricated from its corrupt governor, Sicily will again become the model province. Not only does Cicero identify Sicily here as essential to the Roman Empire, he also describes its current political situation in the context of the Proserpina myth, as his speech against Verres presents him as a latter-day Hades, plundering the island that first made empire desirable:[12]

> Non illi decumarum imperia, non bonorum direptiones, non iniqua iudicia, non importunas istius libidines, non vim, non contumelias, quibus vexati oppressique erant, conquerebantur; Cereris numen, sacrorum vetustatem, fani religionem istius sceleratissimi atque audacissimi supplicio expiari volebant; omnia se cetera pati ac neglegere dicebant. Hic dolor erat tantus, ut Verres alter Orcus venisse Hennam et non Proserpinam asportasse sed ipsam abripuisse Cererem videretur. (*Verr.* 2.4.50.111–12)

(It was not his excessive exaction of tithes, not the plundering of goods, not the unfair courts, not this man's acts of persistent lust, not his violence, not his rudeness, of which these troubled and oppressed people now complained: the holiness of Ceres, the antiquity of her rites, the sanctity of her temple, this is what they wished atonement for through the punishment of this utterly unscrupulous and brazen man: all else they said they were ready to endure and ignore. So great was their distress that one might imagine that Verres, another Orcus, had come to Henna, and not abducted Proserpina but carried Ceres herself away.)

Underlying this myth of empire lies a narrative of a golden age that can be recovered and maintained. Vergil's version of this, as we have seen, is different. While both Cicero and Vergil set Sicily centrally in the question of empire, each presents it differently. Cicero's version of the myth suggests that the loss Sicily has suffered can be repaired, and the ensuing return of the golden age will mark the reconstruction of the empire made perfect by Sicily. Vergil too turns to Sicily, its geography and its history, to suggest an ideal of empire that recovery of past unities might establish. This is the message of *Aeneid* 3. He also, however, points out how such a view of the past and of empire can only be grounded in loss. By setting Aeneas's journey during Proserpina's absence, he captures Ceres in a state of eternal grieving, and plays out, on an epic scale, the ramifications of the anxiety expressed at the start of the *Georgics*. The myth of Proserpina pushes on the edges of the story of empire Vergil tells on Sicily and colors the events with images of loss and the impossibility of recovery: while from one perspective this can be seen as the story of the transformation of the past into a future, from another, it is the story of the persistence of the past in an empire marked by a lack of limits.

Proserpina's Absence Reiterated

The bulk of *Aeneid* 5, however, does not seem to be about absence. Instead, the book revolves around the funeral games played by the Trojans and Sicilians in honor of the anniversary of Anchises' death and, as such, would seem set to present loss as a necessary and natural step toward forward progress.[13] The first of these games, a boat race, draws attention to itself because it is the most detailed and because it refers to numerous authors, Greek and Latin; again, its artificiality would seem to imitate the process of poetic creation and to suggest that Vergil, like the Trojans, is transforming the poetic past into a new Roman future.

While the significance of games per se will be something to which we will return, let us begin by looking carefully at the boat race in its Sicilian setting.

The opening words of the race's description, *Est procul*, invoke a formulaic epic phrase indicating a set piece, a passage that will function, much like an ekphrasis, to comment on the work as a whole. We are thus prepared to read the race metatextually, as guide to the poem.[14] It comes as no great surprise, given this, that the race includes references to earlier passages from the *Aeneid*.[15] Aeneas, as organizer of the competition, establishes the *meta* off the coast of Sicily; *meta* is a word used in *Aeneid* 3.714 to refer to Sicily itself: *hic labor extremus, longarum haec meta viarum*. The race is described as *et longos ubi circumflectere cursus* (*Aen.* 5.131), virtually the same phrase used by Helenus in *Aeneid* 3.430 (*longos et circumflectere cursus*) to advise the Trojans to circumnavigate the island, rather than sailing by Scylla and Charybdis. The fate of two of the boats in the race again echoes Helenus's advice to avoid the rocks of Scylla by leaning on the oars (*insurgite remis* in both *Aeneid* 3.560 and 5.189); one crashing, the other avoiding them too widely, both boats enact the near disasters of the Trojans at the straits of Messina.[16]

That we are to view the boat race as emblematic of the journey of the *Aeneid* seems clear. Yet the race also alludes to other poets. Within the first few lines, the connection with Homer is made explicit: in the first simile of the game the boats are likened to chariots in a race, which takes the reader directly back to the primary source for the passage, the chariot race in *Iliad* 23.[17] And, as Damien Nelis has carefully demonstrated, the race also draws directly on Apollonius. The events of each of the four of the boats entered in the race can be seen to allude to an event in the *Argonautica*. As a result, the Hellenistic tale is refracted through this competition in particular.[18]

The importance of these allusions, however, lies in the way Vergil transforms them. The emphasis he places on the boat names has no precedent in Homer, where neither the horses nor the chariots are specifically named. The shift from land to sea, logical in the context of the island of Sicily, is also, however, a further metatextual sign: even as Aeneas and his men have been involved in a long sea voyage, so the first race will encapsulate and replay that voyage on some level.[19]

In addition, Vergil uses the race to suggest the kind of changes that are in store for the Trojans. Michael Putnam has argued that the boat race (as well as the prize cloak of Cloanthus) foreshadows the loss of Palinurus and the death of Turnus.[20] Noting that the action of the epic at the start of *Aeneid*. 1 begins "precisely at the moment when the ships leave the boundaries [later] set for the competition," Andrew Feldherr argues that the boat race is the first in a series of spectacles that offers "a new context for understanding how even such radically disparate and destabilizing forces as the anger of Juno and the sorrow of the Trojan women can be accommodated within a larger structure whose aim is to create and actualize an image of order."[21] If the *meta*, then, of the race, is also on some level analogous to the larger *meta* of Sicily, then arguably the helmsman Menoetes who gets thrown overboard during the race is not just proleptic of Palinurus[22] but also reminiscent of Anchises, another "helmsman" who is left on the *meta* of Sicily when he died at the end of *Aeneid* 3. Menoetes is, after all, described as *iam senior* (*Aen.* 5.179) as he climbs onto the rock, a phrase suggestive of the older Anchises.

That the boat race emblematizes change seems clear. Yet the nature of that transformation remains to be discovered and, as we shall see, my understanding of the message of the boat race differs from that of Feldherr. The four boats are introduced as follows:

> Prima pares ineunt gravibus certamina remis
> quattuor ex omni delectae classe carinae.   115
> velocem Mnestheus agit acri remige Pristim,
> mox Italus Mnestheus, genus a quo nomine Memmi,
> ingentemque Gyas ingenti mole Chimaeram,
> urbis opus, triplici pubes quam Dardana versu
> impellunt, terno consurgunt ordine remi;   120
> Sergestusque, domus tenet a quo Sergia nomen,
> Centauro invehitur magna, Scyllaque Cloanthus
> caerulea, genus unde tibi, Romane Cluenti. (*Aen.* 5.114–23)

(They enter the first race, equal in their heavy oars, four chosen from the entire fleet. Mnestheus, soon to be Italian Mnestheus from whose name comes the line of Memmius, with fervent oarsmen drives swift Pristis. Then Gyas huge Chimaera, with its huge mass, as big as a city, which Dardan youth in triple tiers propel; the oars rise up in triple row. And Sergestus, from whom the Sergian house holds its name, rode the great Centauro, and Cloanthus the sea-blue Scylla, the origin of your line, Roman Cluentius.)

Although the captains are all explicitly linked to future Roman families, all four of the boat names are allied with monstrous animals, associated more with the Greek mythological past than with the Roman future. Pristis, Chimaera, Centaurus, and Scylla are all names that show up in Greek natural histories or mythology. Hardie suggests that the reader is to think back to the original cosmic struggles (especially through Chimaera and its association through Gyas to the gigantomachy) and, because they are ships, ahead to the contemporary struggles of Naulochus and Actium.[23]

It seems clear that the boat race, with its turning point, is to be taken as a figurative representation of the kind of realignment necessary for Trojan to become Roman.[24] In addition, when the *meta* is rounded, the order of the boats changes: Cloanthus wins, Sergestus loses. The reorganization of the boats themselves is more significant than the names of the men involved, whom Vergil has already indicated are all founders of prominent Roman houses. But Vergil's choice of boat names is also directly linked to Lucretian and Empedoclean cosmology, and the boat race serves to draw those authors into the poetic conversation as well.

In *De rerum natura*, Lucretius alludes to the boundedness of Sicily to highlight its transformative nature in an effort to rewrite and undermine his predecessor Empedocles:

> quorum Acragantinus cum primis Empedocles est,
> insula quem triquetris terrarum gessit in oris,
> quam fluitans circum magnis anfractibus aequor
> Ionium glaucis aspargit virus ab undis,
> angustoque fretu rapidum mare dividit undis   720
> Aeoliae terrarum oras a finibus eius.
> hic est vasta Charybdis et hic Aetnaea minantur
> murmura flammarum rursum se colligere iras,
> faucibus eruptos iterum vis ut vomat ignis
> ad caelumque ferat flammai fulgura rursum. (*DRN* 1.716–25)

(Of them in the forefront comes Empedocles of Acragas; him that island bore within the three-cornered coasts of its lands, around which flows the Ionian ocean, with large winding inlets, splashing salt foam from its green waves, while with narrow strait a tearing sea sunders with its waves the coasts of Aeolia's lands from its island-borders. Here is devastating Charybdis, and here the rumblings of Aetna threaten to gather once more the flames of its wrath, that again in its might it may belch forth the fires bursting from its throat, and once more dash to the sky its flashing flames.)[25]

The aspect of Empedocles to which Lucretius refers here argues that the origins of things lie in the combining of the four elements. As Bailey notes, Empedocles "held that the 'four roots,' as he called them ... themselves remained permanent and unchanged, but produced the world of things by combining with one another in various proportions."[26] Using Sicily as a counterexample, Lucretius argues that the elements remain distinct: the land is bounded, the sea separates Sicily from Italy, fire is distinct from air. All is closed and confined, even if that distinction is, in the case of the Sicilian straits, only the width of his smallest linguistic *elementa*, a (720–21: *angustoque fretu rapidum mare dividit undis / Aeoliae terrarum oras a finibus eius*).[27]

Strikingly, Vergil's passages in *Aeneid* 3 about Sicily (especially *Aeneid* 3.571–77) counter this passage from Lucretius. The lines surrounding the description of Etna which *atram prorumpit ad aethera nubem ... et sidera lambit* ("breaks through the black cloud to the heavens ... and licks the stars") where even the rocks are *liquefacta*, suggest that, even as Lucretius uses Sicily to rework Empedocles, so Vergil will use Sicily to rework Lucretius. Here Vergil's Sicily is defined not by its boundedness but rather by its permeability, and the shadowy outlines of Lucretius's debate with Empedocles here makes this all the clearer. The suggestion made in Helenus's prophecy that Sicily's relationship to the mainland is emblematic of empire is here expanded as Sicily becomes marked by a complicated exchange among a number of poets: through the lens of Lucretius and Empedocles, the epic poems of Homer, Apollonius, and even Vergil come to be viewed as poetic cosmologies.

That reworking continues into *Aeneid* 5. Throughout the depiction of the boat race, in addition to his interaction with the Greek epic poets Homer and Apollonius, Vergil highlights his place in the literary tradition by direct engagement with the other main Latin treatment of Sicily by Lucretius, and he uses this opportunity to broker that poet's conversation with Empedocles. But in contrast to *Aeneid* 3, where the focus is turned toward the future and the time of Vergil and Augustus, in *Aeneid* 5 the emphasis lies on the past and the role poetry plays in revising our understanding of the world.

For not only do the names of the boats point us back toward Greece, but each of the monsters indicated by the names is associated with one of the four roots outlined by Empedocles (*Physics* 7–11), subsequently glossed by Lucretius in *DRN* 1.714–15 and 783–86 as elements.[28] Those passages are worth looking at more closely:

> ... et qui quattuor ex rebus posse omnia rentur
> ex igni terra atque anima procrescere et imbri ...   715
> et primum faciunt ignem se vertere in auras

aeris, hinc imbrem gigni terramque creari
ex imbri retroque a terra cuncta reverti,   785
umorem primum, post aera, deinde calorem . . .

(. . . and those who think that all can grow up out of four things, [from] fire, earth, wind, and rain . . . hold that fire first turns itself into the breezes of air, that thence is begotten rain, and of rain is created earth, and then all things pass back again from earth, first moisture, next air, then heat . . .)²⁹

Note how the first line of this passage, *et qui quattuor ex rebus posse omnia rentur*, is echoed suggestively in the opening of Vergil's description, *Quattuor ex omni delectae classe carinae*, with *quattuor ex* being followed by a form of *omnis*. Vergil's boats point us back to Lucretius's elements.

Moreover, with the exception of Pristis, the boat names are all associated in Augustan texts with particular elements, and Pristis, though rare as a word, is still clearly linked with water, meaning either shark (or sawfish) or sea vessel. *Chimaera*, in Horace's *Carmina* 2.17.13–14, is linked not only with his helmsman, Gyas, but also with fire (*me nec Chimaerae spiritus igneae / nec si resurgat centimanus Gyges [Gyas] divellet umquam*).³⁰ Centaurus, in Propertius 4.6.49–50, is associated with rocks and earth: *quotque vehunt prorae Centaurica saxa minantes; / tigna cava et pictos experiere metus*. Scylla presents, perhaps, the weakest link, if taken, as Hardie does, to indicate the monster; both mentions of the monstrous Scylla in the *Aeneid* do employ the word *caerulea*.³¹ However, the argument for reading Scylla as Scylla Nisi appears equally strong, since it would seem odd to name a boat after an immovable monster, especially one which had so recently threatened Aeneas and his men, and since Vergil had a history of conflating the two stories: *Eclogue* 6.74 refers to the monster as Scylla Nisi, the traditional term for the bird, which Clausen at least sees as "deliberately conflated."³² Perhaps most striking, however, is the fact that the pseudo-Vergilian *Ciris* refers to the transformed bird in terms of her *caeruleis alis*, thus suggesting that there was at some time a tradition of describing the bird as sea-blue.³³ It seems possible, in fact, that Vergil himself may have been drawing on this tradition in his earlier description of Scylla and Charybdis, which would reinforce, rather than reverse, the identification of the boat with the bird. As Scylla Nisi, the element in question is air. All four of the root elements are thus allegorically represented by the four boats.

On the far western shore of Sicily, at the part of the island, as of the text, where the Trojans have reached a critical turning point, Vergil steps back from the main plot to look at that story symbolically, as a synopsis of the journey the Trojans have taken, as well as a foreshadowing of what is yet to come. In this highly artificial context, the boats are given names that seem at the start allied in form and content, via allegory and action, with the elements found in Lucretius: fire, air, water, and earth, and in the order he presents them:

> Effugit ante alios primisque elabitur undis
> turbam inter fremitumque Gyas; quem deinde Cloanthus
> consequitur, melior remis, sed pondere pinus
> tarda tenet. Post hos aequo discrimine Pristis
> Centaurusque locum tendunt superare priorem; 155
> et nunc Pristis habet, nunc victam praeterit ingens
> Centaurus, nunc una ambae iunctisque feruntur
> frontibus et longa sulcant vada salsa carina. (*Aen.* 5.151–58)

(Fleeing the others in the first waves Gyas slips away from the pack amid the turmoil and noise; whom Cloanthus follows closely, better with oars, but the slow ship is held back by its weight. After them, Pristis and Centaurus at equal distance try to gain the lead: now Pristis holds it, now huge Centaurus outstrips her, conquered, now both together, with matched prows, and they are borne along and furrow the salt water with long keel.)

Moreover, the adventures of each boat reflect its element. On the Chimaera, which calls up Lucretian fire, Gyas, angry over his cautious helmsman Menoetes' unwillingness to hug the *meta*, *exarsit ossibus* ("burns in his bones," *Aen.* 5.172). Mnestheus, captain of the fishlike Pristis, is the one Trojan in the race to pray to Neptune, and he does so via an aposiopesis in 195 that recalls the god's own in *Aeneid* 1.[34] He causes his men to work so hard that *sudor fluit undique rivis* (*Aen.* 5.200), and he is the first to reach the open sea. Sergestus, on the earthen Centaurus, runs famously aground; his return is described through the simile of a snake, with its chthonic overtones, struggling to move after having been run over by a chariot's wheel (*Aen.* 5.273–79). Cloanthus, the victor, and owner of the Scylla, flies *citius volucrique sagitta* ("faster than a swift arrow," *Aen.* 5.242).[35]

When the race is over, the winners are clear. While Gyas and Cloanthus compete for the lead, Cloanthus, sneaking through the space between Gyas and a rock, a space Gyas's helmsman refused to close up, darts out in front. Of the back two, Sergestus gains but does not overtake Mnestheus, and then grounds his boat on a reef, putting him out of commission. Having passed Sergestus, Mnestheus then overtakes Gyas (who is floundering, having thrown his helmsman overboard), and then aims to overtake the one remaining competitor, Cloanthus. He almost succeeds, but Cloanthus invokes the god of harbors, Portunus, who, in turn, calls on the nearby Nereids to work together and speed him to shore ahead of Mnestheus.

But while the boats begin in the same order Lucretius argues the elements held at the beginning of the cosmos, they end up differently.[36] Air and water clearly win, ahead of the other two. Vergil suggests that, like the boats, the elements of Aeneas's universe are, at this *meta* in their journey, rearranged. The Trojan world, the world of origin, through the adversities and mishaps of the first four books of the *Aeneid*, has been reorganized to become or to create the proto-Roman world indicated by the names of the boat owners and suggested by the *lusus Troiae* played by the young, future Romans, at the end of the book.

Yet I would suggest that it is Empedocles, rather than Lucretius, who offers the context for understanding the outcome of the race, a reading that brings us back to Proserpina in the process. Even as Lucretius uses Sicily to confront his Greek forebear, so Vergil, in his book about the island addresses and confronts his Greek inheritance. In so doing, he revises the Greek notion of the island as a Greek outpost and claims it for Rome. Joseph Farrell has pointed out that Vergil's aim here is to align himself with Empedocles in order to improve on the original. Farrell's argument rests on the way in which Lucretius's efforts at distinction are here undermined; Vergil distorts the "fact of physical geography" by suggesting that Acragas is just across this strait and that the "Ionian" sea circles the island. "The island itself is presented as if it were composed of Empedocles' four elements," interacting much as Empedocles, not Lucretius, would have understood them.[37] Beyond citing Lucretius, then, Vergil is also, it would appear, offering a verbal cosmology comparable to the worldview offered by Empedocles. Even as the elements exist in flux, constantly interacting, so Vergil's language, especially in the presence of Etna, but also again in *Aeneid* 5, speaks of Empedoclean flux and recombination.[38]

As we have seen, the emphasis on flux in *Aeneid* 3 confirms the theme of accommodation that runs throughout that book. A different message surfaces in *Aeneid* 5. While Empedocles' four roots quickly become glossed in the tradition as the four elements, largely because of the way they are presented at the opening of Lucretius's poem, they are not identified that way originally. Instead, in Empedocles' work, the four roots are identified with gods: Zeus, Hera, Aidoneus, and Nestis.[39] The first three are readily identified in Roman mythology as Jupiter, Juno, and Hades; the fourth, Nestis, is little attested even in the Greek, and the identity remains uncertain. However, the few references that do exist gloss her as either Proserpina or "a Sicilian goddess" and align her with water, or a combination of air and water.[40] In this context, then, the order of the race becomes particularly interesting. At its start, Gyas and Cloanthus, Juno and Jupiter, lead, with Sergestus and Mnestheus, Hades and Proserpina, following behind. At the end, Jupiter wins by pulling rank, while Proserpina outstrips Hades and comes in second. Juno loses. Putting aside Juno's loss at this point—something we will return to later—we need to look carefully at the progress of the other three. In particular, we should look at the race of Mnestheus on the Pristis, the one most closely allied with Proserpina, or at least "a Sicilian goddess."

The Pristis begins at the back, tied with Sergestus on the Centaurus (*Aen.* 5.186–87: *nec tota tamen ille prior praeeunte carina; / parte prior, partim rostro premit aemula Pristis*). Yet, at the turning point, Mnestheus's boat shoots past as Sergestus crashes on the rocks and is described through the following simile:

> qualis spelunca subito commota columba,
> cui domus et dulces latebroso in pumice nidi,
> fertur in arva volans plausumque exterrita pennis   215
> dat tecto ingentem, mox aere lapsa quieto
> radit iter liquidum celeris neque commovet alas:
> sic Mnestheus, sic ipsa fuga secat ultima Pristis
> aequora, sic illam fert impetus ipse volantem. (*Aen.* 5.213–19)

(just like a dove suddenly disturbed from her cave, one whose home and dear nestlings lie in the sheltering pumice, is borne flying into the fields and, terrified from her home, gives a huge clap with her wings; soon, slipping through the quiet air, she skims on a smooth path and does not flap her swift wings. Thus Mnestheus, thus Pristis herself cuts across the remaining water in flight, thus drive itself carries her, flying.)

Many, including recently Fratantuono and Smith, have commented on how this simile introduces the dove who will later be the focus of the archery contest.[41] There is no question this pairing is intentional on Vergil's part, but as we read through *Aeneid* 5, we do not yet know of this event; it is only in retrospect that we see these two passages together. More fruitful a comparison can be drawn between Vergil and Apollonius. In particular, in book 2 of the *Argonautica*, a dove is sent ahead of the Argo at the crashing rocks to see the way and test the safety of the journey.[42] That dove, like this one, is terrified; that one, like this one, makes it through safely, as do the Argonauts who follow in her wake. Apollonius places the crashing rocks in a strait similar to that at Messina, but I think we need to see this event also as a harbinger of what is to come. Drawing on Apollonius, Vergil is suggesting that the boat likened to the dove will make it safely through its journeys.

That boat, however, is also the one allied, via Empedocles, with Proserpina. If we understand Vergil as commenting on Apollonius, as revising that story in the context of Empedocles, then perhaps we can understand the simile in a different context: the dove simile calls up Apollonius, but in a way that points up the differences between the two authors. This dove does not prevail, although it does survive. Beating the boat it is first paired with, it nonetheless is not the out-and-out winner. But it makes sense that the journeys be distinguished. The Argonauts sailed before the Trojan War, and Apollonius's tale provides the back story to the Homeric epics. Vergil's poem tells of the aftermath of that same war, of what happens in the wake of such destruction and displacement. We are, in other words, at a different point on the mythic timeline. In Apollonius, the Argonauts visit an island where Proserpina is characterized in line 897 as "still unbroken":

νῆα δ' εὐκραὴς ἄνεμος φέρεν· αἶψα δὲ νῆσον
καλὴν Ἀνθεμόεσσαν ἐσέδρακον, ἔνθα λίγειαι
Σειρῆνες σίνοντ' Ἀχελωΐδες ἡδείῃσιν
θέλγουσαι μολπῇσιν, ὅ τις παρὰ πεῖσμα βάλοιτο.
τὰς μὲν ἄρ' εὐειδὴς Ἀχελωΐῳ εὐνηθεῖσα   895
γείνατο Τερψιχόρη, Μουσέων μία· καί ποτε Δηοῦς
θυγατέρ' ἰφθίμην ἀδμῆτ' ἔτι πορσαίνεσκον
ἄμμιγα μελπόμεναι· τότε δ' ἄλλο μὲν οἰωνοῖσιν,
ἄλλο δὲ παρθενικῆς ἐναλίγκιαι ἔσκον ἰδέσθαι. (*Arg.* 4.891–99)

(The brisk wind propelled the ship, and soon they spotted the beautiful island of Anthemoessa, where the clear-voiced Sirens, the daughters of Achelous, enchanted anyone who moored there with their sweet songs and destroyed him. Beautiful Terpsichore, one of the Muses, had slept with Achelous and bore them. At one time they looked after Demeter's mighty daughter and played with her while she was still unbroken.)[43]

By contrast, in the *Aeneid* the Trojans visit a Sicily bereft of Proserpina and Ceres, at a time when a mother's loss is reiterated. We catch a glimpse of Proserpina outstripping Hades, but not quite winning out over her father Jupiter. Instead, he prevails, as he will when the deal is struck in the myth:

Proserpina will return to earth, but it is Jupiter who will ultimately determine the terms of the compromise.

We would not want to push this argument too far, but at Drepanum a race between forces allied with nature and the elements ends up with a boat allied with Proserpina escaping while terrified. If we return to the elemental level, it also seems to point to the future of Rome in a way that suggests, further, how Vergil perceived Proserpina. The second half of the *Aeneid* begins with the burial of Caieta whose name, as Servius notes, ad *Aeneid* 7.2, links fire and land explicitly.[44] Yet fire and land are also elements associated with Ceres, particularly in her period of mourning when she blights the soil by withholding water from the crops, linking fire and earth. As long as Proserpina is away, fire and earth are joined, crops are made impossible, the earlier balance is disrupted.

As we have seen, the message of Vergil's proem to *Georgic* 1 is that Proserpina's failure to return would disturb the order of the seasons, which are readily translated into the elements; Ovid's version is perhaps even more illuminating. As we will examine in detail in the next chapter, it is on Mt. Erice, adjacent to the location of the games and overseeing the precise stretch of ocean where the boat race takes place, that Venus asks Cupid to cause Hades to abduct Proserpina. Ovid presents this decision as an expansion of Venus's realm, but the erasure of limits it implies is introduced here in *Aeneid* 5. An empire that expands to include Hades, an empire defined by the abduction of Proserpina, is an empire that knows no bounds.[45]

The Sicilian boat race, when read carefully, suggests that the journey of this epic speaks to a cosmological shift that moves from a certain order to an undoing of that order, from an old balance of forces to a system in which hegemony rules and in which limits are ignored in the name of empire.

Reorganization and Limits

What I am suggesting is that we see *Aeneid* 5 as a book that takes place after Proserpina is abducted, but before any resolution or compromise has been reached, an action hinted at by the result of the boat race. It is a book that plays out the concerns Vergil voices in the proem to the first *Georgic*, one that sets the risks of empire in the context of the myth of Proserpina. It is also, thus, a book about permeability, about the impossibility of segregating the past, the tradition, death, and difference from the future in Rome. But it is also clearly a book about games.[46] Why games are associated with empire is explained not only by reference to Homer and Apollonius but also by internal reference to

Vergil's own definition of the Roman empire. In the first book of the epic, Jupiter explains to Venus that Aeneas will make it to Rome, and empire will be founded: *his ego nec metas rerum nec tempora pono: / imperium sine fine dedi* ("I set neither limits nor times for these things: I grant empire without end," *Aen.* 1.278–79). In this formulation in *Aeneid* 1, that empire will be defined without limits of time or space, Vergil distinguishes his version from other such descriptions, all of which focus on the eternity of the city. Austin, ad *Aeneid* 1.278–79, lists a number of such descriptions of Rome, including those found in Tibullus, Livy, and Tacitus, yet none of these uses the terms Vergil employs; all, instead, refer to Rome as eternal. In using words that first and foremost refer to games, Vergil borrows language of Augustus from the *Res Gestae* (*auxi fines*), elaborates on it by including *meta*, and then literalizes it by having Aeneas and his men work their way toward a limitless empire through a series of games marked less and less prominently by limits. While always read metaphorically, these two key terms, *meta* and *finis*, both have literal first meanings of edge, boundary, limit, especially in the context of games.

Yet, strikingly, the games in *Aeneid* 5 become increasingly about the lack of edges and limits, the failure of the rules to conform to the results.[47] If we follow the games through *Aeneid* 5, we find that the edges and limits become increasingly porous, and the lack of distinction, the failure of rules and limits, increasingly foregrounded. *Aeneid* 5, in other words, plays out for us the gradual move towards empire as defined by Jupiter in *Aeneid* 1, even as it moves from a literal to a metaphoric sense of the key terms through an increasing emphasis on permeability. Even as the book takes us from past to future, and from Trojan to Roman, so it walks us through the history of these key words as a means of understanding the difference between Republic and Empire. By the end we are in a situation where distinctions are blurred, where the rule of *sine fine* assumes a new negative valence. *Aeneid* 5, in other words, on Sicily, not only demonstrates the transition from Trojan to Roman, it also enacts the transformation of Republic to Empire, from civil war, with its implicit hopes of empire, to a harsh reality, where the lack of distinctions often proves chaotic, if not disastrous.

After Aeneas and his men are greeted by Acestes (whom, it is made clear in *Aeneid* 1, they encountered on Sicily earlier [*Aen.* 1.549–58], and who is by birth both Sicilian and Trojan [*Aen.* 5.38–41]), and after the boat race, which is on sea and manned only by Trojans, the competitions that follow—the foot race, boxing match, and archery competition—all include a mixture of Sicilians and Trojans. Moreover, the Sicilians do well: of the two in the foot race, Helymus and Panopes, Helymus comes in second, after Euryalus; in the boxing match, between the Sicilian Entellus, who is older, and the Trojan Dares, Entellus wins. As victor, the Sicilian Entellus is granted a bull, which he kills in one fell swoop. In the archery contest, the Sicilian Acestes, their host, is kept from competing as the dove is struck by Eurytion, yet he shoots his arrow off anyway, where it bursts into flame and appears like a comet in the sky. As with Entellus, Aeneas acknowledges the presence of the gods in this action and rewards Acestes with the best gift, a bowl that was given to Anchises by Cisseus as *monimentum et pignus amoris*. So too the *lusus Troiae* involves all Sicilian horses, with the exception of the one Ascanius rides, a white horse Dido gave him, and the riders are drawn from Trojan and indigenous peoples (*Trinacriae... Troiaeque iuventus* [*Aen.* 5.555]). The emerging Roman would appear to be in debt to the Sicilians.

The language of the games likewise suggests a development through the book: the games all revolve, as games do, around limits. Yet given the resonance of *metas* and *fines* in the discussion of Vergil's depiction of empire, the lack of limits takes on a particular resonance. We have seen how the word *meta* recurs in the boat race and the poem; the same is true for *fines*: each race refers to its limits, yet each race shows how the limits are erased. In the boat race, adding to its programmatic quality, the *meta* and the *finis* work together: the competitors jump from the starting gates, *finibus suis*, and race toward the *meta*. In the boxing match, Aeneas imposes a *finem* when it is clear that Dares will be killed by Entellus's mania. Yet in other competitions the rules as they are laid out are not followed: exceptions are made, rules are broken. The games become increasingly unruly, and the trend seems headed toward chaos. One need only think of the series of exceptions made in awarding the prizes in the archery contest, or the way the *lusus Troiae* moves from a stately dance—

>olli discurrere pares atque agmina terni   580
>diductis solvere choris, rursusque vocati
>convertere vias infestaque tela tulere.
>inde alios ineunt cursus aliosque recursus
>adversi spatiis, alternosque orbibus orbis
>impediunt pugnaeque cient simulacra sub armis;   585
>et nunc terga fuga nudant, nunc spicula vertunt
>infensi, facta pariter nunc pace feruntur. (*Aen.* 5.580–87)

(They galloped apart in step, the three troops breaking their line and dividing into separate teams, then, having been given the signal, they turn about and charge with threatening weapons. Then they make moves and countermoves, opposing one another in the arena, and weave circle within circle and drive the game of war with arms. Now they show their backs in flight, now, on the offensive, they point their weapons, now they ride side by side in peace.)

—to a genuine melee:

> primus et Ascanius, cursus ut laetus equestris
> ducebat, sic acer equo turbata petivit
> castra, nec exanimes possunt retinere magistri.
> "quis furor iste novus? quo nunc, quo tenditis" inquit 670
> "heu miserae cives? non hostem inimicaque castra
> Argivum, vestras spes uritis. en, ego vester
> Ascanius!"—galeam ante pedes proiecit inanem,
> qua ludo indutus belli simulacra ciebat. (*Aen.* 5.667–74)

(And first Ascanius, happy as he was leading the equestrian troops, now fierce, sought the troubled camp on his horse, nor can his fearful leaders hold him back. "What new madness is this? Where now, pitiful citizens, where do you go? Alas," he said, "this is not the enemy or the opposing camp of the Argives that you burn, but your own hopes. Look, I am your own Ascanius!" and he threw at their feet his empty helmet, which he wore in the game as he set in motion the mock image of battle.)

The ideal order of the mock battle becomes chaos in the face of real confrontation.

Neither Separate nor Equal

Time and again the myth of empire that surfaces in *Aeneid* 5 is one of the loss of distinction and the impossibility of balance, coupled with the persistence of the past in the formation of the future. Vergil's reasons for emphasizing Sicily's permeability—in the wake of overt discussion of its isolation—point toward the complex treatment of Sicily in the poem overall. Vergil makes this point by altering several known stories from their original location to the other side of the straits: so, in fact, Daedalus, whom Vergil has land at Cuma, is traditionally shown as landing in Sicily, near Mt. Erice.[48] The burning of the ships, by contrast, is often discussed as occurring on Italy proper, instead of on the western shores of Sicily.[49] The shifting of locations reinforces the notion that Sicily, though separate, is on some level fused with the mainland.

Sicily would seem to offer up a literary model to Vergil as it did for Lucretius, though the goals are markedly different. Sicily, especially as it infiltrates the middle of the text, suggests a movement within the poem as a whole from division to compromise, from caesura to commonplace, but also from identity to hegemony. From the action on Sicily in *Aeneid* 5 to the uneasy pairing of *Aeneid* 6 and 7, in which the strangely sunlit world of the underworld is answered by the darker forests of mainland Latium and the parade of male heroes is complemented by the array of female figures from Caieta to Camilla; in which mainland Latium appears as the supplement to the future of the underworld, to, finally, *Aeneid* 8, where it is not only Vulcan who ties the two halves of the book together—it is on his two "products," Cacus and Aeneas's shield, that the book pivots—but the island of Sicily as well recurs in both a direct and suggestive way. The shield is said to be made near Sicily, thus reiterating precisely what Cicero summarizes in the *Verrines* about the island: it provides the products that Rome needs. More tentatively, perhaps, we have Cacus, son of Vulcan, whose mountain lair echoes the workshop of the Cyclops and turns the Aventine into a type of Sicily: it is Hercules' subduing of Cacus that enables the Arcadians to live peacefully across the Circus on the Palatine. Between the two stories we have images of the two sides of colonization: the benefits they provide and the necessity for subjugation. When Augustus, on the shield, is shown to be reviewing the spoils brought him by his conquered people, his actions echo exactly those of Cacus, who also hung human faces on doorposts.[50] The reordering of the elements in the fifth book speaks to a hierarchization that continues through the poem and, more importantly, control of those forces that underwrite progress.

Identified with Sicily at the start of both halves of the epic, as we have seen, Juno is also situated in the position of a prototypical colony: allied to the ruling power of Jupiter, yet separate from him, she struggles throughout the poem with questions of power and self-identification.[51] Through the compromise at the end of *Aeneid* 12, her people will be transformed into a hybrid provincial state: through this, empire is asserted as the mode of Rome's future, and the poem, in retrospect, is shown to be a site, like Sicily, for the exploration of the elements of empire. What Sicily offers geographically at the start of the poem, the compromise offers conceptually at the end, and the inclusion of Juno in the worldview of the final lines establishes an imperial mode for the future that acknowledges her presence, even as it resonates with the reordering of the boats in *Aeneid* 5. It also, though, undermines that mode in forcing compromise upon her. The imperial model she proposes, that the dress and language of the colonies remain unchanged, is exactly what is shown to have occurred on the proleptic account on the shield, where the conquered people parade in front of Augustus *quam variae linguis, habitu tam vestis et armis* (*Aen.* 8.723).

In addition, the force of the compromise Juno reaches with Jupiter is made clear by the final skirmish of the poem, one that recalls precisely the terms laid out above, as Turnus's final act of strength involves a question of the erasure of limits, and agricultural ones at that:

> nec plura effatus saxum circumspicit ingens,
> saxum antiquum ingens, campo quod forte iacebat,
> limes agro positus litem ut discerneret arvis.
> . . .
> ille manu raptum trepida torquebat in hostem (*Aen.* 12.896–98; 901)
>
> (Saying no more, he looks around and spots a huge stone, an ancient huge stone which, by chance, was lying on the plain, placed in the ground as a marker to keep dispute from the fields. . . . with a shaking hand, [Turnus] seized it and hurled it at his enemy.)

Turnus does not throw just any rock: he uproots a boundary stone and in an act that recalls the proem to *Geo.* 1, erases the limit the stone defines, which is none other than the boundary of plowed land, a boundary loss that recalls Proserpina's absence. We are back in the realm of limitlessness, and the inclusion hinted at in Juno's compromise, the pact that will launch the Roman empire, is shown yet again to be rooted in a loss of distinction.[52] In response, Aeneas, too, does not honor limits as he does not follow the advice of his father to spare the suppliant, but instead kills Turnus on seeing the baldric of his friend and protégé Pallas. The language here is telling, since it is filled with mention of fire and, perhaps most strikingly, ends the poem with a reference to the underworld (*sub umbras*). Turnus's shade joins the others in the realm where Proserpina resides and, as Vergil suggested at the start of the *Georgics*, an empire that extends to the underworld is an empire that has overreached its limits.

The town Aeneas has built on Sicily for the Trojans who remain has nothing distinctive about it. It is called Troy and Ilium; the river is renamed Xanthus. It takes us back to Trojan origins without any sense of context or awareness of location. Even though it is said to be in the shadow of Mt. Erice, sacred to Idalian Venus, and near the tomb of Anchises, none of these features are incorporated into the town itself: the marks of distinction are erased or, at the least, blurred.[53] As if to reinforce this message, the lament of the women, far from being calmed by the decision to stay on Sicily, is reinforced at the beginning of *Aeneid* 7, first with the death of Caieta, Aeneas's nurse, and then in the powerful speech Juno gives to launch the second half of the poem. Juno, seeing the Dardanian fleet *Siculo . . . ab usque Pachyno* ("all the way from Sicilian Pachynus"), laments the efforts wasted on land and sea to keep the Trojans from reaching Italy. The attempt to segregate the mourning women on Sicily does not work, and the theme of loss persists.

The question of why enact the games on Sicily, then, can be answered quite simply in terms of the proposal made in the introduction to this study: that Vergil associates the origins of empire with the island of Sicily and that he sees poetry as a locus for the exploration of political complexity. In *Aeneid* 5 he identifies those origins with the role of edges and limits and the lack of limits in empire. He also responds to the literary drive to posit Sicily as a location of poetic etiology.[54] Because of his belief, made clear throughout the poem, that poetry is a space of experimentation, complexity, contradiction, and debate, the fact that he sets the highly poeticized games on Sicily leads to a further association between Sicily, poetry, and empire. Poets who come after Vergil read the metatextuality of the book not as imperial but as poetic; Vergil's efforts open the door to poets like Ovid and Dante who see Sicily as a locus for the intersection of poetry and empire, a space for the display of imperial tensions and exploration of its essential elements through an enactment of the competition among poets. After Vergil, Sicily becomes a space for poetic competition that mirrors even as it affects the tensions of empire.

3

Venus's Other Son

CUPID AND OVID'S EMPIRE OF POETRY

AS WE have seen, the reach of Vergil's epic parallels and even helps define, while questioning, the reach of Augustus's empire: the journey Aeneas takes maps out the scope of Augustus's developing *imperium* even as it suggests difficulties with the proposed plan. In addition, in the preceding chapters we have witnessed how Cicero's identification of Sicily as the conceptual start of empire made its way into the rhetorical and literary tradition. To talk about Sicily in the Latin tradition after Cicero was to talk, on some level at least, about empire.

But we have also noted how Cicero's approach to Sicily was answered in the first century by Quintilian's assertion that speeches not only affect politics, but that an oration itself can be viewed as a form of empire. In the first chapter we looked at the way that Sicily offered Quintilian a model for digression, which we posited was rooted in an assertion about the role of the island in the burgeoning empire. As oratory expands to include education as well as declamation and politics, the association between speech and empire shifts focus, and texts not only affect politics, they reflect it as well. This is a complex step, since it would seem to suggest, first, that the nature of empire, and the position of Sicily in that empire, are firmly established and, second, that rhetorical texts offer a shadow reality patterned on and influential for the political arena.

Quintilian's assertion of a textualized empire, however, does not begin with him. Instead, I would argue that it is available in Ovid as well, and that in the *Metamorphoses*, his epic collection of myths, Ovid reworks the relationship between poetry and empire and uses Sicily to make a very different point: rather than using his poetry to question or explore the goals of empire, he suggests instead that the true contribution of empire lies in the poetic realm. Consequently, Ovid's epic is a narrative empire of constant fertility and transformation, and of regeneration and regrowth rooted in the absence of decay that, at the same time, critiques the politics of the real world. As Andrew Feldherr has summarized it, "the historical and cultural changes of the period when he wrote led Ovid to investigate the political role of literature and the ways in which reality and representation configure one another with particular energy and brilliance."[1] Rather than seeing epic as a space for the exploration of imperial ideals, Ovid sees empire as the creation of poetic possibility, and Sicily continues to provide a key landscape for such an argument.[2]

The reasons for the difference between the two poets are many. Vergil occupied a powerful post as poet of the rising empire; Ovid, by contrast, while praised at first, was finally exiled most likely for things he had written (*carmen et error*, *Tristia* 2.207). While Vergil continues to insist that poetry and empire go hand in hand, Ovid does not. Instead, as the world appears to turn its back on him and his writings, and sends him to end his life at the outer edge of the Roman Empire by the Black Sea, Ovid experiences a sharp break between the world that surrounds him and the world he creates through his poetry.

Scholarship of early modern texts often alludes to a republic or empire of letters, which describes the interaction and interplay of authors across space and time that mimics the expanding global nature of the Renaissance world.[3] Ovid, too, participates in an empire of letters, but of a very different sort. For while the notion of empire—the same empire Vergil writes of—appalls Ovid as he becomes its victim, it also appears to appeal to him as an author. His is an empire of poems that bridges space and time in conversation and competition with earlier authors and contemporary ones, yet it is a poetics born out of a complex relationship with the world. Ovid shares with Vergil the view that empire differs depending on where you stand, yet he realizes that the power dynamic of the political empire that causes his subjugation can be adopted fruitfully for him as author and creator of his own empire of words.

Empire of Words

At the beginning of the *Metamorphoses*, Ovid sets his poem in motion in explicitly imperial terms:

> In nova fert animus mutatas dicere formas
> corpora; di, coeptis (nam vos mutastis et illa[4])
> adspirate meis primaque ab origine mundi
> ad mea perpetuum deducite tempora carmen. (*Met.* 1.1–4)[5]

(My intention is to speak of forms changed into new bodies; gods, breathe into my undertakings (for you also changed them) and draw down a continuous song from the first beginning of the world to my times.)

For Vergil, imperial expansion is spatial. For Ovid, in the *Metamorphoses*, the imperial expansion, while present, applies more to the text than the world. As Hinds notes, *deducere* is a verb used in discussions of empire as well as poetry:[6] a verb used of the process of moving colonists to the provinces, it also appears in poetry with a meaning akin to "make fine-spun." (Here, for example, see *Eclogue* 6.5: "*pastorem, Tityre, pinguis / pascere oportet ovis, deductum dicere carmen.*" "A shepherd, Tityrus, should feed plump sheep, but sing a fine-spun song." It is perhaps worth noting that the word occurs here in the context of *Syracosio versu*, Sicilian song.) While the *Aeneid* mimics the spatial growth of empire in its reach, the *Metamorphoses*, by contrast, suggests that the spatial dimension of growth applies to the narrative itself. Seen in this light, the odd structure of Ovid's poem seems more reasonable: it is not the agonistic battlefield structure of the *Iliad* or the journey-based structure of the *Odyssey, Argonautica*, or *Aeneid*, all of which insist on the spatialization of time as the primary factor of narrative. Narrative for Ovid is a product of the temporalization of space, which accounts for its almost lyric feel.[7] It is chaotic only if seen in terms of the earlier epics: if approached instead on these other terms, it starts to make sense.

In other words, while the logic of the *Aeneid* is determined by geographic proximity, with the organization of space determining the order of the plot, the logic of the *Metamorphoses* is determined by temporal proximity: stories lead to stories because they happened at neighboring times.[8] The overall organization of the epic, after all, is primarily chronological, not geographic. In this context it makes sense to argue that change is the only constant, as many have done; narrative change is what stitches these times together, and metamorphosis is the physical representation of that change.[9]

As a result, the tale of Proserpina becomes relevant. A myth of seasons, initially, it is therefore also a myth of time. Through this story, as we shall see, Ovid shows how empire reaches into the future and claims both the perpetual and the eternal for itself.

Sicily in the *Metamorphoses*

Ovid's imperial poetics is laid out in the discussion of Sicily in *Metamorphoses* 5, then enacted in his stories about Sicily in books 13 and 14. Sicily remains the location for the poetic discussion of empire, even as the understanding of empire changes. In addition, the extension of empire caused by Proserpina's abduction in Vergil comes to provide the etiology for the immortal success of Ovid's wide-ranging poem.

Ovid's version of the story of Proserpina offers a curious test case for the problem of Sicily. On the one hand, as Stephen Hinds has shown, Ovid's treatment of Sicily, especially in *Metamorphoses* 5 and the fourth book of the *Fasti*, speaks to a clear poetic impulse. Hinds argues that the description of Enna recalls the stereotypical landscapes invoked by Theocritus and other Greek pastoral poets, a *perpetuum ver* in which peace and security are to be expected, while the stagnant nature of its beauty, along with, as we shall see, the clear allusions to Cicero's *Verrines*, anticipate disaster.[10] The detail which Ovid employs creates a backdrop against which the violence and confusion that will only momentarily characterize Proserpina's disappearance are juxtaposed; thus he is able to build anticipation for his audience, and add gravity to the myth, by drawing on a variety of literary precedents from distinct genres. As we shall see, Ovid draws on numerous tales about Sicily, and Enna in particular, to foreground his poetic prowess and placement in the tradition.[11] On the other hand, as Patricia Johnson has argued, Ovid's use of Sicily in *Metamorphoses* 5 remains linked to questions of empire as a locale identified with the failures of politics and the insistence on aggression and annihilation. The abundance of political language and the evocations of both the *Aeneid* and the *Verrine* orations that characterize *Metamorphoses* 5 are seen to establish a correlation between dominance in sexuality and magisterial power. By making evident the fear of rape and abuse in which Proserpina, Cyane, Arethusa, and the nymphs of Calliope's audience are forced to live under the unusually imperial regime of Venus and Cupid, Ovid hints at a similar atmosphere of repression under their historical descendants, Julius and Augustus Caesar.[12] These two views are not incompatible. Rather, what we shall see is that Ovid draws on Sicily's dual heritage as a poetic and political locus to suggest that poetry, while not always capable of changing the world, nonetheless remains able to transcend it. Ovid's poetry about Sicily shows a literature that at once condemns the world and saves itself.

It will be my argument that Ovid's understanding of poetics is directly related to his understanding of imperialism;[13] that, like Vergil, he sees the epic as a space in which to confront complexities of empire;[14] and that, finally, unlike Vergil, he believes that imperial dynamics can be redeemed if applied only in poetry:[15] Ovid condones an imperial poetics even as he condemns imperial politics. As Andrew Feldherr has argued, "the connections Ovid's techniques establish between poem and reality invite reexamination of how real a text can become, of how dynamically it can shape the readers' response to and participation in the world around them."[16] The language of his final claim at the end of the *Metamorphoses* points us back not only to the start of the poem but, more importantly for our purposes, to the language of Proserpina in *Metamorphoses* 5. Moreover, Ovid's poetics is established in the course of his discussion of Sicily, in books 5 and 13–14, which links Sicily to imperial questions raised from Cicero on. But most importantly, Ovid uses the location of Sicily to point to the right and wrong uses of empire, the one in poetry, the other in politics. If Ovid ends up endorsing the imperial, it is in the context of asserting that politics is useful only in creating the need for poetry. In this he has, as in so many other places, succeeded in upsetting the pieties of Vergil: where Vergil sees poetry as a place to work out the dynamics of politics, Ovid presents politics as the place to work out the details of poetry. Politics recedes into the distance at the end of the poem as Ovid the poet rises victorious, and poetry is shown to be as, if not more, quintessentially imperial as politics.

A World Apart

In Ovid's *Amores*, Cupid famously removes a foot from the second line, thus creating the elegiac couplet out of epic hexameter:

> Arma gravi numero violentaque bella parabam
>   edere, materia conveniente modis.
> par erat inferior versus; risisse Cupido
>   dicitur atque unum surripuisse pedem. (*Amores*, 1.1.1–4)[17]

(I was planning to write of arms and violent wars in an authoritative meter, subject matching form. The lower line was equal [to the upper]: Cupid is said to have laughed and snatched away one foot.)

With this move, Ovid stakes his claim both to form and content: he will write in a different meter about a different topic. Yet he also suggests that elegy is a response to epic and, more particularly, that his elegy is a response to Vergil's epic.[18] This particular symbiosis is significant, both in the *Amores* and, later, in the *Metamorphoses*; throughout this chapter we will examine ways in which Ovid not only responds to Vergil, but, more, critiques Vergil's stand on key issues, including love and empire.

Through the course of the *Amores*, Ovid makes clear one particular theme: because love is destructive in the world it becomes creative to the poet.[19] He makes this point in many ways, and the relationship between the two has been analyzed through many lenses, including military imagery (in 1.2, Ovid presents himself as a hostage in Cupid's triumph); erotic parallels (in 2.18, Ovid's resolve to free himself from both his poetry and his girlfriend is broken by the latter's kisses; and in 3.1, Elegy's wanton attire seduces Ovid away from matronly Tragedy) and his emphasis on the erotic elements of mythological stories (in 2.14, he attempts to dissuade Corinna from an abortion by recalling Venus's illegitimate pregnancy of Aeneas).[20] Throughout, Ovid asserts that the very destructiveness of love in the real world is linked, causally, to the fertility of love for poets. There is nothing particularly Vergilian about this argument, except at its start. In this Ovid seems to be staking a separate claim, positing that whereas Vergil wrote in hexameter, Ovid will write in couplets; Vergil wrote about empire, though Ovid will write about love. But in the *Metamorphoses*, these two worlds collide, or, rather, Ovid forces them to smash into each other, and the seeming gentleman's agreement between the two poets becomes instead an out-and-out brawl on Sicily.[21] For in the fifth book of the *Metamorphoses*, Ovid echoes the first line of the *Aeneid*, only this time he does not have Cupid drop a foot, but add an empire.

"arma manusque meae, mea, nate, potentia" dixit,   365
"illa, quibus superas omnes, cape tela, Cupido,
inque dei pectus celeres molire sagittas,
cui triplicis cessit fortuna novissima regni." (*Met.* 5.365–68)

("My arms and hands, son, my power," she said, "take those weapons, Cupid, with which you conquer all things, and wield swift arrows into the heart of the god to whom fell the latest lot of the triple kingdom.")

Moving from a tone of demurral to one of antagonism, Ovid here shifts from love to empire and from elegy to epic. While use of the word *arma* at the start of a line of hexameter is not rare, it is certainly not common in this exact form. It occurs only three other times in Latin poetry before Ovid, all in Vergil: *Aeneid* 1.1, *arma virumque cano*; *Aeneid* 2.181, *arma deosque parant*; and *Aeneid* 11.747, *arma virumque ferens*. The palimpsest on the story of the *Aeneid* is clear: in both stories a son of Venus is to use his powers to conquer unconquered lands. Both are stories of imperial vision: Vergil's the story of the claiming of Italy for the Trojans, Ovid's the claiming of the underworld for Venus. Both begin in Sicily. But they are also echoes of each other, and the lessons of the *Amores* need to be remembered as we move into the *Metamorphoses*. In particular, the prominent theme of the *Amores*, that destruction in love leads to creation in love poetry, is one that is recalled and reinforced by this echo here,[22] even as it is expanded upon to suggest that destruction inherent in empire leads to the creation of an imperial poetics.

Moreover, this point of resonance between *Aeneid* 1.1 and *Amores* 1.1 begins Ovid's account of the abduction of Proserpina from Sicily, and even if we did not have Cicero and Vergil's associations of Sicily with empire in our minds, Ovid would remind us, in Venus's plea: "*cur non matrisque tuumque / imperium profers?*" ("Why don't you extend your empire and that of your mother?" *Met.* 5.371–72). Venus commands Cupid to cause Hades to become infatuated with Proserpina in order that Venus's empire be extended into the underworld and the afterlife. In this, as Johnson has argued, Venus reenacts the role played by Verres in Cicero, who, as we have seen, is likened to Hades in his stealing of the statue of Ceres from the temple at Enna. Johnson is right: Ovid stands with Cicero here in condemning the actions of the aggressors. Emperors, Johnson argues, are like Venus, like Verres, like Hades, and empire itself is aggressive and destructive.[23]

But there is a complication to Ovid's argument that this reading does not fully address, which stems from both the Verrine orations and Sicily. While Cicero does indeed link Verres with Hades, he does not say that empire, as a result, is a bad idea. On the contrary, as we have seen, Cicero's point in the *Verrines* overall is to suggest that empire is both useful and productive when handled correctly—and that Sicily is the example of just such a promising province. If there are governors, like Verres, who approach empire in terms of rapine and greed, empire will founder and wreak havoc on its citizenry. But the idea of empire in and of itself is anything but a bad idea, as Sicily itself has shown time and again: Sicily is the breadbasket and center of provisions for Italy, as well as a place of business[24] and the source of good people, reminiscent of the early days of Roman history.[25] As the first province, Sicily also set an example of loyalty and friendship which other states would then follow,[26] while her resources and harbors assisted in military campaigns against rival civilizations, such as Carthage, thus stabilizing the power of Rome.[27] Empire is not at fault, the ruler is.

It is, then, in this context that we need to approach the story of Ceres and Proserpina, and look closely at the way Ovid tells this particular story as an index of Ovid's interest in rewriting the imperial myths of Vergil.[28] While Vergil's empire is a mixed vision of hope and loss, Ovid's is one ostensibly of greed.[29] Yet even in Ovid's hands, such acquisition retains a sense of possibility, at least for narrative, and it is this aspect that will become crucial to the medieval development of the thread we are following here. It is in Ovid's tale of Proserpina that he responds most directly to Vergil's poem of empire.

The story itself begins with a description of Ceres and her powers which, by extension, are powers associated with Sicily:[30]

> Prima Ceres unco glaebam dimovit aratro,
> prima dedit fruges alimentaque mitia terris,
> prima dedit leges; Cereris sunt omnia munus.
> illa canenda mihi est; utinam modo dicere possim
> carmina digna dea! certe dea carmine digna est. (*Met.* 5.341–45)

(Ceres was the first to overturn the clod with a curved plow. She was the first to give grain and fruitful crops to the lands. She was the first to give laws: all these things are the gift of Ceres; she must be sung by me. Would that I could sing songs worthy of the goddess! Surely the goddess is worthy of a song.)

These powers of Ceres are what are disrupted by Hades' abduction of Proserpina, and Venus's insistence on the expansion of her domain into the underworld. These attributes need to be remembered, even as Sicily's strength in the *Verrines* as a province, and as proof of the potential power of empire, should not be neglected. But notice how these very lines call up Cicero's description of Sicily from the Verrine orations:

> ... primum quod omnium nationum exterarum princeps Sicilia se ad amicitiam fidemque populi Romani applicavit. Prima omnium, id quod ornamentum imperi est, provincia est appellata. Prima docuit maiores nostros quam praeclarum esset exteris gentibus imperare. (Cicero, *Verr.*, 2.2.1.2)

(... the first of which is that Sicily was the premier of all foreign nations to offer herself in friendship and loyalty to the Roman people. She was the first of all to be called province, that embellishment of empire. She was the first who taught our forefathers how splendid it is to govern foreign peoples.)

Mark the repetition of *primum ... prima ... prima*, which Ovid echoes through anaphora at the start of three successive lines, *prima ... prima ... prima*. Ceres is here the personification of Sicily, and it is her song that must be sung (*canenda est*), a song that is above all the song of empire.

The two, in fact, are linked in a way that is familiar to us coming from the *Amores*. There it is the destruction by Cupid in the real world that causes the imaginative world of love poetry to flourish; here, the destruction caused by Venus's other son, Aeneas, and his heirs causes the imaginative world of epic poetry to flourish. The two, of course, are linked by Venus, as her two sons, Cupid and Aeneas, are arguably personifications of two main branches of Latin poetry, elegy and epic. The *Amores* showed us in detail how the very destructiveness of love in society created room—psychic, imaginative, poetic—for elegy. The *Metamorphoses* will show rather how the ravishments of empire create the need, even as they provide the material, for the reach of epic poetry.

Empire of Poetry

Sicily is the location Vergil chose, as we have seen, for the discussion of the potential and risks of empire. Focusing on the straits of Messina and the western cape at Drepanum, *Aeneid* 3 and 5 sketch out—and then question—the abstract notion of the potential of empire as a space for cooperation and enrichment, an area in which competition both is and is not fruitful, differences are acknowledged, strengths are endorsed.[31] Like the island once joined to the mainland, provinces and provincial people share a deep bond with the imperial center, a bond which ultimately may become a shackle or, worse, an erasure of anything indigenous.[32] The poem of the *Aeneid* overall explores the potential and limitations of this notion.

The *Metamorphoses* also explores the potential and limitations of empire in the context of poetry and Sicily. Whereas Vergil uses the poetic space of his epic to juxtapose the pros and cons of the imperial ideal, Ovid uses his poem to make quite a different statement. The very chaos caused by empire, which is never sugarcoated by Ovid, is nonetheless the source of the power of his epic poetry. I do not mean that his epic merely condemns or celebrates empire; like Vergil, Ovid is too good a poet to reduce his epic to the level of propaganda. Instead, Ovid follows his own example from the *Amores* in suggesting that destruction in the real world creates poetic opportunities and, more, that precisely those things that make empire destructive are fruitful in the poetic realm. While Ovid criticizes Augustus for imperialism, he also celebrates its poetic possibilities.

This argument runs throughout the *Metamorphoses*, but it is clearest, and most germane to our overall argument here, in the books that relate to Sicily, *Metamorphoses* 5 and 13–14. *Metamorphoses* 5, as we have seen, offers the story of Ceres and Proserpina, while books 13–14 include the retelling of the tale of Aeneas and so respond most directly to Vergil's epic. Both discussions include uses of Sicily that exemplify Ovid's interest in the empire of poetry. Let us begin with Proserpina.

As we have seen, Vergil does not tell the tale of Proserpina. Ovid, by contrast, rehearses Proserpina's story in full, from the abduction to the compromise and return, while Vergil's focus is on the edges of the island, as Aeneas sails around it. Ovid, ignoring the edges, focuses on the center, and on the central story that Vergil omits.[33] Moreover, his focus on the Proserpina tale is couched, as we have seen, in Vergilian language: "'*arma manusque meae, mea nate, potentia' dixit*" (*Met.* 5.365). Not only does this echo the opening lines of the *Amores*, and suggest Ovid is expanding his own domain, it also echoes the opening line of the *Aeneid* to suggest just which direction this expansion will take.[34] Here meter is critical, as if to reinforce this echo, for not only does the line begin with *arma*, but the first two feet of the line are identical to that of the opening line of the *Aeneid*. Ovid's response to Vergil's epic is rooted on Sicily, and the prominence he grants Proserpina responds directly to Vergil's silence about her myth.

Ovid's Proserpina story is a story of rape.[35] As Johnson sums it up:[36]

> While in the first half of Venus' speech Pluto and Proserpina are the unwitting victims of the "empire of Eros," placing them on par with the narrators of Roman elegy, in this second half the true nature of Venus' *imperium* is revealed: compulsory sexuality. The virgin goddesses Minerva and Diana are perceived as dissidents, rebels from her authority. Venus disregards any right to sexual self-determination Proserpina might have in a single-minded pursuit of two goals: the extension of her empire and the suppression of dissidents against it, those who renounce Love. Proserpina apparently has similar aspirations, which Venus is eager to crush. The two halves of her speech recast an old elegiac metaphor regarding the *castra* of Cupid within the framework of imperial ambitions and thus draw a remarkable parallel between the victims of rape and of expansionist imperial power.

But the context of this tale needs to be examined as well, and it is this I wish to emphasize here. The story of the abduction is told in the context of narrative competition, and it bursts with tales.[37] One story follows hard on the heels of another; one story explodes into another so fast that one tale, that of Arethusa, has to be postponed until the primary tale has been resolved.[38] This fertility of tales runs against the grain of the aridity Ceres imposes while searching for her daughter; the abundance of stories hatched on Sicily creates a complex counterpoint to the context of imperial strictures.

As Johnson has carefully shown, Ovid draws not just from Cicero's description of the rape of Proserpina in the *Verrines* but also, and perhaps more, from theft—of the statue of Ceres in Enna.[39] The specific naming of Venus in this myth as *Erycina* (*Met.* 5.363) recalls the goddess's ancient cult on Sicily, and its role in the corrupt administration of the island under Verres.[40] Venus Erycina became a pawn in whose name the governor was able to conduct massive seizures of property and, consequently, to subjugate the Sicilian people. According to Cicero, Verres' theft of the ancient statue of Ceres particularly epitomized his avarice, leaving nothing untouched by his desire for wealth and power, even those items most valued and held as most sacred.[41] In the *Metamorphoses*, Ovid, by locating the rape of Proserpina on Sicily, rather than in its more traditional Greek setting, evokes the same relationship between Venus Erycina and Proserpina as Verres, and his patron Venus Erycina, had with Ceres. Just as the statue was victim of Verres' insatiable greed, so do the goddesses fall victim to Venus's imperialism. Johnson's point is a strong one: Ovid's allusion to Cicero and to the Verrine orations in particular enables him to discuss imperial aggression. I would push her observations even further and suggest that Ovid's reason for citing the *Verrines* is to reintroduce the description of Sicily as the origin of empire into the discussion, and thereby insist on Sicily as the site of imperial debate.

However, Ovid differs from Cicero in the slant he takes on the issue. While Venus does begin the episode from Erice, the abduction takes place halfway across the island in Enna, followed by the reentry into the underworld from outside of Syracuse. These are important locations, since they suggest a panoramic view of the island as a whole, from west to east, and one that takes into account the interior of the island, not just its coastline.[42] The association with Cicero is clear, but so is the distinction from earlier authors, most notably Vergil.

Moreover, by focusing attention on the interior of the island, we are made more aware of the disturbance Hades causes when he arrives. Compared to Vergil's use of Sicily as a model of former unity, and of a relatively recent break that hints at the possibility for reunification, Ovid's treatment of Sicily suggests something quite different. Here the imperial model is one of rupture and displacement. The land is torn apart, and the innocence and beauty that formerly characterized it is destroyed.[43] It is significant that the action of Hades echoes that of Etna: Venus has Cupid cause Hades to fall in love when he is checking on the giant trapped beneath the volcano, the giant that causes the volcano to erupt. Yet this giant is also a reminder of a former pre-Olympian age; his eruption is a result of his suppression by the Olympians.[44] The Saturnian age, reenacted through the blissful early life of Proserpina, is destroyed by the Olympians; their actions in each case lead to violent disturbance and disruption. The political message is made clear: from the beginning of the first book of the *Metamorphoses* the Olympians are likened to the current regime: Augustus is allied with Jupiter explicitly as Olympus is likened to the Palatine Hill.[45] The actions of the Olympians, be they Venus or Hades, are shown to be violent and aggressive.

The reasons for this change are detailed in the stories that surround the myth, and they are important to our argument here. According to Ovid, as we have seen, Venus complains that Hades is the only one left who has not been struck by love. How different this is from the myth as told either in the *Fasti* or the *Homeric Hymns*, where it is a sort of locker-room dare that gets Hades interested in Proserpina. Here it is Venus, whose interest is her own: her powers, she says, could be universal;[46] her reach could be not only expanded but eternal if only Hades would fall in love.[47] Love thus becomes the focus of the Proserpina tale for Ovid, which ties the story more tightly to his own shorter poems and, as we will see in later chapters, becomes critical in medieval versions of the myth.

The tale of Ceres is told by Calliope in competitive response to a challenge by the nine Pierides, whose story is told in shorthand, almost list form, directly before that of Calliope and includes the story of Typhoeus, the giant trapped under Etna. William S. Anderson has critiqued the tale told by Calliope, saying it is every bit as rambling as that of the competitor;[48] I would disagree, suggesting instead that Calliope's tale is intentionally structured as a series of interlocking tales and so is a tale about violation that also demonstrates narrative ingenuity. As such, it serves as a key example of the way content affects style but, more, how the fruitful elaboration of narrative can derive from the violence of theme.

A further example of this phenomenon can be seen in the tale of Arethusa. While Vergil mentions this story as Aeneas and his men sail by the fountain of Arethusa on the southeastern coast of Sicily, he does not go into detail.[49] Ovid does. Ceres learns of the location of her daughter from Arethusa who first refuses to explain why she had visited the underworld, then later in the book recounts her story:

"Exigit alma Ceres, nata secura recepta,
quae tibi causa fugae, cur sis, Arethusa, sacer fons.
conticuere undae, quarum dea sustulit alto
fonte caput viridesque manu siccata capillos   575
fluminis Elei veteres narravit amores." (*Met.* 5.572–76)

("Nurturing Ceres, her daughter safely recovered, asks you, Arethusa, what was the cause of your flight, why are you a sacred spring. The waves fell silent as their goddess raised her head from the deep spring, dried her green hair with her hand, and narrated the tale of the old love of the Elean river.")

Arethusa arrives in Sicily pursued by Alpheus. The gods protect her, but not from exile. Nonetheless grateful for this, she claims Sicily as her newfound home, yet the fact remains that she has been displaced because of pursuit. Her journey from east to west was not one she would have taken willingly, and her transformation from human to spring stigmatizes her. The fact that her journey mirrors that of Aeneas traveling from Troy to Rome—that it, too, sketches out the reach of empire—is only further evidence that here, too, we have a story of empire. But what a different empire: Ovid's version is one based on greed, rape, unmatched expansion. Venus wants to lay claim to all parts of the universe: heaven and earth are not enough, she must conquer the realm of the afterlife as well,[50] *agitur pars tertia mundi*. Arethusa offers a glimpse of the effects of such a grandiose scheme.[51] Her world has been expanded and her home has been moved through no will of her own. She has been forced out, forced west, where her pursuer follows her, through the underworld, all the way to Sicily. This is not love, but rape, and this imperial expansion is not one of generosity but of greed.

But her entreaty to Ceres complicates this reading:

> atque ait: "o toto quaesitae virginis orbe
> et frugum genetrix, inmensos siste labores,   490
> neve tibi fidae violenta irascere terrae;
> terra nihil meruit patuitque invita rapinae.
> nec sum pro patria supplex; huc hospita veni,
> Pisa mihi patria est et ab Elide ducimus ortus.
> Sicaniam peregrina colo, sed gratior omni   495
> haec mihi terra solo est; hos nunc Arethusa Penates,
> hanc habeo sedem—quam tu, mitissima, serva." (*Met.* 5.489–97)

(And she speaks: "O you, mother of the girl sought throughout all the earth and of produce, now stop your endless efforts and don't be so thoroughly wrathful against the land which has been good to you. The land has deserved none of this; against its will it opened to the theft. It is not for my own country that I pray, for I arrived here as a stranger: Pisa is my native country, and from Elis I claim my roots. I live in Sicily as a foreigner, but this land is more pleasing to me than every [other] place; I, Arethusa, now have these Penates, this dwelling-place—which, I pray you, save, O most merciful.")

Here, while pointing out that she came to Sicily as a stranger, and lamenting the loss of her native land, Arethusa also states that she loves Sicily above all (*gratior omni / haec mihi terra solo est, Met.* 5.495–96), and without Sicily she would not be able to tell Ceres of Proserpina's whereabouts or of her own life and journey. In other words, Arethusa would not have a role in this story without her exile. The very journey she laments provides the source of her role in the epic. And, even more to the point in the context of the Proserpina story overall, Arethusa's own tale, delayed due to the recovery of Proserpina, is derived from Ceres' negotiation and return of her daughter.

What becomes apparent in Ovid's retelling of the myth of Proserpina is that her recovery and the negotiation that leads to it—precisely that aspect of the tale omitted by Vergil—are linked directly to narrative fertility and abundance. But they are also tied to a forward-looking view, one that we will see in some detail in the other Sicily stories Ovid tells.

Narrative Straits

The same contradiction is apparent, perhaps even more so, in the stories set on Sicily in *Metamorphoses* 13–14, where the very structure of the tales makes this clear. Here, on the one hand, we have Ovid causing Aeneas and his men to sail directly through the mythically hazardous straits of Messina, thus undermining both Vergil's plot and interpretation;[52] on the other, the break between books 13 and 14 enacts precisely the space of the straits: stories that end 13 are on Sicily, while those that begin 14 are on Italy.[53] As with the abduction of Proserpina, the break or rift caused by empire or geology, while not sutured over by poetry or time, is shown to be productive of stories and poetry.

The straits of Messina pose no threat to Ovid—in direct contrast to Vergil— in terms of the plot of the *Metamorphoses* and bear none of the weight they do in the *Aeneid*. Instead, the aspect of Sicily that plays out the imperial theme is the one ignored by Vergil, even though Ovid continues to use Sicily as the landscape of empire, only to redraw its nature in the stories he chooses to tell.

In *Metamorphoses* 13–14, during the so-called "little *Aeneid*," Ovid covers the same ground as Vergil, discussing the journey of Aeneas from Troy to Italy. Yet, as we have come to expect, his iteration of the journey is rooted in critique of Vergil and, by extension, of empire.[54] While Cicero is missing from Ovid's later discussion of Sicily, the points made in the fifth book of the *Metamorphoses* are far from absent. In particular, Vergil's use of the straits as exemplum of the model for empire is deconstructed and put to a new use.

Even if mention of Cicero and the Proserpina story from the *Verrines* is absent in these books in the *Metamorphoses*, however, Cicero's presence is felt through the emphasis placed on rhetorical prowess at the start of book 13, which begins with a competition over arms. Given that Ovid has made it clear that *arma* for him is a trigger word signaling Vergil and Vergil's poem, this is significant indeed. Much like the boat race at the start of *Aeneid* 5, the opening gambit of the little *Aeneid* serves to introduce the reader to issues at the center of this competition.[55]

Ajax begins. The opening words, *Consedere duces* (*Met.* 13.1), recall the beginning of *Aeneid* 2, *Conticuere omnes*. Identified from the start with his shield, much as Aeneas's shield in *Aeneid* 8 becomes at times a metonym of the epic, Ajax then makes the following points: he is known for his courage and brute skill in contrast to Ulysses' wiliness with words. But he queries whether the arms are denied him because he was the first to take up arms ("*An quod in arma prior . . . veni*," *Met.* 13.34) and, more than that, fought hard while Ulysses pulled back. Ulysses responds by pointing out that while Ajax is known only for his prowess in battle, Ulysses does so much more: he fights, but he also strategizes and persuades, in many different contexts.

It seems plausible to suggest that this debate over *arma* is a debate over poetry, and the contest, which ends in Ulysses' favor, serves to characterize Vergil as a writer with one theme, who asserts he should prevail because he wrote of empire first, while Ulysses is portrayed as having many strings to his bow: he can prevail in any number of contexts: many of the events he relates are ones Ovid writes about in *Amores* and *Fasti* as well as the *Metamorphoses* itself. The debate between Ajax and Ulysses that begins the book is, in effect, a poetic competition between Vergil and Ovid, which Ovid wins handily.[56] The two face off over the *arma* of Achilles, the opening word of Vergil's epic, and Ulysses' victory points to the superiority of argument over action, while Ajax's suicide that follows handily moves Vergil out of the way.[57] The remainder of books 13 and 14 plays out this victory, as Ovid retells the story of the *Aeneid* in his own terms, emphasizing things Vergil chose to gloss over, and skipping things Ovid found unimportant.[58]

The fact that this is set as a competition, not unlike the games in *Aeneid* 5, is perhaps suggestive. If we see the little *Aeneid*—note that Ovid's version begins in book 13, just where Vergil's poem left off at the end of book 12—as Ovid's response to Vergil, it is even more striking how much of these books is spent on Sicily, and how different the use of Sicily is.[59] To begin with, Vergil's repeated assertion that the straits offer geographic proof for the potential of empire is absent. Helenus's prophecy is all but omitted and certainly doesn't include the detail that is repeated in Vergil and then enacted as Aeneas and his men fail to sail through the straits not once but twice, first before picking up Achaemenides, then with Achaemenides on board (*Aen.* 3.558–69, 682–99).

In Ovid, Helenus's advice is mentioned in *Metamorphoses* 13.722–23, but it is ignored. As we have seen, Aeneas and his men sail through the straits with no struggle, marking, not masking the divide:

> Hunc ubi Troianae remis avidamque Charybdin   75
> evicere rates, cum iam prope litus adessent
> Ausonium, Libycas vento referuntur ad oras. (*Met.* 14.75–77)

(When the Trojan ships with their oars had overcome this [rock=Scylla] and greedy Charybdis, and when they had now approached the Ausonian shore, they are borne off to the Libyan coast by the wind.)

Moreover, the division represented by the straits is emphasized on the narrative level of the tale as well: Sicily's geography is replayed in the lay-out of books 13 and 14. Book 13 interrupts the tale of Aeneas to tell the tales first of Polyphemus, Galatea, and Acis, then of Glaucus and Scylla. The story of Polyphemus in particular marks a distinction from Vergil: rather than the pathetic image provided in *Aeneid* 3 of the wounded monster thrashing through the waves to try to capture the Trojans, *Metamorphoses* 13 draws its details from the *Odyssey*, filling in the full story of Ulysses' clever escape. The final tale of *Metamorphoses* 13, that of Glaucus and Scylla, continues into book 14, with Glaucus's appeal to Circe and the transformation of Scylla occurring there. But the break between the two books coincides precisely with Scylla leaving Sicily at the end of *Metamorphoses* 13 and, at the beginning of book 14, the story of Glaucus's journey as he sets out to follow her:

> Iamque Giganteis iniectam faucibus Aetnen
> arvaque Cyclopum quid rastra, quid usus aratri
> nescia nec quidquam iunctis debentia bubus
> liquerat Euboicus tumidarum cultor aquarum;
> liquerat et Zanclen adversaque moenia Regi   5
> navifragumque fretum, gemino quod litore pressum

Ausoniae Siculaeque tenet confinia terrae.
inde manu magna Tyrrhena per aequora uectus
herbiferos adiit colles atque atria Glaucus
Sole satae Circes, variarum plena ferarum. (*Met.* 14.1–10)

(And now Etna, piled on the Giant's throat, and the fields of the Cyclops, which knew nothing of the rake and the use of the plow, which neither knew nor owed anything to yoked oxen, the Euboican reaper of the swelling waves had left behind, and he had left behind also Zancle [Messina] and the walls of Rhegium, opposite, and the ship-wrecking straits, pressed by twin shores, that marks the limits of the Ausonian and Sicilian lands. From there, borne through the Tyrrhenian sea by his great stroke, Glaucus arrived at the grass-bearing hills and halls of Circe, daughter of the Sun, full of a variety of wild beasts.)

The straits of Messina are enacted through the break between books 13 and 14, and the divide is thereby emphasized. In direct contrast to the earlier treatment of Sicily in book 5, in which emphasis was placed on the inland part of the island, rather than the coast, books 13 and 14, which purport to retell the stories of the first half of the *Aeneid*, draw our attention to the part of Sicily focused on first by Vergil, the straits. But unlike the *Aeneid*, which mentions the separation at the straits only to lead discussion to an underlying and recoverable unity, Ovid points to the straits as a point of separation and rupture. There is no effort on Ovid's part to mask the break or suture it over. By contrast, the break is highlighted by the division between *Metamorphoses* 13 and 14.[60]

This approach to the straits as a place of division echoes the reiterated motif of interruption seen in the tales about Sicily in *Metamorphoses* 5. In the context of the later books, though, this pattern of interruption speaks to Ovid's understanding of empire overall, which is rooted in metaphors of acquisition and rape. There is no underlying unity that empire will or may recover for Ovid. Instead, empire is a system of pursuit and abduction, as can be seen in the tales of Polyphemus and Glaucus, where the straits resurface as setting and refuse to be bridged in the narrative structure of these tales. And yet, as we have seen often with Ovid, the rupture of empire enables the proliferation of narrative, as it offers the opportunity for the wonderfully ornate and detailed stories of Polyphemus and Glaucus.

Most telling, however, is the story of Achaemenides, for here the distinction from Vergil is marked precisely in terms of locations near the straits. In

Vergil, Achaemenides appears as a Greek abandoned to the Cyclops by Odysseus:

"sum patria ex Ithaca, comes infelicis Vlixi,
nomine Achaemenides, Troiam genitore Adamasto
paupere (mansissetque utinam fortuna!) profectus." (*Aen.* 3.613–15)

("I am from the land of Ithaca, a comrade of unlucky Ulysses, called Achaemenides. Since my father Adamastus was poor (would my lot had remained!), I departed for Troy.")

Despite his Greek heritage, the Trojans pity him and take him on board, where he helps orient them in their journey around Sicily. Ovid, however, introduces Achaemenides after they have reached the Italian mainland, and has him tell the whole story of Polyphemus's attack on Ulysses and his men:

Talia convexum per iter memorante Sibylla
sedibus Euboicam Stygiis emergit in urbem   155
Troius Aeneas sacrisque ex more litatis
litora adit nondum nutricis habentia nomen.
hic quoque substiterat post taedia longa laborum
Neritius Macareus, comes experientis Vlixis.
desertum quondam mediis qui rupibus Aetnae   160
noscit Achaemeniden improvisoque repertum
vivere miratus... (*Met.* 14.154–62)

(Along the curved way, as the Sibyl continued to speak of such things, Trojan Aeneas emerges from the Stygian holdings at the Euboican town [of Cuma] and makes customary sacrifices, and lands on the shore that does not yet bear his nurse's name [Caieta]. Here also Neritian Macareus, comrade of tested Ulysses, had stayed after the long weariness of his labors. He recognizes Achaemenides, once deserted among the rocks of Etna, and is astonished suddenly to find him alive.)

The change is drastic, but the effect is telling: through this series of events Ovid turns our attention away from the Vergilian version of the Cyclops story and relates instead the story of Ulysses' escape as told in the *Odyssey*. This version of Polyphemus's tale is a striking contrast to the one just seen in book 13, as the forlorn lover becomes the man-eating monster. Moreover, the tale Achaemenides tells leads into a retelling of subsequent tales of Ulysses' travels, rather than Aeneas's.[61] Ulysses has surfaced as important, and his tales trump those of Aeneas.

The reasons for this are several. On the one hand, by emphasizing Ulysses over Aeneas, Ovid is able to play out the victory announced at the beginning of book 13: Ulysses beats Aeneas just as Ulysses beats Ajax, both avatars of the poetic competition between Ovid and Vergil. On the other, Ulysses is a character dear to Ovid's heart due to his rhetorical prowess.[62] His verbal cleverness distinguishes him from Ajax, but also from Aeneas, and he stands as a model to Ovid of the powers of the word. Whereas, however, Ulysses' strength lies in the spoken word, Ovid's power lies in the written: it is his tremendous ability with written wordplay that pervades the *Metamorphoses*, and, he would suggest, distinguishes that epic from the *Aeneid*.[63]

There is, in fact, a sharp juncture between the image of empire presented in *Metamorphoses* 5 and that of the stories that Ovid tells about the island of Sicily. For as much as the narratives seem to focus on the disintegration of community, the stories themselves are joyous and playful. The world they describe—the imperial world that surrounds them—does not match the stories that continually regenerate.[64] It would not, I think, be going too far to suggest that whereas Vergil urges us to see Sicily's former union with the mainland of Italy as model for empire, Ovid urges us time and again to see that there are no unities of any lasting sort except those of narrative, and time as played out by narrative. What lies behind the immediately visible and tangible is one story and then the next. Empire as a political ideal is to be condemned, even as it is being mocked, because it is founded on nothing that lasts.[65] Stories, however, created out of language can grow and regenerate and, as a result, will survive.

There is a further aspect to Ovid's allusion to the Verrine orations that should be brought out here, an aspect underplayed by Johnson. Underneath Cicero's argument about Verres is the clear assertion that if justice is brought to bear, if Verres is found guilty and the statues returned, the golden age will be restored, Proserpina will be returned to Enna, and the rape and all its consequences will be undone.[66] One could see this as a variant of Vergil's understanding of empire: that underneath rupture lies continuity, which grants authority to—even as it offers a warning about the homogenizing dangers of—empire. But Ovid's particular take on this is different. While empires rise and fall, and the ages decay from golden to iron (and beyond), poetry speaks eternal truths, truths that do not suffer decay, that cannot be stolen, abducted, or violated.[67] In contrast to Vergil, whose greatest fear is the lack of limits created by Proserpina's absence, in Ovid, Proserpina's negotiated return, possible only in poetry, ensures the lack of change. While Proserpina is never present in the *Aeneid*, she is never missing from Ovid's poem.

More to the point, however, Venus is never missing from this poem either. It is Venus and her children that define Roman literature, starting with Ennius, perhaps, but definitely with Lucretius, played out in the elegists, and culminating in Vergil, whose story of Venus's heroic son provides the basis for the *Aeneid*. Venus is the one who extends her imperium; imperium is associated with rifts, rape, and displacement in Ovid, but it is also associated with stories that emerge from those rifts, of the tales of Venus's other son, Cupid, who sets in motion so many of the stories. It is Venus's role at the start of the tale of Proserpina that is ultimately so telling for understanding Ovid's perception of the role of Sicily in his tale as she extends her imperium into the afterlife, erases difference between life and what comes after, and extends the range of poetry into the future.

While on a political level Venus's challenge to Cupid in *Metamorphoses* 5, to cause Hades to fall in love, does indeed speak of extending imperium beyond its bounds, it also, and perhaps more importantly, speaks of the continuity of poetic imperium from the past to the present. In the political world, such imperial expansion entails avarice in one form or another. In the poetic world, it is something quite different, as poets draw on each other, reworking and revising the texts that have come before. As we have seen, the very abduction of Proserpina leads directly to the telling of a spate of stories. There is nothing absent here.

Ovid's view is perhaps clearest in the final passage of the epic:

> Iamque opus exegi, quod nec Iovis ira nec ignis
> nec poterit ferrum nec edax abolere vetustas.
> cum volet, illa dies, quae nil nisi corporis huius
> ius habet, incerti spatium mihi finiat aevi:
> parte tamen meliore mei super alta perennis   875
> astra ferar, nomenque erit indelebile nostrum;
> quaque patet domitis Romana potentia terris
> ore legar populi, perque omnia saecula fama
> (siquid habent veri vatum praesagia) vivam. (*Met.* 15.871–79)

(And now I have finished my work, which neither the wrath of Jove, nor fire, nor sword, nor consuming age can destroy. When it wishes, let that day, which has power over nothing except this body, end the reach of my uncharted life. Nevertheless, in my better part, I will be borne above the high stars, immortal, and my name will be unerasable. Wherever Rome's power stretches over the tamed lands, I shall be read by the lips of the people and, thanks to renown, (if the prophecies of seers have any truth) I shall live through all ages).

Ovid is the emperor of his poetic domain, and his empire will outlast all others.[68] His poetic empire will, in fact, accomplish exactly what Venus asks of Cupid in *Metamorphoses* 5, as it will live on into the future, beyond the scope of his life, conquering all limits.[69] In this Ovid responds to Vergil's concern about an empire without limits (in *Geo.* 1.37–42 and *Aen.* 12.951–52),[70] by suggesting that true empire is poetic, not political, and temporal rather than spatial. Ovid's use of *deducere* at the start of the epic (*Met.* 1.4) points to this, since in the poetic realm last is always best as it engulfs and transforms what came before.[71] Ovid's celebration of poetic tradition is an inversion and critique of political rule. The empire of love is the empire of poetry; both are an empire of time and of a *perpetuum carmen*. While empire is indeed initially a political idea or ideal, in Ovid's mind it fails there, even as it provides the most fertile model for the relationship of a poet to his fellow poets.[72] In Ovid's hands, political empire becomes a metapoetics that describes and lays out the ideal relationship between a poet and his predecessors and imitators.

The relationship between Sicily and empire becomes, through Ovid, a textual one, as Sicily becomes seen as a location that exists as much in the eyes of the poets as in the real world. Empire, too, is reconceived to respond to and celebrate the needs of the poets. Ovid focuses our attention on the textual past and poetic opportunities Sicily has offered, rather than its geography: in his stories about Sicily, Ovid competes with Vergil, above all, but also Cicero as he suggests that the concept of empire—of expansion, competition, even hegemony—has its true place in the world of letters. Sicily remains identified with empire, but poetic empire, and the new world Venus claims as her own as she gazes out across Sicily from the top of Mt. Erice, is not so much Hades as the afterlife of poetry. Sicily, through Ovid, becomes associated with the capacity of poetry, especially love poetry, to be "borne above the stars" and remain immortal. The expansion without limits that is of such concern to Vergil—the expansion identified with the abduction of Proserpina from Sicily—offers Ovid his final, celebratory metaphor. His body may die, *incerti spatium mihi finiat aevi*, but his poetry will live forever. Empire without limits is redefined by Ovid as a poet's dream. Such a conclusion would be too bleak to acknowledge except for one thing: Proserpina's return. In a brief but important passage, Ovid does something critical, again in response to Vergil. His story of Proserpina does not end with her abduction to Hades. She is not trapped in the underworld, as she would appear to be for Vergil. Instead, she is returned to earth, albeit for only half the year, having been reported as eating seven pomegranate seeds in the underworld:

> ... cultis dum simplex errat in hortis, 535
> puniceum curva decerpserat arbore pomum
> sumptaque pallenti septem de cortice grana
> presserat ore suo ... (*Met.* 5.535–38)

(While the innocent wanders in the cultivated gardens, she had plucked a red fruit from the curved bough and had pressed to her lips seven seeds taken from the pale rind.)

This action, seen by just one character, Ascalaphus, is reported to Jupiter who, in turn, tells Ceres that Proserpina can only return to earth for six months.[73] This negotiation, reported in *Metamorphoses* 5.564–71, is dwelt on further in *Fasti* 4.607–18. What is usually taken as an agricultural myth to explain the cycle of seasons, in the context of the *Metamorphoses* and the rest of the stories on Sicily, can be read slightly differently. Here we have Venus, who succeeded in extending her empire to the afterlife through the abduction of Proserpina. Proserpina's tale transforms the matrix of epic from space to time as its geographical structure is, in Ovid's hands, replaced by a literary one. Ceres' journey, reported by Ovid in both *Metamorphoses* 5.438–45, 462–63, and *Fasti* 4.569–72, one that points out the geographical borders of the empire, fails since it does not include the underworld; success is sketched by Jupiter's negotiation, which is temporal. Love poetry, in Ovid's hands, will reign into the future, borrowing and adapting what it inherits from the past.[74] But there remains the need for interacting with, if not affecting, the world, a need that provides the substance of the stories. The poetry that results from this cyclicality—the *perpetuum carmen*—is poetry that is fed by its hunger for the real and the present, provided by Proserpina in her six months on earth visiting Enna, that original *perpetuum ver*, even as Ovid's stories comment on and critique the world that surrounds him. The failure of empire leads to a successful narrative strategy that both transcends and engages with the world.

4

Claudian, Etna, and the Loss of Proserpina

AFTER OVID, the story of Proserpina on Sicily fractures along a number of lines. In this chapter and the next I will trace two itineraries which the tale follows: in this chapter I will follow one from Italy north, consolidated around the reception of Claudian's *De Raptu Proserpinae*; in the next, I will explore another from Paris south, focused on Cicero's version of the tale in the Verrine orations as rediscovered in the eleventh century, as well as an anomalous, yet important, later version of the story: the return of Proserpina in the *Ovide Moralisé*. Disparate routes with different aims, these itineraries nonetheless end up sharing traits, and the tale of Proserpina and its setting on Sicily come to be charged with a new imperial purpose.

Although the early vernacular literature of Sicily itself often included allusions to its classical sources, this particular myth does not surface as important. As Julie Van Peteghem has recently shown, and others have corroborated, the earliest vernacular works from Sicily demonstrate clear familiarity with Ovid and his works, yet they are not focused on questions of empire. Tales that focus more on love than politics, such as those of Pyramus and Thisbe and of Narcissus, recur in the poems of authors from the court of Frederick II. Those texts that do address politics, such as the *Liber ad Honorem Augusti* by Pietro da Eboli, which specifically evokes Vergil, Lucan, and Ovid, nonetheless show little influence of the passages analyzed here. The influence of Vergil's fourth *Eclogue* is more prominent than any part of the *Aeneid*.[1]

The disparate versions of the tale of Proserpina take different paths. On the one hand, *De Raptu Proserpinae* of Claudian (370–404) comes to feature prominently in medieval classrooms as one of the *sex auctores*.[2] The second itinerary, though, which we will investigate in the next chapter, addresses the reemergence of Sicily in the context of empire that results from the Norman conquest of the island, followed swiftly by its role in the First Crusade. These events, I will argue, cause the texts already studied in the classroom to take on new meaning, even as they coincide with—or perhaps occasion—a renewed interest in Cicero's *Verrines*, a text marginalized throughout the early Middle Ages.[3] As a work that argues, as we have seen, that Sicily was "the first of all to be called province, that embellishment of empire, . . . the first who taught our forefathers how splendid it is to govern foreign peoples," this text takes on new importance with the growing interest in a renewed political system as Sicily comes, once again, to offer a space for the discussion of empire, even as the tale of Proserpina offers a narrative structure for that discussion.

We have seen how the myth of Proserpina is treated by Cicero, Vergil, and Ovid; we have noted how her abduction is located on Sicily and with Cicero, and Ovid in his wake, becomes situated at Enna in the center of the island. We have also seen how Ovid responds to Vergil's anxiety about the unrestricted expansion of empire, causing Sicily to become even further identified with imperial discussions. The following will focus only on changes Claudian makes, changes that affect the tradition of the myth. In particular, we will focus on the location of the abduction and the narrative arc of the story, including the mapping of Ceres' journey in pursuit of Proserpina.[4]

As we move through texts that debate increasingly the idea—rather than the reality—of Sicily we find significant changes in its perception which are then folded into the use of the island as locus of a new form of political debate. As with Vergil and Ovid, certain locations on Sicily are highlighted over others. In Vergil the emphasis lies on the impassability of the straits of Messina and the transitional nature of the turn at Drepanum; in Ovid, the focus turns to the significance of Enna, in the center of the island and the narrative potential of the straits; in medieval texts the focus rests largely on that same eastern shore, especially on the volcanic Mt. Etna and the strangely calm straits. Moreover, it is in this narrow space that Ovid's dual theme of the politics and poetics of empire continues to be played out.

That empire, though, is changed from the one whose meaning Vergil and Ovid debated through texts involving Sicily. As we follow the paths the Proserpina story took, we will also interrogate the transformation of the poetic landscape of Sicily, and we will show the changing role of language especially in relation to the afterlife. The narrative of Sicily we will follow is eventually a story of *translatio studii et imperii* shot through with the redemptive language of the High Middle Ages. But at first it is a tale of loss and abandonment.[5]

De Raptu Proserpinae

Claudian's *De Raptu Proserpinae* (c. 395–397) is his version of the Proserpina myth, widely available in the Middle Ages.[6] Based on Ovid's version, Claudian's narrative is accessible from the fifth century on, and by the thirteenth century had become a staple in the curriculum of schools in the north, as Rita Copeland and others have demonstrated.[7] The *sex auctores*, or *Liber Catonianus*, provided university students with a Latin curriculum that extended beyond Vergil and Ovid with, it has been argued, the goal of introducing those students to the concept of *Romanitas*.[8] But that tale, as transmitted, includes two important differences from the earlier versions: though her story is still set on Sicily, Proserpina is abducted from the slopes of Mt. Etna rather than from the center of the island, and the story breaks off at the moment when Ceres begins her search for her daughter. While the ancient versions of the tale all resolved Proserpina's abduction through a negotiation between Pluto and Ceres (with Jupiter sometimes weighing in), Claudian's version and its commentaries omit that negotiation. As a result, the myth of Proserpina both unfolds in a different location, and it comes to serve as a myth of departure.[9]

Location of the Abduction

As we saw in the last chapter, Ovid is clear that Proserpina's abduction takes place at Enna. In the *Metamorphoses* (5.388–92), but especially in *Fasti* (4.419–44), Enna is described in detail as the location of an eternal spring, a *locus amoenus* par excellence:

> terra tribus scopulis vastum procurrit in aequor
>   Trinacris, a positu nomen adepta loci,   420
> grata domus Cereri: multas ibi possidet urbes,
>   in quibus est culto fertilis Henna solo.
> . . .
> valle sub umbrosa locus est aspergine multa
>   uvidus ex alto desilientis aquae.
> tot fuerant illic, quot habet natura, colores,
>   pictaque dissimili flore nitebat humus.   430
> quam simul aspexit, "comites, accedite" dixit
>   "et mecum plenos flore referte sinus."
> praeda puellares animos prolectat inanis,

> et non sentitur sedulitate labor.
> haec implet lento calathos e vimine nexos, 435
>   haec gremium, laxos degravat illa sinus:
> illa legit calthas, huic sunt violaria curae,
>   illa papavereas subsecat ungue comas:
> has, hyacinthe, tenes; illas, amaranthe, moraris;
>   pars thyma, pars rhoean et meliloton amat; 440
> plurima lecta rosa est, sunt et sine nomine flores;
>   ipsa crocos tenues liliaque alba legit.
> carpendi studio paulatim longius itur,
>   et dominam casu nulla secuta comes.[10]

(The Trinacrian land runs out into the wide ocean on three cliff-bound sides, having earned its name from its geographical position, the favorite home of Ceres. She owns many cities there, including fertile Enna with its cultivated soil. . . . In a leafy valley there is a spot damp with the abundant spray of water falling from on high. As many colors as nature has were there, and the earth, as if painted, was sparkling with a variety of flowers. As soon as she saw this, [Proserpina] said "Approach, friends," she said, "and, along with me, bring home laps full of flowers." The trivial bounty attracted their youthful spirits, and toil was not felt with the task. This one fills baskets woven of supple reeds, this one fills her lap, that one the loose fabric; this one gathered marigolds, this one paid attention to beds of violets; that one cut off poppy blossoms with her nails; you held the attention of these, hyacinth, you caused those to delay, amaranth; some love thyme, others cactus and melilot; many a rose is plucked, as are flowers without a name. [Proserpina] herself picked slender crocuses and white lilies. Focused on gathering, she, little by little, strayed away, and, by chance, no companion followed their leader.)

Enna, or Henna, Ovid situates specifically in the center of the island, while Mt. Etna, described in *Metamorphoses* 5.442 and *Fasti* 4.491–96, is at a remove, located near the straits of Messina. The mention of Arethusa in the lines immediately preceding these suggests the poetic roots of this description in Theocritus as she served as the muse of the earlier Greek's bucolic poetry.

In a notable swerve from the previous version, however, Claudian places Proserpina's abduction on Mt. Etna, described as *parens florum*, and shown begging Zephyrus to make the fields bloom, *forma loci superat flores*: "The beauty of the spot surpasse[s] the flowers" (2.101). Ceres herself is said to be from Etna (1.122) and she has hidden Proserpina in a castle near Etna, weaving a "cosmic cloth" while she is away.[11] Note that the description comes from the ancients, but the focus now is placed on Etna, rather than Enna:

> ... Trinacria quondam
> Italiae pars una [iuncta] fuit, sed pontus et aetas
> mutavere situm. rupit confinia Nereus
> victor et abscissos interluit aequore montes   145
> parvaque cognatas prohibent discrimina terras.
> nunc illam socia raptam tellure trisulcam
> opponit natura mari: caput inde Pachyni
> respuit Ionias praetentis rupibus iras;
> hinc latrat Gaetula Thetis Lilybaeaque pulsat   150
> bracchia consurgens; hinc indignata teneri
> concutit obiectum rabies Tyrrhena Pelorum.
> in medio scopulis se porrigit Aetna perustis,
> Aetna Giganteos numquam tacitura triumphos,
> Enceladi bustum, qui saucia terga revinctus   155
> spirat inexhaustum flagranti vulnere sulphur
> et quotiens detractat onus cervice rebelli
> in dextrum laevumque latus, tunc insula fundo
> vellitur et dubiae nutant cum moenibus urbes. (*DRP* 1.142–59)[12]

(Trinacria was formerly one part of Italy, but sea and time changed the location. Nereus broke the confines as victor and poured through the cut off mountains with water, and a small distance separates similar lands. Now nature has set against the sea that three-pointed island broken from its kindred soil: from there the headland of Pachynus regurgitates the Ionian wrath by its overhanging cliffs; from here Gaetulian Thetis barks and, rising up, beats against the Lilybaean arms; from here the rabid Tyrrhenian, enraged at being contained, shakes the reef of Pelorus. In the middle, Etna extends itself with half-burned cliffs, Etna which will never remain silent about the victory over the Giants, the pyre of Enceladus, who, bound at his wounded back, breathes inexhaustible sulphur from the flaming wound and whenever he shifts the burden with his rebellious neck towards the right and left side, the island is then plucked from the foundations and the uncertain towns nod with their walls.)

And it is from here that Hades abducts Proserpina:

hic ubi servandum mater fidissima pignus
abdidit...
     iam linquitur Aetna
totaque decrescit refugo Trinacria visu. (*DRP* 1.179–80; 190–91)

(Here's where the most faithful of mothers has hidden her loved one for safekeeping... now Etna is left behind and all Trinacria grows smaller as the view recedes.)[13]

In most of the ancient Roman versions of the story, Etna served as just one of two key locations in the myth as the spot where Ceres lights her torches as she begins her search for her daughter, abducted from the other key spot, Enna. The medieval version of Claudian's account merges these two events, as Etna serves as both the idyllic site of abduction and the nightmarish location of raging fires. Here, far from that fair field of Cicero's Enna, we move back east to Etna: in Claudian, as it is received the entire tale takes place on the volcano.[14]

Stephen Hinds has suggested that this change may well not have been made as early as we had thought.[15] Rather, he argues that for Claudian the rape was still set at Enna, following Ovid and others, and suggests that it is not until the later tradition that the abduction moves to Etna. Our purpose here, though, is to examine the text that played a part in medieval culture. As a result, the timing of the changes is not as crucial as the fact of their existence. In the school texts and their related commentaries, the abduction takes place on Etna.[16]

Moreover, the shift of location is not unique or original: the alteration appears to occur as early as the *Fabulae* of Hyginus (c. 64 BC–AD 17). A work written in the first century AD, Hyginus's *Fabulae* remains influential through the course of the Middle Ages. It is therefore significant that we find the following:

Pluton petit ab Iove Proserpinam filiam eius et Cereris in coniugium daret. Iovis negavit Cererem passuram ut filia sua in Tartaro tenebricoso sit, sed iubet eum rapere eam flores legentem in monte Aetna, qui est in Sicilia, in quo Proserpina dum flores cum Venere et Diana et Minerva legit, Pluton quadrigis venit et eam rapuit; quod postea Ceres ab Iove impetravit ut dimidia parte anni apud se, dimidia apud Plutonem esset.[17]

(Pluto asks Jupiter permission to marry Proserpina, his daughter by Ceres. Jupiter said that Ceres would not allow her daughter to go to darkest

Tartarus, but he orders him to snatch her while picking flowers on Mount Etna, which is in Sicily; on which, while Proserpina picks flowers with Venus, Diana, and Minerva, Pluto came in his chariot and snatched her; which is why afterwards Ceres convinced Jupiter that she should be half the year with her, half with Pluto.)

Hyginus here identifies the site of the abduction as Etna, which is now characterized by flowers (*in quo Proserpina dum flores... legit*). The two locations of Ovid's version that clearly distinguished the beauty of Enna and its flowers from the fires of Etna are here conflated. In some ways this shouldn't surprise us: Theocritus and the pastoral strands that derive from his *Idylls* likewise placed beautiful flowers on Etna.

The substitution of Etna for Enna recurs elsewhere, including in the Second Vatican Mythographer:

Venus, indignata quod Proserpina Iovis et Cereris filia coniugia sperneret, Plutoni propter terrorem Tiphei evomentis Ethnam ab inferis emerso intulit amorem ut Proserpinam Iovis et Cereris filiam circa cacumen Ethne flores legentem eriperet. (chap. 115)[18]

(Venus, offended because Proserpina, daughter of Jove and Ceres, spurned marriage, brought love to Pluto, having emerged onto Etna from the underworld out of fear of the vomiting of Typhoeus, so that he might abduct Proserpina, daughter of Jove and Ceres, picking flowers near the summit of Etna.)

The third Vatican Mythographer, otherwise known as pseudoAlbrecht, also makes this substitution.[19]

Juxta Aetnam rapta eius dicitur filia, quod, ut testator Lucanus, Sicilia frugum est feracissima.

(It is said that her [Ceres'] daughter was seized near Etna because, as Lucan claims, Sicily is most fruitful in crops.)[20]

The move to Etna, whenever it actually occurs, coincides with the growing importance of the volcanic mountain in many varied texts, even as it corresponds to a growing suspicion of the town name of Enna.[21] As we have seen, the earlier mentions of Etna contrast it starkly to the lush fields of Enna. Starting with Seneca the Younger (4 BC–AD 65), though, the mountain itself gains prominence and becomes the focus of the island, even outside of the myth of

Proserpina. The rocky climb to truth and virtue is a favorite metaphor for Seneca, but there is one rocky climb that he describes in detail, situated on a specific mountain: *Si haec mihi perscripseris, tunc tibi audebo mandare, ut in honorem meum Aetnam quoque ascendas*; "If you will write me a full account of these matters," he says, "I shall then have the boldness to ask you to perform another task: also to climb Etna at my special request" (to Lucilius, *Epist.* 79.2).[22] Etna, he continues, offers the quintessential challenge for an author because so many poets have written about it. The cragginess of the mountain—its height, its challenge—is compared in this essay to the difficulty of attaining the sublime style, a difficulty made all the more challenging by the fact that so many had attempted it before: Ovid, he says, could not be prevented from using this theme simply because Vergil had already covered it.[23]

> Quid tibi do ne Aetnam describas in tuo carmine, ne hunc sollemnem omnibus poetis locum adtingas? Quem quominus Ovidius tractaret, nihil obstitit quod iam Vergilius impleverat; ne Severum quidem Cornelium uterque deterruit. Omnibus praeterea feliciter hic locus se dedit, et qui praecesserant non praeripuisse mihi videntur quae dici poterant, sed aperuisse. [Sed] Multum interest utrum ad consumptam materiam an ad subactam accedes: crescit in dies, et inventuris inventa non obstant. Praeterea condicio optima est ultimi: parata verba invenit, quae aliter instructa novam faciem habent. Nec illis manus inicit tamquam alienis; sunt enim publica. . . . Aut ego te non novi aut Aetna tibi salivam movet; iam cupis grande aliquid et par prioribus scribere. Plus enim sperare modestia tibi tua non permittit, quae tanta in te est ut videaris mihi retracturus ingenii tui vires, si vincendi periculum sit: tanta tibi priorum reverentia est.
>
> Inter cetera hoc habet boni sapientia: nemo ab altero potest vinci nisi dum ascenditur. Cum ad summum perveneris, paria sunt; non est incremento locus, statur. Numquid sol magnitudini suae adicit? numquid ultra quam solet, luna procedit? Maria non crescent; mundus eundem habitum ac modum servat. Extollere se quae iustam magnitudinem implevere non possunt. . . . An Aetna tua possit sublabi et in se ruere, an hoc excelsum cacumen et conspicuum per vasti maris spatia detrahat adsidua vis ignium, nescio: virtutem non flamma, non ruina inferius adducet; haec una maiestas deprimi nescit. Nec proferri ultra nec referri potest; sic huius, ut caelestium, stata magnitudo est. Ad hanc nos conemur educere.[24]

(Indeed, what do I offer you so you don't just sketch Etna in your poem, don't just brush on this topic, required of all poets? Ovid could not be kept from treating this because Vergil had already covered it; nor could either of these writers deter Cornelius Severus. Moreover, this topic has given itself to them all happily, and those who had gone before seem to me not to have precluded what could be said, but to have opened the way. Much depends on whether you undertake material that is already harvested or newly sown, where the topic grows daily and what has been argued does not stand in the way of what will be argued. Furthermore, the best situation falls to the last; he finds prepared words which, when arranged differently show a new face. He does no violence to those [words] of others. For they are public property.... Either I don't know you or Etna makes your mouth water. You have been wanting to write something in the grand style and equal to your forebears. Your modesty does not allow you to hope for more, which is such a great factor for you that you seem to me to be about to rein in the force of your natural talent, if there should be any risk of outstripping others, so great is your reverence for the earlier writers.

Among others, wisdom has this advantage: no man can be outstripped by another, except during the climb. But when you have reached the top, they are the same, there is no place for further distinction, the contest rests. Is it possible for the sun to add to its size? Can the moon advance beyond what is accustomed? The seas do not grow. The universe keeps the same character, the same limits. Things which have attained their due size cannot grow higher.... Whether your Etna can collapse and fall in ruins, whether the assiduous force of the flames diminishes this lofty summit, even visible for many miles over the deep sea, I do not know; flames or ruin will not diminish virtue. This is one greatness that knows no diminution. It cannot be raised or lowered further. Its magnitude, like that of celestial objects, is so. To this level let us try to raise ourselves.)

Etna's prominence becomes the hallmark of these late antique and early medieval texts about Sicily even as it becomes affiliated with discussions of poetic competition.

Other works students and commentators might have read would feed into this very notion of Etna as a place of increased attention. In the sixth century we find a critical passage for our argument in Gregory the Great (*Dialogue* 4.35) that focuses on Etna in a way that will have lasting impact, as he makes the link between the volcanic flames and fires tormenting the damned[25]:

GREGOR: Sed idem Eumorphius ad extrema vitae veniens, vocavit puerum suum, eique praecepit, dicens: "Vade citius, et dic Stephano

Optioni, ut concitus veniat, quia ecce navis parata est ut ad Siciliam duci debeamus..."

PETR.: Terribile est valde, quod dicitur: sed quaeso te, cur egredienti animae navis apparuit, vel cur se ad Siciliam duci moriturus praedixit?

GREGOR: Anima vehiculo non eget: sed mirum non est, si adhuc homini in corpore posito illud apparuit, quod per corpus assueverat videre, ut per hoc intelligi daretur quo ejus anima spiritualiter duci potuisset. Quod vero se ad Siciliam duci testatus est, quid sentiri aliud potest, nisi quod prae ceteris locis, in ejus terrae insulis eructante igne tormentorum ollae patuerunt?[26]

(GREGOR: Now, when Eumorphius himself was nearing the end of life, he called his servant and ordered him, saying, "Go quite quickly and tell Stephen Optio to come quickly, since, behold, the ship is ready that we need to be transported to Sicily..."

PETER: What is said is truly shocking. But I ask you, why did a ship appear for the departing soul, or why did he foretell that he, about to die, will be taken to Sicily?

GREGOR: The soul has no need for transportation. But it is not surprising if at this point a man in his corporeal state saw that which he is accustomed to see through the senses, so that through this he was given to understand how his soul could be transported spiritually. As to what is attested, that he should indeed be transported to Sicily, what else can be meant but that, more than anyplace else, on the islands of that land, pits lay open with spewing fire of torment?)

Once established in the literature, this identification of Etna with Gregory's understanding of it as a place of fire and brimstone becomes standard. Translations of Gregory's *Dialogues* are widespread: the Sicilian translation, *Libru de lu dialagu de Sanctu Gregoriu*[27] adds that souls go not only to Sicily but also to *Bulcanu e Stronguli e li autri,* that is, the other volcanic islands off the coast north of Etna; all of the translations of this dialogue I have seen identify Sicily with its volcano, Etna, and Etna with purging fires.[28] In this dialogue, Gregory the Great links Etna with the afterlife, and identifies it as the place where the body waiting to die or be reborn will be purged of its sins. Later, Etienne de Bourbon[29] (1180–1261) will state that *locus purgatorii prope civitatem Cathenam [est]* ("the location of purgatory is near the city of Catania").

Yet even before the development of Purgatory as a fixed location, as Jacques Le Goff has clearly shown, Gregory's dialogue nonetheless speaks to the longstanding biblical belief that there are places on earth where sinners go to be purged of sin and readied for the last judgment. As Claire Honess has noted, early Purgatory was affiliated with Hell.[30] Le Goff concludes that Sicily fails to become the terrestrial model for Purgatory because "[e]n Sicile la grande tradition infernale n'a pas permis au Purgatoire de s'épanouir. L'antique Enfer a barré la route au jeune Purgatoire."[31] ("on Sicily the grand tradition of hell does not extend to Purgatory. Ancient Hell barred the route to youthful Purgatory"). In this, however, Le Goff downplays a strain that recurs in texts about Sicily, that of the recovery of a lost paradise. While it is indeed true, as Le Goff demonstrates, that Etna is affiliated with punishment of sin in the underworld, it is also true, as we shall see, that it is associated with tales of redemption as Enna, the location on Sicily that had been associated with lost paradise, becomes unable to play that role.

The concept of a place and state of purgation that precedes death had biblical origins. Identified as Gehenna, with its development into a place of fleshly purgation, this location continues to be identified throughout the relevant literature. The similarity of the two names, Enna and Gehenna, seems to rob the plateau of its earlier innocence. Enna's alternative name, *Henna*, comes even closer to the biblical Gehenna, and so to a place associated not with flowers and beauty but, rather, with punishment.[32] Isidore (560–636) writes that Etna is where Scylla and Charybdis are to be found, mentions the constant fire and smoke, and ends with: "Mount Etna is so-called from fire . . . and sulfur; Gehenna likewise" (XIV.viii.14).[33] Moreover, in his *De natura rerum* 47.4, he adds:

> De monte Aetna . . . Constat autem ad exemplum gehennae, cuius ignis perpetua incendia spirabunt ad puniendos peccatores, qui cruciabuntur in secula seculorum. Nam sicut isti montes tanta temporis diuturnitate usque nunc flammis aestuantibus perseverant, ita ut numquam extingui possint, sic ignis ille ad crucianda corpora damnatorum finem numquam est habiturus.
>
> (About Mount Etna. . . . It, however, is an example of Gehenna, whose fires will exhale perpetual flames for the punishment of sinners, who will suffer for age after age. For even as these mountains persist with roiling flames from the very beginning of time to now in such a way that they may never be extinguished, just so that fire of Gehenna intended for the suffering of the damned will never come to an end.)

To this encyclopedist, these two locations are paired. Bede (672–735) echoes this sentiment with: *Inde montis Aetnae ad exemplum gehennae* (PL 90, col. 0276A) ("From the [instance] of Mount Etna [we find] the example of Gehenna").[34]

Later texts are more explicit. *La conquesta di Sichilia per li Normandi* suggests a link between the two: *Nota chi Mungibellu si chamava intandu Gibel, lu qualli nuy ora per littra chamamu Ethna, quasi munti di focu, oy di lu Infernu, sive Gehenne.*[35] ("Note that Mongibello was then called Gibel, which now in writing we call Etna, that is a mountain of fire either from the Inferno, or Gehenna"). There is an apparent blurring of the two, and even when Gehenna is not mentioned, the two locations become joined because of their linguistic similarity. Enna and Etna, especially in manuscripts, are morphologically close enough to encourage confusion if not conflation. The eighteenth-century *Lexicon topographicum Siciliae* under *Enna* includes:

> Quamquam vero Scriptores alii raptam Proserpinam in Aetna monte evulgent, ... nolim hic funem trahere. "Mirum dictu," scribit Cluverius, "quoties in antiquorum libris duo ista vocabula Enna et Aetna confundantur. Hinc factum, ut alii raptum illum in Aetna, alii ad Ennam obtigisse, affirment."[36]

> (Although indeed some writers claim that Proserpina was raped on Mt. Etna, ... I don't wish to concur. "It's amazing," writes Cluver, "how often in books of the ancients the two words Enna and Etna are confused. From this they affirm that some hold that the abduction took place on Etna, others at Enna.")

The same text also cites "Strabo 2.103" (book 6, chap. 2) as an example of an alternate reading: *"Juxta Aetnam Siciliae montem fluere..." et legunt nonnulli: "Juxta Ennam"* ([The rivers] "'flowed near Mt. Etna in Sicily' and some read: 'near Enna'").[37]

Medieval maps—the Hereford *mappa mundi* (c. 1300) in particular—bear this out. In the image reproduced here, we see Mt. Etna in the center of the island, replacing Enna.[38] In addition, the triangular shape of both mountain and island echo the name Trinacria and their similar orientation reinforces the notion found in the literature that the island is all but identified with the volcano.[39]

Arguably, through the linguistic similarity between Enna, or Henna, and Gehenna, the location develops from the *locus amoenus*, as in Ovid, to its very opposite, a land of punishment and hell on earth. Yet since that is what Etna already offers with its volcanic history, the two are frequently conflated.[40] And the reworking of the island does not end there. There remains a need for a site that speaks of perpetual spring, a setting for, among other things, Proserpina's

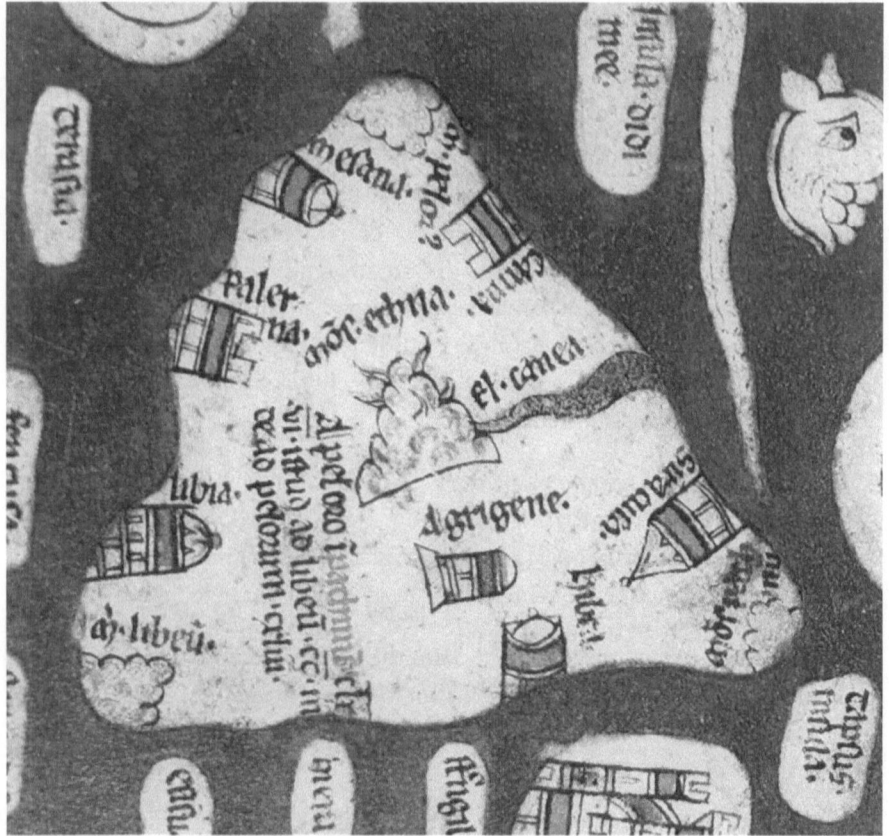

FIGURE 1. Hereford *mappa mundi*, detail of Sicily (c. 1300). 1.58 × 1.33 m (5 ft. 2 in. × 4 ft. 4 in.). © Hereford Cathedral. Reproduced with permission.

innocence. Etna, thanks perhaps to Theocritus and the pastoral tradition, perhaps to the polarities associated with Sicily in general, becomes a place known not just for terror, but for beauty as well. The two approach each other and, in many instances, merge, as in the *Fabularius* of Conrad of Mure (1210–1281), who argues that Pluto snatched Proserpina *circa cacumen Ethne vel Ennei campi flores legentem cum puellis coevis* ("around the summit of Etna or of the Ennean field when she was picking flowers with girls the same age").[41]

As a result, the descriptions of Etna—and the myths they conjure up—come increasingly to draw greater attention to Etna as a place marked by an unearthly combination of charm and horror, a location characterized by countervailing tendencies. This fusion is particularly notable among writers who have not visited the island.

For the most part it is Etna's intermittent blasts of fire that continue to attract the attention of writers. The treatment of Etna as a place of fiery purgation continues into the high Middle Ages, with, for example, Goffredo Malaterra (fl. eleventh c.) referring to Etna as a place marked by lava flows, snow, floods, and hail.[42] Likewise, Peter Damian (1007–1072) writes in the *Vita Sancti Odilonis* of the horrors heard on Sicily:[43]

> Sunt, inquit, vicina nobis loca, ex quibus gravissima flammarum furentium evomuntur incendia, in quibus etiam locis animae reproborum diversa luunt pro meritorum qualitate tormenta. Ad quorum semper exaggeranda supplicia innumerabiles sunt daemones deputati, qui intolerabiles eorum poenas quotidie renovant; et eos ad rediviva supplicia indesinenter instaurant. Quos tamen ego frequenter audivi querulis lamentationibus ejulantes et lacrymabili vociferatione deflentes, quod orationibus et eleemosynis quorumdam adversus eos infoederabiliter concertantium frequenter ex eorum manibus eriperentur animae damnatorum.

> (There are, he said, places near us from which are spewed forth the harshest fires of raging flames; in these places also souls of reprobates undergo diverse torments according to what they deserve. Countless demons, who renew the intolerable penalties daily for these men, are assigned for heaping up punishments of these men forever; they expose them to renewed penalties indefinitely. Nevertheless, I frequently heard those men screaming with plaintive lamentations and crying with a tearful plea, because by the prayers and almsgiving of certain people striving relentlessly on their behalf, the souls of the damned are frequently snatched from the hands of the demons.)

Around 1173, Peter of Blois, having returned from Sicily, wrote a similar letter from the safety of England to a bishop still abroad:

> Terra siquidem vestra devorat habitatores suos nec parcit aetati, nec sexui defert, nec personam considerat, nec favorem conditionis, nec gratiam dignitatis acceptat. Triginta et septem animae cum domino Stephano Siciliam sunt ingressae, omnesque in morte conclusi sunt, praeter me et magistrum Rogerium Northmannum, virum litteratum, industrium et modestum. Nos solos eduxit Dominus per misericordiam suam de medio umbrae mortis in

fortitudine manus suae. Cumque vix aut nunquam permittatur egressus his, qui semel ingressi sunt: nolo ingredi; . . . Quis, quaeso, ibi securus inhabitat, ubi praeter caeteras passiones, montes ignem infernalem semper evomunt, et fetorem sulphureum evaporant? Nam ibi procul dubio est porta inferi, de qua dictum est: A porta inferi erue, Domine, animam meam. Portae, inquam, mortis et inferi sunt montes Trinacriae, ubi absorbentur a terra homines, et descendunt in infernum viventes . . . Sed ad vos, amantissime Pater, in Siciliam non revertar. Fovet Anglia me jam senem, quae vos fovit infantes. Utinam relinqueretis terram illam, Pater, montuosam et monstruosam, et ad nativi aeris dulcedinem rediretis . . . Fugite, Pater, a montibus flammivomis, suspecta sit vobis Aetnae vicinitas, nec vos morientem videat regio infernalis.[44]

(Indeed your land devours its inhabitants without thought of age or deference to gender, nor does it take character into consideration, nor does it accept the favor of condition or the influence of dignity. Thirty-seven men went to Sicily with lord Stephen and all are imprisoned in death except myself and our leader Roger the Norman, a literate, industrious, and modest man. We alone the Lord led out through his pity from the middle of the shadow of death by the bravery of his hand. Since this departure was permitted rarely or never for these who had once gone in, I do not wish to go in. . . . Who, I ask, is secure living there, where in addition to other suffering, the mountains always spew forth infernal fire and steam with sulphurous stench? For there, without a doubt, is the gate of hell, about which it is said: "Rescue my soul from the gate of hell, Lord." The mountains of Sicily are the gates of death and hell, I say, where men are absorbed by the earth and descend living into hell. . . . But to you, dearest Father, in Sicily I will not return. England nurtures me as an already old man, even as it did you as a child. Would that you would leave that land, Father, mountainous and monstrous, and return to the sweetness of your native air . . . Flee, Father, from the flame-spewing mountains: the vicinity of Etna should not be trusted by you, and that infernal region should not witness you, dying.)

He continues: *Scitis quod Aetna mons frequenter ignes suos in immensum circumquaque diffundit: et adhuc per spatium diaetae unius undique combusta et deformata est tota facies regionis* (PL 207, cols. 135A–B: "You know because Mt. Etna frequently pours forth its own fires in immense and enveloping waves; and besides in the space of a single day the entire appearance of the region is on fire and disfigured everywhere"). Through descriptions such as these, Etna becomes identified as a place of both beauty and terror, an identification that continues throughout the Middle Ages.

We find a parallel description in the work of Hugo Falcandus, who in both his *Liber de regno Sicilie* and his *Epistola . . . de calamitate Sicilie* (c. 1200) refers to Etna in comparable terms. The author is reacting to the volcano's recent eruption in 1169,[45] which destroyed Catania; nevertheless, we find in Hugo's writings first a description of the eruption (sect. 53C), then, both there and in the *Epistola*, an interpretation of the event:

> His aliisque prodigiis curie familiares eorumque fautores perterriti, arbitrabantur novitatem hanc rerum magnam Siculis calamitatem portendere. timebant ergo ne cancellarius, ope et consilio Constantinopolitani imperatoris, qui legatos eius, ut ferebatur, benigne susceperat, regnum Sicilie, collectis viribus, occuparet.[46]

(Having been terrified by these and other signs, the servants of the curia and their supporters were judging that this newness of things signified great calamity for the Sicilians. They were therefore afraid lest the chancellor, with his strength gathered together, might occupy the Sicilian kingdom, by the power and council of the emperor of Constantinople, who, as it was said, had received his ambassadors kindly.)

In the preface to his history, the connection is made even clearer:

> quod si nostri temporis mala et que ipsi vidimus volumus recensere, nuper te vehemens terre motus tanta concussit violentia ut cunctis ruentibus edificiis haud facile numerabilem utriusque sexus multitudinem lignorum ac lapidum moles oppresserit. nunc autem, ut sic fortune lentescat improbitas, post multa et varia calamitatum genera turpissime tandem addiceris servituti. (*Epistola*, sect. 56A)

(But if we wish to recall the ills of our time and those which we ourselves have seen, recently a vehement earthquake shook you with such violence that, with all the buildings falling down, a mass of wood and stone covered an indeterminate number of both sexes. Now, however, as the wickedness of fortune thus weakens, after many disasters of various kinds, you will finally be termed most foully as slaves.)[47]

But the opposite is true as well. For every story that exists about the infernal fires of Etna there is one about its heavenly qualities. Early on we find evidence that Deucalion and Pyrrha were believed to have restarted the world from Etna: Hyginus, in *Fabula* 153, "Deucalion et Pyrrha," offers the following:

> Cataclysmus, quod nos diluvium vel irrigationem dicimus, cum factum est, omne genus humanum interiit praeter Deucalionem et Pyrrham, qui in montem Aetnam, qui altissimus in Sicilia esse dicitur, fugerunt.[48]

(Cataclysm, which is what we call flood or inundation, when it happened, erased the entire human race except Deucalion and Pyrrha, who fled to Mt. Etna, which is said to be the tallest in Sicily.)

While the story of Deucalion and Pyrrha is usually set on Parnassus, the conflation of disaster and hopefulness that the story tells is characteristic, as we have seen, of Sicilian myths.[49] But taken together this tale hands to the Middle Ages a possibility that is swiftly capitalized on: the story of Deucalion and Pyrrha is read as a type of Noah's flood, which, in turn, is seen as a type of the fall and a forerunner of the resurrection. And all of it happens on Mt. Etna. In the ninth century (850), Freculphus makes this point, quoting Josephus, who cites Manaseas's ninety-sixth book of the history of the flood:

> Sed et Manaseas Damascenus in nonagesimo sexto historiarum libro ita de hoc diluvio dicit: Est et super Muniadam excelsus mons in Armenia, qui Baris appellatur, in quo multos fugientes sermo est diluvii tempore liberatos, et quemdam simul in arca devectum in Siciliae montis venisse summitatem, lignorumque reliquias multo tempore ibi conservatas ferunt. Fuit autem ista arca quam etiam Moses Judaeorum legislator scripsit.[50]

(Manaseas the Damascene in the ninety-sixth book of his histories says thus about this flood: there is indeed a lofty mountain over Minyas in Armenia, which is called Baris, where the story is that many fleeing in the time of the flood were freed and that at the same time a certain man borne in an ark had come to the summit of the Sicilian mountain and they say that scraps of wood were conserved there for a long time. This moreover was the very same ark that Moses, lawmaker of the Jews, also wrote of.)

This identification of Etna with the origin of the renewed world fits well with the examples of Etna's identification with the earthly paradise.

This fact is reinforced by a wealth of stories about hidden paradises found on Etna. It is in the *Otia Imperialia*, however, that we get the most striking adaptation of this myth.[51] There Etna is described as having a cave on one of its shoulders where Arthur lives:

In Sicilia mons est Ethna . . . Hunc autem montem vulgares Muntgibel appellant. In huius deserto narrant indigene Arcturum magnum nostris temporibus apparuisse. Cum enim uno aliquo die custos palefridi episcopalis Catheniensis commissum sibi equum depulueraret, subito impetus lascive pinguedinis equus exiliens ac in propriam se recipiens libertatem fugit. Ab insequente ministro per montis ardua precipitiaque quesitus, nec inventus, timore pedissequo sucrescente, circa montis opaca perquiritur . . . Artissima semita sed plana inventa, puer in spatiosissimam planiciem iocundam omnibusque deliciis plenam advenit, ibique in palatio miro opere constructo repperit Arcturum in strato regii apparatus recubantem.[52]

(Mount Etna is in Sicily . . . The local people call this mountain Mongibello. They relate that in our own times the great Arthur has appeared in an unfrequented region of it. For one day the man who looked after the bishop of Catania's palfrey was rubbing down the horse entrusted to his care, when suddenly in a burst of playful exuberance, the horse, leaping up on its own, broke free, and fled. Sought, but not found, by the pursuing groom through the steep and dangerous reaches of the mountain, with his fear growing with every step, he probed the dark recesses of the mountain. . . . Having found a very narrow but level path, the servant came out onto a hugely wide and beautiful plain, full of every delight; there in a palace constructed with marvelous worksmanship, he discovers Arthur reclining on a couch of royal splendor.)

This tale creates a tradition of its own, with the Italian version, "Detto del gatto lupesco" repeating the story of Arthur and introducing him into Italian folk lore.[53]

From the loss of innocence, then, found in early discussions of Etna we move to stories that present the mountain as also an earthly paradise, such as the stories of those in the *Otia*, Deucalion and Pyrrha, and Noah. These texts mark both a connection to the Ovidian identification of Sicily with the Proserpina myth and a divergence from it: here, as opposed to Ovid, the image of the golden age is not destroyed. Instead, the texts are clear that it remains, hidden perhaps, yet intact. Medieval stories set on Etna, then, do not tell of the loss of innocence alone but rather the story of its embeddedness.

Not only does the reception of Claudian succeed in conflating Enna and Etna, but Hades' dramatic rending of the earth to abduct Proserpina absorbs within it the separation stories of the island from the mainland. In this, the separation is transferred from Scylla and Charybdis to Etna, and the violence of the break becomes a locus for discussion of innocence rather than unity. In other words, whereas for Vergil the break between the two landmasses rested on the assertion that there had been a unified land at some point in the past, for Claudian, responding to Ovid, the big break tore open what had been a heaven on earth to create a situation of post innocence shadowed by the possibility of innocence restored.

The text of Claudian that we work with, and the text available during the Middle Ages, posited Etna, in all its complexity, as the location of the abduction. In this, it resonates with the growing interest, in Italy and elsewhere, in the volcanic mountain, and suggests that Enna has been first marginalized arguably because of its association with Gehenna, then reconceived as part of Etna. Yet there is one further anomaly in Claudian's text to make note of: the narrative arc of the myth.

Narrative Arc

The most astonishing thing about Claudian's text is where it ends. The myth as told by Cicero and Ovid, drawing from the earlier versions including the *Homeric Hymn to Demeter*, is essentially tripartite: it tells of the agreement made with Hades to abduct Proserpina (although the reasons vary: for his power, for Venus, for Jupiter), the abduction, and the negotiated return. While Claudian includes the first two, he omits the third: his is a grim tale of abduction, a tale without resolution that ends with Ceres finally getting word, through a dream, of Proserpina's location, but before her journey there or subsequent negotiation. There is no resolution. As a result, the story Claudian tells serves a very different purpose from that served by Cicero or Ovid: this is a myth of loss, not recovery; and of the hollowness of home once it is devoid of family.[54]

Through Claudian, the myth of Proserpina changes from a narrative of negotiation to one of loss and from a story about the triangular island of Sicily to one about a mountain known increasingly as a place of transition. These differences from the tale in Cicero do more to change the nature of the tale than might first be apparent. As the story is transmitted, it is a tale in which Etna is the only location that matters, a location marked by both beauty and terror, and it is a tale of loss. While in the ancient versions of the tale, from the *Homeric Hymns* through Ovid, Proserpina's abduction is resolved through a negotiation between Pluto and Ceres with Jupiter weighing in, in Claudian's version that negotiation never takes place. It is his tale that offers the most important and available version of the myth to be transmitted to the Middle Ages. For those educated in France, who had most likely never visited Sicily, and who had precious few other texts about the island to compare it to, the image they have is influenced by this text: Sicily is identified with Etna. Etna is a place known both for its raging flames and its surpassingly beautiful landscape. And Sicily, with the tale of Proserpina, comes to be a land associated with loss, since nowhere in the text of Claudian does Sicily's connection with negotiation appear.

In addition, this is a story that portrays the notion of empire as a space defined by ever-increasing edges and growth, yet one that is chaotic, without a true center. This is suggested in the description of the cosmic cloth, or tapestry, Proserpina is described as weaving in the first book, but even more clearly in Ceres' description of her proposed journey:

> non Rheni glacies, non me Riphaea tenebunt
> frigora, non dubio Syrtis cunctabitur aestu.
> stat fines penetrare Noti Boreaeque nivalem
> vestigare domum; primo calcabitur Atlans
> occasu facibusque meis lucebit Hydaspes. (*DRP* 3.321–25)

> (Not the ice of the Rhine nor the Riphaean cold will hold me back, nor will the Syrtes delay me with its uncertain tides. I am resolved to penetrate the bounds of the South Wind and to track down the snowy home of the North; I will trample upon Atlas where the sun first sets and Hydaspes will shine bright with my torches.)[55]

Ceres may light her torches at Etna, but she travels to the ends of the earth searching for her daughter. In the course of the text, Sicily has moved from being an out-of-the-way location where her daughter was safely stashed to the center against which all faraway edges are measured. If there is a renegotiation present here, it is in the definition of empire, where Sicily moves from province to center.[56]

That the tale of Proserpina was perceived as a tale of loss can be traced through a number of texts in the tradition following Claudian. Gregory of Tours (538/9–94) likens Proserpina's fate to that of Dido:

> Taceo Cupidinis, non Ascanii dilectionem emeneosque, lacrimas vel exitia saeva Didonis, non Plutonis triste vestibulum, non Proserpinae stuprosum raptum, non Cerberi triforme caput.[57]

> (I remain silent about [affairs of] Cupid: not the love and marriage of Ascanius or the tears or harsh departure of Dido, not the sad foyer of Pluto, not the libidinous abduction of Proserpina, not the triple head of Cerberus.)

So, too, Fulgentius (fl. late fifth / early sixth c.), in *Expositio Virgilianae continentiae*, writes: *Sicut enim inferni Proserpina regina est, ita scientiae regina memoria est, quae in elisis proserpens dominatur perenniter mentibus*. (For as Proserpina is queen of the underworld, so memory is the queen of knowledge, which, gliding, reigns perennially in unfettered minds).[58]

The fact that these versions of the Proserpina myth do not progress beyond the abduction—as we have seen, Claudian's tale does not tell of the return,[59] and none of the examples speak of her recovery—means that the focus of this tale remains on the events leading up to Proserpina's disappearance, not on her return. How we prepare ourselves for the fiery judgment of Etna is read through the ancient tale that touches on that very topic: Proserpina's abduction by Hades on Etna. Marjorie Woods has argued eloquently for the need to interpret such partial stories as complete narratives, since they were processed that way at the time.[60] It is indeed true in this case that an essential myth such as that of Proserpina that also offered a partially veiled critique of empire would have served an essential purpose. A story of loss, and of empire redefined in the presence of loss, is a story that would have resonated and struck a chord. This is a tale of no recovery and no return, a tale of an empire gained through loss, a tale that denies a fruitful future.

The myth suggests repeatedly that the response to the abandonment inherent in this story is punishment. The story of Proserpina, ending with Ceres' search rather than discovery and renegotiation, serves as an allegory of the fall. Yet as times change, and the interest in expanding the Christian empire both territorially through the Crusades and spiritually via the ramifications of regular confession instituted by the Fourth Lateran Council started infiltrating daily life, the question of the return, with its built-in need for negotiation, became more pressing. To put it another way, the process of negotiation, of establishing a balance between action and confession, meant that Claudian's version of the tale failed to have sufficient agency. As a result, in the high Middle Ages, tales that featured the return of Proserpina, set in the landscape established in the texts just reviewed, come to supplement the version Claudian offered. In addition, the very texts that offered discussions of her return also situated the myth more squarely in the context of empire, a context that spoke directly to both public and private concerns of the days of the early Crusades.

5

The Redemption of Proserpina

AS WE saw in chapter 4, Claudian's *De Raptu Proserpinae* focused on Proserpina's abduction. Texts that draw from Claudian's version confirm Sicily as the setting for the Proserpina myth and tell only of her abduction, not the negotiation that led to her return. The fact that such an approach fits with Vergil's concerns in the opening of the *Georgics* as well as transitional events preceding the afterlife, gleaned from texts such as Gregory's *Dialogues*, reinforces this reading. This strand of the Proserpina myth is a myth of loss.

Yet the form of the tale appears to lose its appeal. Instead, as the imperial issues of the Norman conquest of Sicily and the Crusades begin to crystallize there is growing interest in other aspects of the myth, including negotiation, return, and redemption, and the shape the tale takes changes, both in terms of what is activated from the past and what is told of in the present. An index to these changes is provided by the descriptions of the straits of Messina. In his *Chronicon*, Richard of Devizes refers to the straits as the River Del Far or Farus and writes that King Richard, *transmisso flumine magno del Far, quod a Sicilia Calabriam separat* ("having passed over the great river Del Far, which separates Calabria from Sicily"), entered Calabria in arms.[1] Goffredo Malaterra, writing in the first chapter of book 2 about Roger I's approach to Sicily, refers to the journey across the straits as most dangerous, yet narrow (*periculosissimo quamvis brevi*[2]) and eminently crossable. From the extraordinary impassability of the straits in Vergil's text to a river (perilous, but a river nonetheless), the description of the straits has changed, as has their metaphoric purpose. While there is still mention of terrible weather and tides in the straits, the fact that the passage has been described as a river is significant. One sees the same effect in the illustrations that accompany the twelfth-century epic of Frederick II by Peter of Eboli (fl. 1196–1220), where the straits are a navigable river, easily crossed, and filled with plentiful marine life.[3]

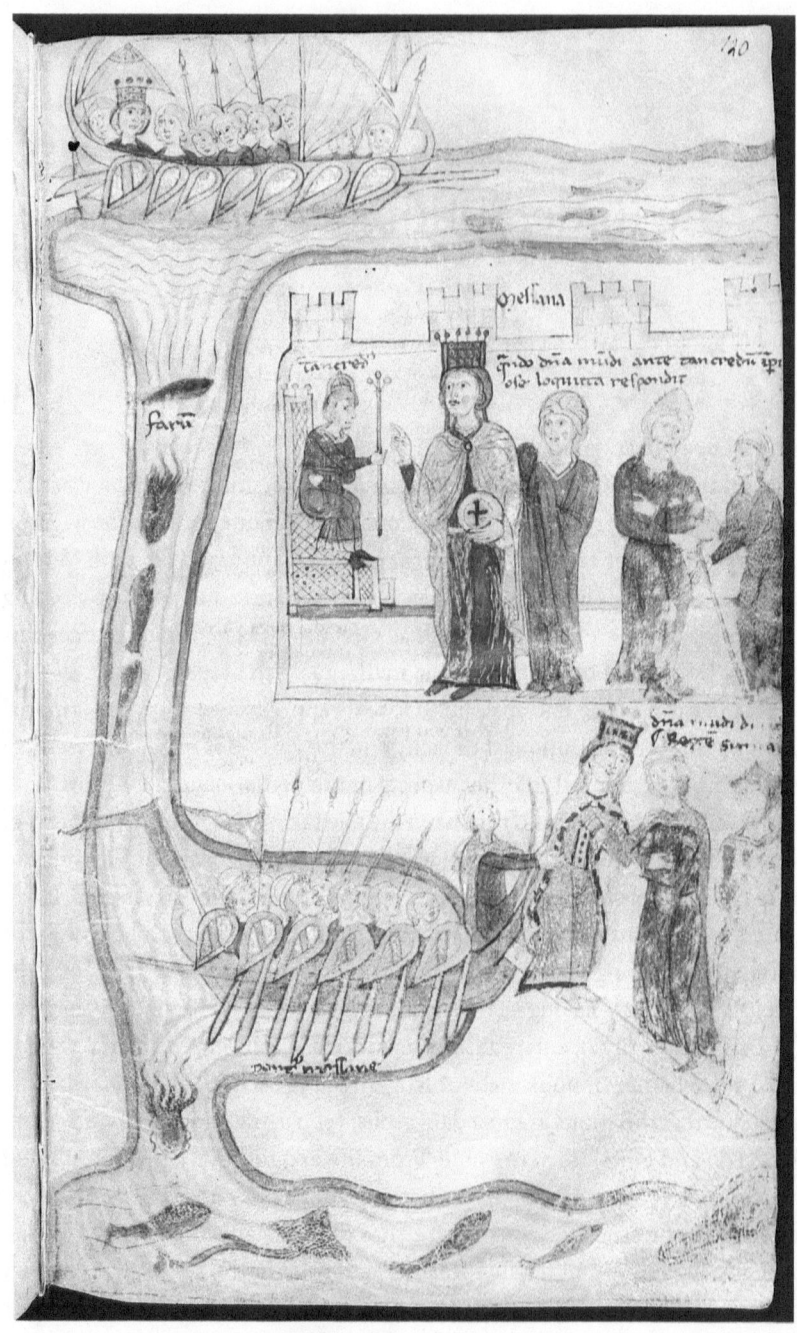

FIGURE 2. Peter of Eboli, *Liber ad honorem Augusti*, lat. Bern, Burgerbibliothek, Cod. 120.II, f. 120r (c. 1195–1197): (https://www.e-codices.ch/en/list/one/bbb/0120-2). Creative Commons license.

The difference is so drastic one is led to wonder if there were geological events to account for it. There were a cluster of eruptions from Etna in the late twelfth century, and the flow from those extended the shelf near the straits out farther into the bay.[4] Time of year may affect tides, which would in turn affect the flow of water in the straits. More important than either of these factors, however, is the fact that these accounts and images depict the straits from the north, while the earlier accounts have had the reader approach the straits from the south. There are in fact two tides at the straits, one flowing south from the Tyrrhenian Sea, the other north from the Ausonian Sea. The two coincide at the point where the lands are closest, and, when both tides are full, the straits roil. But when the northern tide is stronger than the southern one, the effect would be something like that of a river, especially to those coming from the north. The most likely explanation of the difference between the ancient and medieval descriptions is that the straits, like the stories that surround them, are being viewed from a different angle. From the south, the straits are to this day tricky to navigate; from the north, they pose far less of a problem.[5]

Overall, then, while there remains mention of the straits as impassable,[6] the stories that come from the north, particularly those of the Normans and the Germans, present the straits as a river. Hugo Falcandus (Chapter 1, section 1, "The King crosses to Salerno"), talks about the straits as if they did not exist (*rex Farum transire disposuit, ac primo Messanam, dehinc, paucis post diebus, Salernum proficiscitur*; "the king decided to cross the straits, and he advances first to Messina then, after a few days, to Salerno"); the progress of the king is described as if Sicily were joined to the mainland. From the absolute division of Vergil, then, we have moved to a situation in which it is not so much the island's relationship to the mainland of Italy that is at stake, but rather its importance to the countries to the north. It is, in short, Sicily's role as a port to travelers headed south and east, rather than its function as a province, that energizes these descriptions.

Even as the description of the straits changes radically, so the story of Proserpina takes on a new shape and purpose when viewed from the north, particularly after the Norman conquest of Sicily in 1061–91. While the use of Claudian in the classroom continues well into the thirteenth century, by the eleventh century it is accompanied with competing tales that emphasize the importance of Proserpina's return. The tale is set again in a context of empire, but one that is very different from the empire of Cicero, Vergil, or Ovid. Yet those texts come to have increased resonance. In this chapter let us turn to two examples of this changed perspective. We will look first at the reappearance of Cicero's *Verrines* and their subsequent influence, then turn to a case of Ovidian influence.

As we have seen, the story of Proserpina is brought to bear at a critical point in Cicero's *Verrines*. I would like to look more carefully at the text of the Verrine orations that survived into the Middle Ages, both separately and embedded in other, mostly rhetorical, texts.[7] Passages from the *Verrines* were available throughout the Middle Ages via quotation, but also in two families of manuscripts, one circulating in northern France and Germany, the other in Italy. Few contain the complete text of the Verrine orations. The northern group contained, among other things, the Proserpina story; the oldest member of the Italian group was inserted into Montecassino 361 and contains a tenth-century copy of "the portion of the *Verrines* dealing with lands in Sicily."[8] The other manuscripts in this family contain the Proserpina story as well. During the high Middle Ages, then, 2.4—which includes the Proserpina section—seems to have been especially available.

It is worth remarking again that the Proserpina section of the *Verrines* is mostly a meditation on the need for her return. That is, the thrust of that speech is focused, as we have seen, on Cicero's plea to return the stolen goods to Ceres' shrine, which will happen when the Hades-like governor Verres has been removed. In *Verrines* 2.4.50.111–12, as we have seen in chapter 2, it is "the holiness of Ceres, the antiquity of her rites, the sanctity of her temple, [that] they wished atonement for through the punishment of this utterly unscrupulous and brazen man: all else they said they were ready to endure and ignore. So great was their distress that one might imagine that Verres, another Orcus, had come to Henna, and not abducted Proserpina but carried Ceres herself away." As we have seen, atonement in the form of return is the goal of the speech.

Evidence of interest in adapting the *Verrines* comes from an eleventh-century manuscript (c. 1075) now in the Bibliothèque Nationale de France, MS Lat. 7776. In the fourth section of the second speech, we find a curious emendation that ties in precisely with the questions we have been considering. While the original Cicero reads that Ceres lit her torches *his ignibus qui ex Aetnae vertice erumpunt*, this text clearly emends the words to: *his ignibus qui ex ennae vertice rumpunt*, a correction made all the stranger when we consider the beginning of the following sentence, where the word is left intact (*Henna autem ubi eaque . . .*).

We cannot know for certain whether the manuscript originally read that Ceres lit her torches at Etna, as in standard texts of Cicero, but what we do

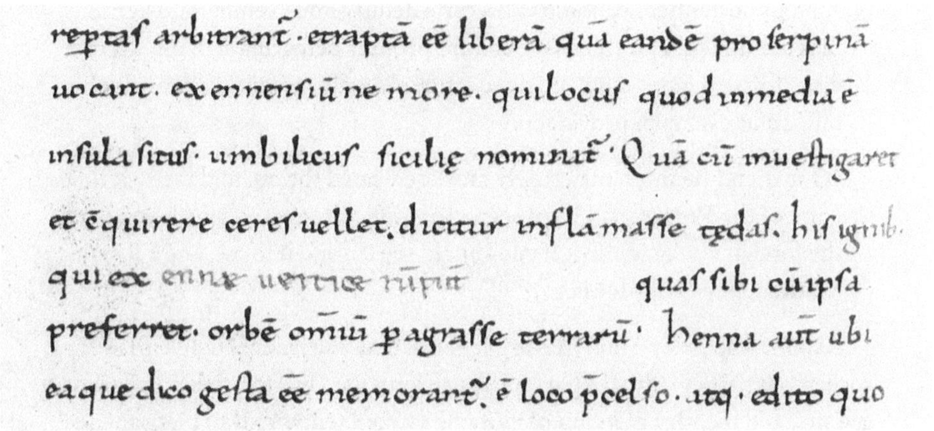
reptas arbitrant· ereptā ee liberā quā eandē proserpinā
uocant. ex ennensiū ne more. qui locus quod inmedia ē
insula situs· umbilicus siciliæ nominat· Quā cū inuestigaret
et ēquirere ceres uellet, dicitur inflāmasse tedas. his ignib.
qui ex ennæ uertice rūpit quas sibi cū ipsa
preferret· orbē omiū pagrasse terrarū· henna aut ubi
ea que dico gesta ee memorant. ē loco pcelso· atq· edito quo

FIGURE 3. Cicero, *Verrine Orations* (c. 1075). Paris, BnF, lat. 7776, f. 132v (detail).

know is that this manuscript has been emended at this point into something that makes no sense, either in terms of context—you cannot light torches at Enna—or consistency—*Enna* is called *Henna* in the lines that follow. We have seen in the previous chapter that Claudian's tale, as transmitted, moved the story of Proserpina entirely to Etna; this manuscript version appears to be a hypercorrection that moves it all back to Enna. It seems probable that the re-emergence of the Ciceronian text here causes later readers to correct the story from the medieval, Claudian-inspired setting on Etna to the Ciceronian setting of Enna. It seems plausible that the hypercorrection is spurred on by an awareness of conflict between Claudian's version of the story and a resurgence of interest in and accessibility to the original Cicero text.

In addition to—or perhaps as a result of—this increased availability, the *Verrines* were a topic of discussion among the faculty and students of Rheims during the late eleventh century, just at the time when Odo, who would become Urban II, the pope who launched the first Crusade through his speech at Clermont-Ferrand in 1095, was enrolled. Urban was educated at the cathedral school of Rheims, under the tutelage of a certain Bruno, whose mentorship continued into Urban's papacy, when the pope brought him to Italy as an advisor to the Holy See. Bruno, in turn, was a colleague with a master Herimann; Bruno most likely attended Rheims to study under Herimann, then returned there to teach with him; both were active on the faculty around 1076.[9] While none of Herimann's writings survive, he is the addressee of letters dated 1057–67 by a follower of his and Bruno's, which include the following request:

Amicus noster Benno, homo vobis certe deditissimus, retulit mihi Verrinas illas subdifficiles ad transscribendum propter peregrinam illam litteram visas fuisse. Unde, si ita vobis videatur, eas nobis remittite, et ego vobis humanius exemplar providebo.

(Our friend Benno, a man surely most dedicated to you, told me that that copy of the *Verrines* had been seen, very difficult to transcribe because of the foreign way of writing. If you should see it, send it to me, and I'll make a more refined copy for you.)[10]

As Jonathan Riley-Smith has argued, the Crusade launched by Urban II's speech was particularly striking for its goal. Jerusalem had long been a pilgrimage site, and the very mention of its name evoked sentiments of piety and redemption; the place itself

> was a relic, having absorbed the *virtus*, the sacred power, of the prophets and holy men of Israel, the apostles and first Christians and above all Christ himself, the incarnate God. He had walked there. He had been baptized in the waters of the Jordan. He had been crucified on Golgotha, where the ground had soaked up his blood. He had been laid to rest in the Holy Sepulchre, from which he had risen. . . . It was the goal of Jerusalem that made the crusade a pilgrimage.[11]

We do not, of course, have the actual speech that launched the first Crusade, but the extant versions speak to the claim that going on the Crusade will incur forgiveness, penance that will be rewarded by grants of indulgence. For instance, Fulcher of Chartres, writes in the *Historia Hierosolymitana*:

cunctis autem illuc euntibus, si . . . vitam morte praepeditam finierint, remissio peccatorum praesens aderit. Quod ituris adnuo, dono isto investitus a Deo . . . ituris autem mora non differat itere, sed propriis locatis sumptibusque collectis, cessante bruma vernoque sequente, Domino praevio tramitem acriter intrent. (1.3.5, 8)

(There will be immediate remission of sins to all those going there, if they have finished this life. This I grant them through the power of God with which I am invested. . . . Let those who go not put off the journey, but rent their lands and collect money for their expenses; and as soon as winter is over and spring comes, let them eagerly set out on the way with God as their guide.)[12]

And Robert the Monk, writing perhaps twenty-five years after the speech, in his *Historia Iherosolimitana*, exhorts his audience to take up the pilgrimage:

> Viam *sancti Sepulcri* incipite, terram illam nefariae genti auferte, eamque vobis subjicite, terra illa filiis *Israel* a Deo in possessionem data fuit, sicut Scriptura dicit, *quae lacte et melle fluit*. . . . Iherusalem umbilicus est terrarum, terra prae ceteris fructifera, quasi alter Paradisus deliciarum. Hanc redemptor humani generis suo illustravit adventu, decoravit conversatione, sacravit passione, morte redemit, sepultura insignivit. Haec igitur civitas regalis, in orbis medio posita, nunc a suis hostibus captiva tenetur, et ab ignorantibus Deum ritui gentium ancillatur. Quaerit igitur et optat liberari, et ut ei subveniatis non cessat imprecari. A vobis quidem praecipue exigit subsidium, quoniam a Deo vobis collatum est prae cunctis nationibus, ut jam diximus, insigne decus armorum. Arripite igitur viam hanc in remissionem peccatorum vestrorum, securi de immarcescibili gloria regni coelorum.[13]

> (Set out on the road to the Holy Sepulchre, deliver that land from a wicked race, and take it yourselves—the land which was given by God to the sons of Israel, as Scripture says *a land flowing with milk and honey* . . . Jerusalem is the navel of the Earth. It is a land more fruitful than any other, almost another Earthly Paradise. Our Redeemer dignified it with his arrival, adorned it with his words, consecrated it through his Passion, redeemed it by his death, and glorified it with his burial. Yet this royal city at the center of the world is now held captive by her enemies and enslaved by those who know nothing of the ways of the human race. So she begs and craves to be free, and prays endlessly for you to come to her aid. Indeed it is your help she particularly seeks because God has granted you outstanding glory in war above all other nations, as I said earlier. So seize on this road to obtain the remission of your sins, sure in the indestructible glory of the Heavenly Kingdom.[14]

In particular, the version included by William of Tyre (1130–1186)—based in part on the account of Fulcher of Chartres (c. 1059–1128)—is worth a careful look.

> Hec igitur nostre salutis **incunabula**, domini patriam, religionis matrem populus absque deo, ancille filius Egyptie possidet violenter et captivatis libere filiis extremas imponit conditiones, quibus versa vice merito servire tenebatur. Sed quid scriptum est? *Eice ancillam et filium eius!* Sarracenorum enim gens impia et inmundarum sectatrix traditionum loca sancta, in

quibus steterunt **pedes domini**, iam a multis retro temporibus violenta premit tyrannide. . . . Ingressi sunt canes in sancta, prophanatum est sanctuarium, humiliatus est cultor dei populus, angarias patitur indignas genus electum, servit in luto et latere regale sacerdotium, **princeps provinciarum** facta est sub tributo civitas dei. Cuius non liquefiat anima, cuius non tabescant precordia, his ad animum recurrentibus? Quis hec siccis oculis audire potest, **fratres karissimi**? Templum domini, de quo zelans dominus vendentes eiecit et ementes ne domus patris eius fieret spelunca latronum, facta est sedes demoniorum. (*Chronicon* 1.15.31–48; emphasis mine)

(This cradle of our salvation, the native land of our Lord, and the mother of religion, is now forcibly held by a people without God, the son of the Egyptian handmaiden. Upon the captive sons of the free woman he imposes desperate conditions under which he himself, the relations being reversed, should by right have served. But what is written? "Cast out this bondwoman and her son." For many years past, the wicked race of Saracens, followers of unclean superstitions, have oppressed with tyrannical violence the holy places where the feet of our Lord rested. . . . Dogs have entered into the holy places, the sanctuary has been profaned, the people, worshippers of God, have been humbled. The chosen race is now enduring undeserved tribulations, the royal priesthood slaves in mud and bricks. The city of God, the chief over provinces, has been rendered tributary. Whose soul is not softened, whose heart does not melt, as these indignities recur to his mind? Who, dearest brethren, can listen to this with dry eyes? The temple of the Lord, whence He, in His zeal, drove those who bought and sold, that the house of His Father might not become a den of thieves, has been made the home of demons.)[15]

Identifying Jerusalem as a sacred space, William asserts that its holiness was due to the presence of the godhead: God had stood there. That space has been violated, he says, by invaders, an act that causes the speaker to shudder with fear. The violation of the sanctuary is reiterated, and the crowd is addressed to right the wrongs through their pilgrimage to the Holy Land.

While it is clear from other versions of the sermon, especially that of Robert the Monk, that Jerusalem is perceived in terms reminiscent of Cicero's view of Sicily, the parallels with *Verrines* 2.2.4.48–50 are particularly striking in William's version of Urban's speech, which echoes the structure of the key Proserpina section of the Verrine orations:

Nam et natas esse has in his locis deas et fruges in ea terra primum repertas esse arbitrantur, et raptam esse Liberam, quam eandem Proserpinam vocant, ex Hennensium nemore, qui locus, quod in media est insula situs, umbilicus Siciliae nominatur.... Propter huius opinionis vetustatem quod horum in his locis vestigia ac prope incunabula reperiuntur deorum, mira quaedam tota Sicilia privatim ac publice religio est Cereris Hennensis.... Etenim urbs illa non urbs videtur, sed fanum Cereris esse; habitare apud sese Cererem Hennenses arbitrantur, ut mihi non cives illius civitatis, sed omnes sacerdotes, omnes accolae atque antistites Cereris esse videantur. Henna tu simulacrum Cereris tollere audebas, Henna tu de manu Cereris Victoriam eripere et deam deae detrahere conatus es? quorum nihil violare, nihil attingere ausi sunt in quibus erant omnia quae sceleri propiora sunt quam religioni.

(For they say that these goddesses were born in those places [Sicily], and that corn was first discovered in that land, and that Libera, whom they call the same as Proserpina, was abducted from a wood of the inhabitants of Henna, a place which, located in the middle of the island, is called the navel of Sicily.... On account of the antiquity of this belief—that the footprints, even the cradle, of these gods, were discovered in [Sicily]—there exists throughout Sicily, in private and public gatherings, a devotion to Ceres of Henna that is quite astonishing.... For indeed that city [of Henna] is seen not as a city, but as a sanctuary of Ceres. The people of Henna believe that Ceres lives among them, and to me they do not seem to be citizens of that city, but all priests, all servants and ministers of Ceres. And was it from Henna that you dared to remove the statue of Ceres? At Henna you tried to snatch Victory from Ceres' hand, removing goddess from goddess? Among people for whom everything was closer to sin than to religion, nothing of theirs did they dare to violate, dare to touch.)

In both passages, the desecration of the temple is identified as a violation of sacred area. The sanctity of that space is determined by the fact that the gods actually stood there. The emotional impact of that act is brought out by rhetorical questions. The violation is reiterated, and the crowd is addressed to right the wrongs: *iudices*, in Cicero, *fratres karissimi*, in William. Moreover, the word choice in both texts is similar. Enna and Jerusalem are each shown to be in the middle of their land (*in media est insula situs*, *Verr.* 2.2.4.48; *in medio terre*, *Chronicon* 1.15.18). The temple is the cradle in each case (*incunabula* in both) and the feet—*pedes* or *vestigia*—of the gods offer the proof of sanctity. In

Cicero the abduction of Proserpina occurred in the middle of the island, when Hades appeared from a cave to assault her. In a similar fashion, William of Tyre describes the location of the Holy Sepulchre as a cave in the middle of the land, and the violation includes the fact that there "virgins are compelled to have sex" (*coguntur virgines fornicari*, *Chronicon* 1.15.69).

Perhaps most striking, however, is the fact that embedded in William's description of Jerusalem is the phrase *princeps provinciarum* (*Chronicon* 1.15.42–3), which is a direct quotation from Lamentations 1.1, yet which also echoes the very phrase Cicero uses in the Verrine orations to identify Sicily's importance at the start of the imperial movement, the one quoted earlier and adapted by Ovid:

> Nam cum omnium sociorum **provinciarum**que rationem diligenter habere debetis, tum praecipue Siciliae, iudices, plurimis iustissimisque de causis, primum quod omnium nationum exterarum **princeps** Sicilia se ad amicitiam fidemque populi Romani applicavit. (*Verr.* 2.2.1.2)

> (You owe careful consideration to all allies and all provinces, but especially, judges, to Sicily, for a great many very just reasons: first, that Sicily was premier among all foreign nations to join herself in friendship and trust to the people of Rome.)

Through these echoes—especially this last—the Sicily of the *Verrines* and its imperial purpose to recover the lost holiness, linked through Cicero to the recovery of Proserpina, is activated in this text about the first Crusade. We know William had read Cicero—he quotes him in the introduction to this account—and he may have seen the parallels with the Verrine orations himself, or recognized them in Urban's account, where they may well have occurred.

It would appear that in the story of Ceres as told by Cicero, William, or Urban, finds a myth of redemption. The earlier presence of the *Verrines* at the critical juncture of the future pope's life seems more than suggestive; and the iteration of the argument in at least one of the extant versions of that speech seems provocative indeed. Cicero may well provide the subtext for the language of the first Crusade, as the sermon is filtered through the Verrine orations, especially given that Urban II not only appears to have read the *Verrines* at Rheims but also witnessed the Norman conquest of Sicily, which served in retrospect as a "proto-Crusade."[16]

William of Tyre's version of the sermon also offers a particular understanding of the earlier text. What is of interest to us here is how his text offers a reading of Cicero's speech, which in turn affects the representation of both crusade and empire. While the goal of the first Crusade is to liberate the Holy Sepulchre, the thrust of all the versions of Urban's sermon suggests that this action will return the original holy space to the Christians. Robert the Monk's speech is explicit in this regard, asserting that it is the land of milk and honey that will be recovered through the actions of the first Crusade: this imagined return to the Christian golden age is closely echoed by William of Tyre's suggestion that the Crusade will recover the land of origin for the Christians.[17] That this occurred with tremendous brutality and loss of life, both during the first and subsequent Crusades, cannot be forgotten, however. As with Cicero, the idealized plan and its realization are two very different things, and the reality of the Crusades bears little in common with the speech that launched it.

William—or Urban—appears to identify in the Verrine orations a myth of redemption, a story of empire rooted in a return to origins. Even as the "Saracens" violated the temple at Jerusalem and raided the Holy Sepulchre, so Verres, likened by Cicero to Hades, stole the sacred statue of Ceres.[18] The Crusaders are urged to restore the tomb by means of language that echoes that of Cicero asking the judges to force Verres to return the statue of Ceres and so restore the sanctity of her temple at Enna and, in so doing, Proserpina will be returned; Sicily will regain the beauty that it always deserved and that it knew once before the abduction. Through the language of the first Crusade, not only does crusading come to be seen as imperial, but texts of empire, such as the Verrine orations, become interpreted in the context of medieval thought, even as the Crusades become presented in the language of empire. Through Urban's speech, Sicily becomes affiliated with the capture of Jerusalem. Through at least William of Tyre, the ancient mythologies of Sicily, and the stories that had become accreted to them, take on new potential in Christian universal history. In brief, the ancient myths of Sicily become seen as proleptic of the tales of the first Crusade.[19]

The first Crusade, as we have seen, expanded the understanding of empire to include redemption. The journey to Jerusalem becomes the model for the journey towards salvation through the recovery of a lost paradise. William of Tyre's version of Urban II's speech seems calqued on a reading of the Proserpina myth from the Verrine orations that casts the notions of loss and recovery in terms of guilt and penitence. More than this, the traces of the *Verrines* point to Sicily as the root of this new form of empire, in which the languages of penitence and empire are intertwined.

Sicily's role in the definition and expansion of the Roman empire caused versions of Proserpina's tale to be used to address imperial concerns. High medieval retellings of the myth reinforce an association between Sicily and empire, even as they rework the tale to communicate a new understanding of empire. The significance of the tale is not the aspects found in Claudian but, rather, in the very part he omits, regarding the return of Proserpina. Through the language of at least one version of the sermon that launched the first Crusade, not only does crusading come to be seen as imperial, but discussions of empire, such as the Verrine orations, are reinterpreted in the context of medieval thought and presented as speaking about recovery. Proserpina's link with Sicily transmitted via the *Verrines*, with its associations with empire, causes that myth to become a story of potential redemption, even as the Crusades cause penitence to infiltrate the myth of Proserpina.

Etna the Redemptive: The *Ovide Moralisé*

Through accounts such as that of William of Tyre, Cicero's version of the Proserpina myth, which casts empire as a return to origins and places emphasis on the process of recovery, reenters the conversation. While no longer an agricultural myth, as it was originally for Vergil, the tale of Proserpina's fate changes focus in the later Middle Ages to respond to new discoveries and pressures, events which relate to what we have seen to be a reworked understanding of empire. In addition to the geographical expansion implicit in the imperial efforts of the Crusades, empire comes to have a spiritual dimension that also finds expression through the stories of Sicily and Proserpina.

While the text of Claudian remains available and a staple of liberal arts education throughout the high Middle Ages, it comes to be joined by another thread, that of commentaries on Ovid. The *aetas Ovidiana* of the twelfth and thirteenth centuries includes, as many have shown, a growing fascination with Ovid's topics and storytelling techniques. Within these commentaries and retellings of Ovid's tales, a new strand of the Proserpina myth surfaces, one not only drawn from Ovid but also one that completes the tale as told by Claudian and offers versions of and interpretations of the return and renegotiation.[20]

As we discussed in earlier chapters, Ovid's version of the Proserpina myth is tied to his understanding of empire. For him, in the *Metamorphoses*, political imperial rule and geographic expansion are destructive, while poetic imperialism is not. Throughout the *Metamorphoses* Ovid argues for the need for imperialistic drives in poetry in order to prevail into the future. This emphasis on the power of language over politics is one he ties explicitly to the Proserpina myth, since he presents that myth, as we have seen, as the imperial tale that counters Vergil's account of Aeneas. While Vergil laments empire as the Augustan geographic expansion that ignores limits, Ovid sings of the expansion of love into the future through poetry.

In the high Middle Ages this Ovidian understanding of empire takes on new importance in one particular realm, that of redemption. We have seen how the act of participating in a Crusade offers redemption, yet even for those who do not go on Crusade, verbal redemption becomes key. Culminating in the canons of the Fourth Lateran Council (1215) and the Second Council of Lyon (1274), the paired concepts of confession and redemption become explicitly allied with the concept of Purgatory.[21] The Fourth Lateran requires all faithful to confess: the spoken word of both penitent and confessor causes changes in the future. Likewise, with the second Council of Lyon, the prayers of the living offer the primary means of redeeming the dead. Not only do these texts focus attention on language and grant it tremendous power, they do so in the context of a revitalized understanding of empire, that of the spiritual realm. Even as Ovid saw potential in the power of the poetic word in the future, so these texts point up the power of language for the future of the soul. And even as the Crusades expanded the notion of empire geographically, so redemption applied the concept to the spiritual realm. Redemption offers to expand the realm of life into the future.

Growing interest in the redemptive power of language appears in many contexts during this era, but for our purposes it is of interest that we see it appearing in the tales of Proserpina and accounts of Sicily. Whereas, in the earlier versions looked at in the last chapter, the story often stopped with Proserpina remaining in the underworld, in these later versions, her return starts to be mentioned once again, but often in the context of negotiation. An example is provided in the *Appendix Ovidiana*, where Proserpina is portrayed as being in the underworld, not to return unless she can be with the protagonist-lover:

Respice quod Stigiis Proserpina fertur in undis
nec vult salva fore, nisi me sibi iungat amore. (*De nuntio sagaci*, 23–24)

(Look how Proserpina is borne on the Stygian waves and doesn't wish to be saved unless she joins me to herself in love.)[22]

The narrator, in a conversation with Cupid, boasts that he is an irresistible lover whom even goddesses pursue. For our purposes, the fact that Proserpina is both still in the underworld and amenable to returning—and being saved— under the right circumstances is of interest. Likewise, in the commentary by

Arnulf of Orléans, the pomegranate is glossed as the infernal fruit, pointing the way to Milton's connection of Proserpina and Eve but not specifically explaining how the two stories intersect.[23] In other versions, similar comments are made on the return of Proserpina and her eating of the pomegranate seeds. So, for instance, the *Integumenta Ovidii* (1190–1270; lines 265–72) mentions the seven grains and the seasonal negotiation.[24] Later, in Giovanni del Virgilio (c. 1327), we continue to find detailed mention of the abduction (in the fifteenth transformation of the book) with the identification of Proserpina's sash by Cyane as the sixteenth transformation, and the renegotiation necessitated by Ascalaphus that leads to the seventeenth transformation as he is turned into an owl. The seven seeds are mentioned specifically but not glossed in relation to Proserpina.[25]

All these versions hint at an increased interest in Proserpina's negotiated return, yet none is as explicit as the tale found in the *Ovide Moralisé*. There the story of Ceres and Proserpina is presented as a tale of redemption and purgation, virtually a foundation story of Purgatory that links the seven pomegranate seeds to the seven deadly sins, and the delay in return in terms of confession and redemption. In the *Ovide* Ceres is glossed throughout as the church, first in her role as representing humanity (3053), then, in her brandishing of the torch, as the light that shines in the darkness (3069–73).[26] Her return to Sicily, after her journey "par tout le mont" (3167), is presented as a return to the dry land (*Siccanie* is glossed as *seche terre*, lines 3168–69) or dry heart, as it lacks the humidity of charity. Following a lengthy discussion of the fate of a soul denied redemption, the *Ovide* has Ceres hear from Arethusa, glossed as penitence (3280), that Proserpina is in the underworld; Arethusa's ability to surface from the underworld is shown as proleptic of Proserpina's own fate, rising pure and clear from the depths of hell. On the strength of Arethusa's report, Ceres appeals to Jupiter that her daughter be returned; Jupiter agrees, as long as Proserpina can swear that she hasn't eaten anything; Ascalaphus, who is here likened to the devil (*c'est li deables* [3380]) and presented as more of a scoundrel than Hades himself, tells Jupiter that he has seen Proserpina eat seven *grains*, which are glossed as the seven sins. Proserpina has fallen.

What makes this tale particularly fascinating is the connection it draws between Proserpina's return and the concept of redemption. Jupiter's argument progresses from an either/or, black/white situation (Proserpina will only return if she has abstained from eating anything in Hell; if she has not abstained, she cannot under any circumstances return) to one of mediation and compromise: God, *qui plus veult la convercion / des gens que la dampnacion* ("who prefers conversion [=salvation] of people more than damnation"), comes up with a solution:

> Que l'ame en torment remaindroit 3415
> Une piece et s'espurgeroit
> Et sa penitance feroit
> Des sept grains qu'ele avoit mengiez,
> C'est des sept creminaux pechiez
> Dont elle estoit ains entechie, 3420
> Et, quant el seroit espurgie,
> Si s'en istroit de purgatoire,
> Pour estre em pardurable gloire
> Aveuc l'Iglise trihunphant. (*Ovide* 5.3415–24)

> (That the soul would remain in suffering
> A while to be purged
> And do its penance
> For the seven seeds she had eaten,
> That is, the seven mortal sins
> By which it was stained,
> And when it has been purged
> It will leave purgatory
> To share eternal glory
> With the church triumphant.)

The process of Proserpina's return is presented as the prototype for the experience of Purgatory. One of the manuscripts, C, confirms this reading by replacing line 3417 with *En purgatoire sans doubtance* ("In purgatory without a doubt") to which the scribe adds: *Et la feroit sa penitence* ("And there would do its penance").[27] As in Ovid, Proserpina is abducted from Sicily, and her mother, while searching the world, focuses mostly on Sicily (*Toutes terres escommenie / Et devant toutes Siccanie*, lines 2124–25). The geography of the tale is vague, but it is clear that Hades, having appeared in the valley, not lake, of Pergusa, abducts Proserpina through a break in the land (*La terre est ouverte et fendue: / Par illuec a fete s'entree / Dis a decendre en sa contree*, lines 2019–21). While we cannot assert that this is Etna, it is clear that the tale takes place on Sicily and specifically in its eastern section.

This particular version of the glosses of *Metamorphoses* 5 is, as far as we know, unique. None of the other medieval treatments of the *Metamorphoses* takes this tack. Arnulf's glosses and allegories on the *Metamorphoses* do not link the pomegranate or seeds to the seven deadly sins. He mentions the pomegranate in the allegories and in his glosses on the *Fasti*, at 4.607 and 608, explicating them in sexual terms. The Vulgate Commentary is similarly silent on the pomegranate and redemption, as is Giovanni del Virgilio, both in his allegories and *Expositio*.[28]

Recent work on the *Ovide Moralisé* has focused on the first book, so does not touch on the story of Proserpina.[29] But it is clear even there that the sources and the paths of influence are problematic.[30] And yet the text seems above all to respond to the world in a way that strict intertextual reading impedes. I would suggest, in the case of the tale of Proserpina, that looking for provable paths of sources and influence is less profitable than understanding the cultural context of the tale. As we will see in the next two chapters, this use of the Proserpina myth is not unique—Dante too is fascinated by her return—but, rather than setting the *Ovide* aside and treating it as merely anomalous, we would be better served to see it as one, perhaps maverick, attempt to adjust a classical tale to new surroundings and demands.[31]

By the fourteenth century, the overriding concerns of empire are no longer fully answered by Claudian's truncated version of the Proserpina story, though Etna remains central. Instead, this version of the tale in the *Ovide* speaks to a renewed interest in negotiation and redemption. And yet, it is important to note, continuities remain: the same tale of Proserpina, set on Sicily, is used to narrativize new questions of empire. Whereas the imperial associations of Proserpina's stories originally focused on the role Sicily played in defining empire for Rome, and the expansion first east, then to the underworld, of empire, what these stories show is something different. The story of Ceres, as found in Cicero and Ovid, is here reinterpreted to offer a model for the empire of the soul, one in which prayers can lead to action in the next world. The journey to the otherworld that you make through prayer for yourself and others becomes the model for the journey towards salvation, and both share descriptions of Sicily as a subtext, rooted largely in the myth of Proserpina. This new form of empire, in which the language of penitence is featured, is set on the eastern shore of Sicily.

Ceres and Redemption

By the fourteenth century the return of Proserpina had taken a new turn and was closely allied with the notion of Purgatory, even as the location of Purgatory had been increasingly identified with Etna in the context of this story:

atonement and prayers in this life can lead to positive results for others in the next. The journey to the parallel world of Jerusalem that you make for yourself and for others becomes through time the rhetorical journey to the underworld that you make through prayer, based on the return of Proserpina. William of Tyre's version of Urban II's speech offers a reading of the Proserpina myth from the Verrine orations that casts the notions of loss and recovery in terms of guilt and penitence, a reading supported by later versions such as that of the *Ovide Moralisé*. Moreover, his choice of the *Verrines* points to Sicily as the root of this new form of empire, in which the language of penitence and the description of Purgatory are intertwined.[32]

The echoes of the Verrine orations in William of Tyre's account of Urban II's speech, then, draw on a long association of Sicily with purgation even as they adapt to speak to a new understanding of the Christian mission. It is perhaps relevant at this point to remember that many of the crusading missions left from Messina, near Etna, on Sicily. Sicily was, in so many ways, the starting point of the Crusades. From Sicily—from its myths of purgation, penitence, and redemption—the new Christian mission, the crusading mission, was launched. Ceres rather than Proserpina becomes the focus of the myth, and redemption through language becomes a means for restoring lost innocence in this fallen world. As we shall see, Dante's understanding of Purgatory is guided by these very notions, and redemption in *Purgatorio* continues to be explicitly linked to the story of Proserpina.

I have argued in the preceding chapters that Cicero's Sicily, as mediated through Vergil and Ovid, becomes a site of poetic and rhetorical exploration: good empire for Ovid is an empire of letters, a process of competition and rivalry within the literary sphere. The explosion of stories around the straits of Messina suggests that Cicero's identification of Sicily and empire has become in Ovid's hands a poetic methodology, one that encourages poetic competition as the productive form of empire building. Ulysses' victory over Ajax—a thinly veiled allegory of Ovid's over Vergil—reiterates this point. Poetic rivalry, intertextuality, and expansion of the literary enterprise are all presented as a form of empire. As Cicero's Proserpina myth becomes interpreted by Ovid in terms of Venus's extension of her power into the underworld, so it also becomes a proto-humanist model for literary competition and rhetorical debate across generations of writers. As we saw in chapter 3, the myth of empire, in Ovid's hands, becomes a poetics.

Yet in the medieval accounts of Sicily and tales of Proserpina we have looked at, this turn toward the poetic takes on a renewed value in the real world, as language becomes the means to both education and redemption. That is, Ovid's very insistence on the strength of an imperial approach in the poetic realm, together with the link he draws between the power of love and the power of poetry, feeds into medieval understandings of the power of language in the empire of letters on the one hand and the process of redemption on the other. The penitential language of the first Crusade—go on this journey to become a better person and enter heaven—is read back into understandings of empire and informs treatments of imperial texts, such as the Verrine orations and the *Metamorphoses*. Both the Norman conquest of Sicily and the first Crusade suggest that the mission is a journey for the soul; that journey is seen as one that begins on Sicily, as the tale of Proserpina is read as the foundation text for redemption. In particular, through Proserpina, the concept of crusading becomes seen as an expansion of the interior world—you go on a journey for spiritual as well as nationalistic reasons—and the journey in space is presented as a type of the journey of the soul. Empire comes to include redemption in the context of and through the mythology of Sicily, and it does so through readings of Ovid and Cicero.

Recent scholarship has demonstrated the profound interaction of cultures on Sicily during the Middle Ages.[33] But the imperial structure outlined in the *Verrines* and expanded by Vergil and Ovid is one that deliberately turned the gaze of the world from east to west and asserted the power of the Latin tradition.[34] By returning to the Latin source at this time, the medieval authors engaged in just such a series of choices, asserting the preeminence of the West over the East. In addition, however, we find a gradual move away from viewing the Proserpina myth as a tale of loss to one that presents it instead as a story of reparation and redemption in the context of a world that is expanding both physically and spiritually.

6

Quando n'apparve una montagna

PURGATORY AND THE VOYAGE OF ULYSSES

IT WOULD seem that the literary adaptation of the myth of Proserpina takes two forms in the high Middle Ages: versions derived from Vergil and Claudian, either separately or together, speak of abandonment and loss, while tales told in the Ovidian tradition tell of negotiation and recovery. By the time of Dante (1265–1321), the story of Proserpina's loss has been supplemented by the account of her return, and empire is presented as a myth of renewal, if at a cost. The two variants of her tale co-exist, as Claudian's version is taught in schools with the fuller, Ovidian story developing alongside, through commentaries and vernacular reworkings.

The Proserpina tale studied in the last chapter establishes a cultural association between the myth of Proserpina, her return, and the growing interest in redemption brought about in large part by the Fourth Lateran Council. There we noted that the myth of Proserpina gained prominence through its interest in extending empire beyond the known world, either toward unfamiliar reaches explored through the Crusades or through the expansion into the afterlife promised by medieval Christianity. This cluster of associations guides Dante's *Commedia* as well, particularly in his understanding and representation of the nature of Purgatory.[1] In these final two chapters we will examine the contexts in which we as readers approach the mountain of Purgatory in the *Commedia*. This chapter will focus on its role as seen from afar in *Inferno* 26; the next will view it from up close, as the mountain Dante climbs in the second canticle. Both treatments of the mountain are important for understanding how Dante develops the complex of themes we have followed so far, as well as for seeing how the myth of Proserpina and significance of Sicily play out in Dante's hands.

The overall structure of Dante's *Commedia* (1308–1320) speaks to his interest in recovery of the soul and of the past—especially in *Purgatorio*—and suggests that the Ovidian version of the tale of Proserpina might predominate in his writings. We shall see that this is in fact true, though we will also note that Dante and the commentators are clear that Proserpina is abducted from Mt. Etna, not Enna. Moreover, Dante's fascination with *imperium* indicates that the cluster of topics we have been following here might well surface in the *Commedia*. What we find, not unsurprisingly, is a complex meditation on empire focused on themes of loss, abandonment, exile, and recovery.

Dante's understanding of empire is clearest in *De Monarchia*,[2] but versions of the theory occur in *Convivio* and throughout the *Commedia*. There good empire, or *imperium*, is based on that of the ancient Romans, where church and state were distinct and neither had power over the other. As Sabina Tuzzo has usefully summarized, it is in *Purgatorio* XVI that Dante first spells out the "two suns theory," to which he returns in the third book of *De Monarchia*. In *Purgatorio* XVI Dante clarifies that the power of the true emperor will derive from God, ultimately, and will not depend in any way on the Pope.[3] The papal bull of 1302, which explained the relationship of church and state not as two *luminaria magna* but rather as the sun and moon, is countered here:

> Soleva Roma, che 'l buon mondo feo,
>   due soli aver, che l'una e l'altra strada
>   facean vedere, e del mondo e di Deo. (*Purg.* XVI.106–8)

> (For Rome, which made the world good, used to have
> two suns; and they made visible two paths—
> the world's path and the pathway that is God's.)

Equally clear is the notion that the eternal world and the temporal, though both stemming from God, are or should be ruled by different leaders, the eternal by the Pope and the temporal by the monarch or emperor, and each leader is marked by the clarity of his vision.[4] So, earlier in *Purgatorio* XVI:

> Onde convenne legge per fren porre;
>   convenne rege aver, che discernesse
>   de la vera cittade almen la torre. (*Purg.* XVI.94–6)

> (Therefore, one needed law to serve as curb;
> a ruler, too, was needed, one who could
> discern at least the tower of the true city.)

In *De Monarchia* Dante develops this theory as a result of his desire for imperial restoration even as he spells out his disdain for the papal drive for temporal power. The first two books of *Monarchia* acknowledge the utility and legitimacy of empire. Specifically drawing from the *Aeneid*, Dante recognizes Aeneas as noble and Augustus as the second founder of Rome after Aeneas. Acknowledging that God sides with Aeneas, he argues that his rule produces freedom, which is the mark of good government. In *Monarchia* 3.15, Dante states explicitly that the power of the emperor in no way derives from the church. His is a temporal authority, a rule with a temporal end, and in this limited and secularized context Dante grants a high position to philosophy and, later, poetry. The Roman model stands firm as Aeneas and Augustus represent *imperium* worthy of imitation.

While that *imperium* does not exist in Italy during Dante's time, he finds it in Roman culture, specifically in the rule of Augustus, but extending as far as the reign of Frederick II, even as he hopes for its resurgence in the future: the upper terraces of *Purgatorio* and *Paradiso* speak to its potential revival. As such, it is an *imperium* at a remove: it exists in the past and future only, although, we will see, *Purgatorio* offers a means to its retrieval. As we will see in the next chapter, the expansion of empire beyond the known world that we have reviewed in the last few chapters becomes reshaped in Dante's hands to speak of an *imperium* of a past and future time. Such an empire has no place in *Inferno*, which unfolds in the unremitting present, but it meshes well with the expectations of *Purgatorio*, where past and future come to coexist. The difference between the two canticles turns on one significant feature whose origins we will trace in this chapter: the ability to understand the past as future, and therefore to enable the creation of an *imperium onde Cristo è romano*, requires the capacity to interpret, to read both literally and figuratively, to see something as itself and other.[5] While most figures in *Inferno* lack this skill, it is one that Dante comes increasingly to acquire. The appearance of the mountain of Purgatory in *Inferno* XXVI offers essentially a test case of this issue, as the way the mountain is interpreted varies widely among those who read or hear about it.

It should not surprise us that the tale of Proserpina, a guiding narrative of *Purgatorio*, as we shall see, is all but absent from *Inferno* XXVI. While loss and abandonment are prevalent stories in this canticle, the possibility of recovery is not.[6] Yet to the extent that the later cantos of *Inferno* serve to set the scene for *Purgatorio*, it should be equally unsurprising to find texts of Sicily, the setting of Proserpina's abduction and her return, starting to shape the literary landscape of the *Commedia* as the canticle draws to a close.[7]

Mountain of Purgatory

The mountain of Purgatory appears first in *Inferno* XXVI in the tale Ulysses recounts about his final journey with his men:

> ... n'apparve una montagna, bruna
>   per la distanza, e parvemi alta tanto
>   quanto veduta non avëa alcuna. (*Inf.* XXVI. 133–35)
>
> (... there before us rose a mountain, dark
> because of distance, and it seemed to me
> the highest mountain I had ever seen.)[8]

The mountain later identified as Purgatory Ulysses here discusses is traditionally understood as a geographical marker: Ulysses went so far afield on his journey that he even saw Mt. Purgatory, which Dante situates on the opposite side of the globe from Italy. I propose that we also understand the mention of Mt. Purgatory as signaling that *Inferno* is drawing to an end and that *Purgatorio* is, quite literally, on the horizon. As a result, the text suggests, the differences between the two locales, and the poems that describe them, need to be clarified.

At the opening canto of *Purgatorio*, which we will discuss in detail in the next chapter, we are offered a short, yet complex, phrase about what sets that locale apart, a phrase that proves useful in understanding a key difference between the two canticles:

> e canterò di quel secondo regno
>   dove l'umano spirito si purga   5
>   e di salire al ciel diventa degno.
> Ma qui la morta poesì resurga (*Purg.* I.4–7)
>
> (and what I sing will be that second kingdom,
> in which the human soul is cleansed of sin,
> becoming worthy of ascent to Heaven.
> But here ... let the dead poetry rise again.)[9]

While the entire *Commedia* explores the notion of empire in the region beyond the known world, *Purgatorio* focuses that investigation on the hermeneutic task of revitalizing the dead. Dante makes clear in the opening canto of *Purgatorio* that what distinguishes that canticle is the ability of interpretation to give new life through allegorical reading, which goes hand in hand with the cleansing of the soul and will also bear on Dante's view of empire. For now I just want to point to the defining role Dante here assigns to allegorical interpretation. Successful ascent of Mt. Purgatory, he suggests, entails mastering a hermeneutic process that will enable the pilgrim to conquer sin and overcome death.

This approach offers a way in to *Inferno* XXVI. If we take the opening of *Purgatorio* as indicative of what characterizes that location, the appearance of Mt. Purgatory Ulysses remarks on can be understood as a visual reminder of the need to learn to interpret, an ability that will enable the dead, and their poetry, to rise to new, Christian truths. The canto, in other words, is about the importance of reading and interpretation as much as it is about geography, and the interaction among Vergil, Ulysses, and Dante can be approached as a primer of different types of reading, effective and not. But before entering into an interpretation of these lines, let me just emphasize that we are still in *Inferno*. That is, while Purgatory makes an appearance, no one actually breaches the mountain. It serves as a signal of what is soon to come but does not require the abilities needed to ascend the mountain. Of the three characters, Dante alone will eventually master them.

Inferno XXVI is arguably the most studied canto of the first canticle.[10] In it Dante and Vergil encounter Ulysses in the flame with Diomedes and hear the tale of Ulysses' journey and death. In the *Digital Dante*, Teodolinda Barolini provides an excellent overview of earlier readings of the canto.[11] As she summarizes, the criticism breaks into two camps, roughly that of the two fourteenth-century commentators, Buti and Benvenuto, with Buti being "critical of the Homeric hero," and Benvenuto seeing him as someone who "excit[es] Dante's admiration." Later critics, Barolini argues, follow this divide, with a group of critics arguing on Ulysses' behalf, emphasizing Dante's admiration for Ulysses' desire for knowledge, while others point to his rhetorical deceit and sinfulness. Barolini's own interpretation moves from this either/or approach to suggest that Dante's creation is rooted in classical texts of Cicero (*De Finibus*), Horace (*Ars Poetica*), and Vergil (*Aen.* 2); her more recent readings of the canto point to the importance of interpretation. My reading draws on an additional classical text, 88 of the *Epistulae Morales*[12] of Seneca the Younger, as well as a cluster of medieval works Dante would have been familiar with.

All commentators on this canto assert that Ulysses' story is a new one, different from those that were told of him before. Yet while the story is new to Ulysses, it is not new to literature. Instead, the speech we hear in *Inferno* XXVI is, I will show, a pastiche of many texts which Ulysses ventriloquizes. This serves a purpose: it presents Ulysses as a storyteller and insists that we as readers find a way to interpret it. It is significant, in this context, that the mountain of Purgatory is mentioned at all. With the possible exception of the first canto,[13] nowhere else in *Inferno* is the mountain even alluded to, and there is little reason to mention it here.

My reading of this canto, then, starts from the observation that the speech of Ulysses is highlighted for its presentation as much as its content and so focuses on elements of narration as much as, if not more than, doctrine. More than any other speech in the *Inferno*, the context and strategy of the interchange is reported: Vergil tells Dante that he will speak to Ulysses and asks Dante to be silent. The most common reading of this canto asserts that Ulysses himself explains where he has been and what has happened to his men. The speech is treated as a confession, in which Ulysses is seen as finally admitting to his pride and seeking to rid himself of the stigma of his wrongdoings. However, placed back in context, this canto can be approached rather as an example of the problems of reading and interpretation, and the limitations placed on it by the one posing the questions as well as by the issues of literary reception.

Why Where Matters

This approach to *Inferno* XXVI asserts that the speech acts of the three involved characters, Ulysses, Vergil, and Dante, are each important, but for different reasons: we are asked to pay attention, at different times, to what Ulysses says, what Vergil believes he meant, and what Dante understands him to have said.

In *Inferno* XXVI we find Ulysses with Diomedes in what is later identified as the flame of false counselors.

> Rispuose a me: "Là dentro si martira   55
>   Ulisse e Dïomede, e così insieme
>   a la vendetta vanno come a l'ira;
> e dentro da la lor fiamma si geme
>   l'agguato del caval che fé la porta
>   onde uscì de' Romani il gentil seme.   60
> Piangevisi entro l'arte per che, morta,
>   Deïdamìa ancor si duol d'Achille,
>   e del Palladio pena vi si porta." (*Inf.* XXVI.55–63)

(He answered me: "Within that flame, Ulysses
and Diomedes suffer; they, who went
as one to rage, now share one punishment.

And there, together in their flame, they grieve
over the horse's fraud that caused a breach—
the gate that let Rome's noble seed escape.

There they regret the guile that makes the dead
Deidamia still lament Achilles;
and there, for the Palladium, they pay.")

As Vergil himself says here (though not in the *Aeneid*), it was Ulysses who, through the ruse of the Trojan horse, led not only to the fall of Troy but, more, to the opportunity of the story of Aeneas and Rome, and therefore to the resulting empires and their tales. The pairing with Diomedes is here explained through their twin roles in Vergil's version of their collaboration at Troy in *Aeneid* 2, and Vergil clarifies the importance of the two Greeks' actions in the creation of his own epic.[14] Ulysses, in other words, is critical for the afterlife of Troy, both in terms of the tradition that includes the *Aeneid* and the founding of the Roman empire.

The Ulysses canto, at first, then, would not appear to be about reading. Instead, it would seem to fit into a tradition Dante would have known of, one that debated at length the location of Ulysses' journey, especially given the phrase Vergil uses:

". . . l'un di voi dica
dove, per lui, perduto a morir gissi." (*Inf.* XXVI.83–4)

(". . . let one of you retell
where, having gone astray, he found his death.")

The question Vergil asks—the one he understands Dante wants him to pose—is made clear in the lines "tell me where," with the word *dove* emphasized by its placement at the start of line 84, which in turn echoes a similar one a few lines earlier at the start of line 77:

Poi che la fiamma fu venuta quivi
    dove parve al mio duca tempo e loco,
        in questa forma lui parlare audivi . . . (*Inf.* XXVI.76–8)

(And when my guide adjudged the flame had reached a point
where time and place were opportune,
this was the form I heard his words assume . . .)

The question of where Ulysses traveled is not new with Dante or Vergil but was often debated in Hellenistic writings, as this passage from Aulus Gellius (AD 123–c. 165) makes clear:[15]

> Accipio cupidus et libens, tamquam si copiae cornum nactus essem, et recondo me penitus, ut sine arbitris legam. At quae ibi scripta erant, pro Iuppiter, mera miracula! quo nomine fuerit qui primus "grammaticus" appellatus est; et quot fuerint Pythagorae nobiles, quot Hippocratae; et cuiusmodi fuisse Homerus dicat in Ulixis domo λαύρην; et quam ob causam Telemachus cubans iunctim sibi cubantem Pisistratum non manu adtigerit, sed pedis ictu excitarit; et Euryclia Telemachum quo genere claustri incluserit; et quapropter idem poeta rosam non norit, oleum ex rosa norit. Atque illud etiam scriptum fuit, quae nomina fuerint sociorum Ulixis, qui a Scylla rapti laceratique sunt; utrum ἐν τῇ ἔσω θαλάσσῃ Ulixes erraverit κατ' Ἀρίσταρχον an ἐν τῇ ἔξω κατὰ Κράτητα. (*Noctes Atticae* 14.6.3)

> (I took the book eagerly and gladly, as if I had got possession of the horn of plenty, and shut myself up in order to read it without interruption. But what was written there was, by Jove! merely a list of curiosities: the name of the man who was first called a "grammarian"; the number of famous men named Pythagoras and Hippocrates; Homer's description of the λαυρή, or "narrow passage," in the house of Ulysses; why Telemachus did not touch Pisistratus, who was lying beside him, with his hand, but awakened him by a kick; with what kind of bolt Euryclia shut in Telemachus; and why the same poet did not know the rose, but did know oil made from roses. It also contained the names of the companions of Ulysses who were seized and torn to pieces by Scylla; whether the wanderings of Ulysses were in the inner sea, as Aristarchus believed, or in the outer sea, according to Crates.)[16]

In *Inferno* XXVI, Ulysses essentially enacts this debate in a curious way. On the one hand, he clearly states that he had traveled with the few tired men left him after they visited Circe. They went beyond Caieta: he sees Spain, he says, and Morocco; Sardinia and "the other islands in the Mediterranean" (lines 103–5); then to *Sibilia* and *Setta* (lines 110–11) where they saw the pillars of Hercules, "beyond which no man should go" (line 109). There, after encouraging his men, he turns his stern to the morning and *sempre acquistando dal lato mancino* ("always gaining on the left-hand side," line 126), he rows hard until he sees a huge mountain. As he and his men approach, however, a storm from the *nova terra* (line 137) overwhelms them with turbulent waters three times; on the fourth they capsize and drown.

There is no question that the passage answers Vergil's question, as it focuses on where Ulysses went. Yet that "where" includes suggestive echoes between this passage and others. When Ulysses first says that he travels through the straits, he says *acciò che l'uom più oltre non si metta* (line 109), paraphrasing Helenus's advice to Aeneas to avoid the straits (*Aen.* 3.429–32):

> praestat Trinacrii metas lustrare Pachyni
> cessantem, longos et circumflectere cursus,   430
> quam semel informem vasto vidisse sub antro
> Scyllam et caeruleis canibus resonantia saxa.

> ("Better to round the turning point of Trinacrian Pachynus, delaying, and take the long route round, than once to have seen hideous Scylla in her vast cave and rocks echoing with seagreen dogs.")

Ulysses characterizes his men as *vecchi e tardi* (line 106), a near-translation of Vergil's characterization of the Trojan women left on Sicily in *Aeneid* 5.715: *senes ac fessas*.[17]

Moreover, in the passage from *Aeneid* 3, as we have seen, the Trojans, following Helenus's advice, sail up to the hazards of Scylla and Charybdis and then, leaning hard on their left-hand oars, avoid the straits by sailing back down the straits:

> . . . primusque rudentem
> contorsit laevas proram Palinurus ad undas;
> laevam cuncta cohors remis ventisque petivit (*Aen.* 3.561–63)

> ("First Palinurus turned the screeching prow to the left-hand waves; all the crew sought the left with oars and wind.")

In Ulysses' account of his final journey, he says that he and his men rowed hard, *sempre acquistando dal lato mancino*. Moreover, he describes that *tre volte il fé girar con tutte l'acque* ("three times it turned [the boat] around with all the waters," line 139) in the same way as Aeneas and his men:

> tollimur in caelum curvato gurgite, et idem
> subducta ad Manis imos desedimus unda.   565
> ter scopuli clamorem inter cava saxa dedere,
> ter spumam elisam et rorantia vidimus astra. (*Aen.* 3.564–67)

(We are borne to the heavens by a curved eddy, and again with the wave having ebbed we plunge to hellish depths. Three times within the carved-out rocks the cliffs gave a cry, three times we saw the foam scattered and the dewy stars.)

Like Aeneas, Ulysses works hard to keep gaining on the left, like Aeneas, he is tossed up and down three times by the waves at the straits.

These echoes are made even clearer if we compare Dante's Italian not to the Latin of Vergil but, rather, to a fourteenth-century Italian translation of the *Aeneid*, that of near-contemporary Ciampolo di Meo degli Ugurgieri (written 1312–16):

"O compagni, liberate voi di questi pericoli, e tutti insieme siate alli remi." E non altrimenti che lo' fu comandato, fanno. E Palinuro primo insieme torse le funi della nave e la prora all'onde dalla parte sinistra. Tutta la turba domandòe la parte sinistra colli remi e co li venti. Noi siamo levati in cielo per lo mare curvato, e poi discendiamo a li profondi spiriti per l'onda subtracta. Tre volte gli scogli diedero suono fra li saxi cavati; tre volte la schiuma exclusa e·lle stelle bagnate vedemo. Mentre che erano queste cose, vento con sole ci lasciò istanchi e lassi, ed essendo ignoranti della via, perveniamo alle contrade de' Ciclopi.

("Oh, comrades, free yourselves from these dangers, and apply yourselves altogether to the oars." And they did precisely as they were commanded. And Palinurus first twisted the ropes of the vessel and the prow to the waves on the left side. The entire crew sought the left side with oars and wind. We were raised to the skies by the curved wave, then we descended to the depths with the receding wave; three times the cliffs resounded within the hollow rocks; three times the foam thinned out and we saw the bathed stars. While these things were going on, the wind and the sun left us tired and worn out; and being ignorant of the way, we found ourselves at the land of the Cyclopes.)[18]

This translation suggests a reading of Vergil through Dante as it echoes Dante in the address to the comrades, the emphasis on the left-hand effort, the mention of the participation of the crew with the oars, and the triple rise and fall of the waves, even as it translates the passage from the *Aeneid*.[19]

The importance of the commentary and translation tradition is what I would emphasize, for it is in these texts, both Latin and vernacular, that suggestive resonances occur that guide our reading of Dante's poem.[20] Moreover,

Dante as much as tells us that he is relying on these intervening traditions in the language of Ulysses' speech in *Inferno* XXVI. When he says, in lines 92–93, that he had left Gaeta, before it was named, and, in 110–11, passed by Sibillia and Setta, he is speaking not as Ulysses (or Vergil) but as Hercules in Guido delle Colonne's 1287 *Historia Destructionis Troiae*:

> Hunc locum angustum a quo primum hoc Mediterraneum mare dilabitur nostri hodie navigantes Strictum Sibile nominant sive Secte, et locus ille in quo predicte columpne Herculis sunt affixe dicitur Sarracenica lingua Saphy, quidam locus a quo sufficit ultra non ire.
>
> (Our sailors today call this narrow place from which this Mediterranean Sea first flows away the strait of Seville or Sebta, and that place in which the aforesaid pillars of Hercules are located is called in the Saracen language Safi, a place which it is impossible to go beyond.)[21]

Vergil has Ulysses represent himself in the words of the *Historia* as Hercules going beyond the edge of the world at the *columpne Herculis*. Ulysses' story is based more on text than on experience, and Dante wants us to be aware of this.

But the location of Ulysses' journey—whether it lies in the Mediterranean or beyond—is in fact more complicated than it might first appear. For while Ulysses explicitly states that his journey led him beyond the Mediterranean, and while the external evidence of *Paradiso* will support this assertion, the intertexts suggest otherwise. It is my argument, in fact, that Ulysses does in fact see a tall mountain beyond the pillars of Hercules, but that Vergil believes that that mountain is none other than Etna; it is for this reason so many of the intertexts mention Sicily. To put this slightly differently, we come to know in *Paradiso* that Ulysses is seen to sail beyond the straits of Gibraltar and to a point at the Antipodes, opposite the entrance to the underworld, where the mountain of Purgatory is said to rise. Ulysses speaks of this journey in ways that can be confirmed by this later passage. But looking back at the passages cited from the *Aeneid*, we see that the echoes come from book 3 and refer to places at or near Sicily. Only the pillars of Hercules would seem to undermine this and even that has a Sicilian connection. We have noted that the journey to these pillars is strongly influenced by the text of Guido delle Colonne's description of the journey of Hercules. As it turns out, the pillars there are a moveable target. In the *Historia Destructionis Troiae* Guido suggests that these pillars, or at least pillars also called the pillars of Hercules, were set up not at Gibraltar but rather on the coast of Sicily:

Ex hoc itaque loco illi qui putaverunt provinciam Messe esse Siciliam oppinionem eorum multa firmitate corroborant, asserentes Herculem in Siciliam venisse. Unde dictum est in una parte Sicilie, ex parte barbarorum, Herculem ex causa memorie suas fixisse columpnas. Qui locus adhuc dicitur Columpnarum. . . . In hac igitur terra . . . adhuc supersunt quedam columpne, que vulgo columpne Herculis nuncupantur, et in ea quondam Fredericus Secundus, princeps rei publice Romanorum et rex Sicilie, fecit construi quandam terram, considerans locum ipsum habitantibus utilem propter situm, quamvis in facie pelagi situs sit, carens omni stacione salubri. Que tamen terra, propter situs bonitatem plena populo, usque in hodiernum diem dicitur Terra Nova.

(From this point, those who thought that the province of Messa was Sicily corroborate their opinion with great firmness, asserting that Hercules came to Sicily. Hence it is said that in one part of Sicily, in the barbarians' part, Hercules set up his pillars in order to be remembered. This is called today the Place of the Pillars . . . In that land therefore . . . there survive today certain pillars which are commonly called the Pillars of Hercules, and there Frederick II, prince of the Roman Republic and King of Sicily, once had some land piled up, thinking that this place would be good to live in on account of the strategic site, although it is situated facing the sea, lacking every healthy situation. This land, however, filled with people on account of the good qualities of the location, is up to the present day called Terra Nova.)[22]

Guido corrects his identification of the columns from earlier and places them squarely on Sicily, near Messina, in a land that *usque in hodiernum diem dicitur Terra Nova* ("is up to the present day called Terra Nova"). That Dante has this text and this correction in mind is suggested by line 137, which states that Ulysses, having passed the pillars of Hercules, spots the mountain of Purgatory and is blown off course by a wind from none other than *la nova terra*.

> Noi ci allegrammo, e tosto tornò in pianto;
>   ché de la nova terra un turbo nacque
>   e percosse del legno il primo canto. (*Inf.* XXVI. 136–38)

(And we were glad, but this soon turned to sorrow,
for out of that new land a whirlwind rose
and hammered at our ship, against her bow.)

Not only does the mountain of Purgatory loom in *Inferno* XXVI, but it does so in the context of Sicily. Mention of the pillars of Hercules together with the identification of the land as *nova terra*, both occurring in Guido's second passage on Sicily, suggest that the version of the story we hear indicates that Ulysses did not pass beyond the straits of Gibraltar but, instead, went through straits on Sicily near Messina—the straits of Messina so important to Vergil's epic. The conflation of the two straits is encouraged by other texts: Pliny the Elder tells us that the straits of Messina are known as the Royal Pillars (whence the town name Rhegium);[23] and the chronicle of Richard of Devizes (fl. late twelfth c.) includes, in a passage focused on Messina, the fact that he will fight throughout Sicily all the way to the pillars of Hercules (Section 24: *tota sibi, si jusserit, sudore suo Sicilia subjicietur; totus, si voluerit, usque ad Columnas Herculis, ibit in sanguine*; "all Sicily at his command alone, shall be subjected to him by their labour; all, if he should but desire it, as far as the Pillars of Hercules shall be steeped in blood").[24] Whether or not these are actually the same place is irrelevant: by virtue of their sharing the same name, the straits of Gibraltar and the straits of Messina become conflated through mention of the pillars of Hercules.

Enacting the very question posed in the earlier texts, then, the Ulysses canto thus debates rather than resolves the issue of how far Ulysses went in his journey. While he says he went beyond the straits, the intertextual echoes would suggest he went no further than Sicily. In support of this, there is one additional text that needs to be brought to bear, another of Vergil's own. For although in *Inferno* XXVI Vergil explicitly references only *Aeneid* 2 and the trickery of Ulysses and Diomedes, the pair appear together one other time in his epic. In *Aeneid* 11, as the Latins are struggling to conquer the Trojans, they send an embassy to none other than Diomedes to request his aid. He refuses, explaining that his days of fighting are over, and in support of this, explains what has happened to the other Greek heroes:

"o fortunatae gentes, Saturnia regna,
antiqui Ausonii, quae vos fortuna quietos
sollicitat suadetque ignota lacessere bella?
quicumque Iliacos ferro violavimus agros   255
(mitto ea quae muris bellando exhausta sub altis,
quos Simois premat ille viros) infanda per orbem
supplicia et scelerum poenas expendimus omnes,
vel Priamo miseranda manus; scit triste Mineruae
sidus et Euboicae cautes ultorque Caphereus.   260
militia ex illa diversum ad litus abacti
Atrides Protei Menelaus adusque columnas
exsulat, Aetnaeos vidit Cyclopas Vlixes." (*Aen.* 11.252–63)

("O blessed peoples of ancient Ausonia, kingdom of Saturn, what fate troubles you, peaceful, and persuades you to wage unknown wars? We who violated the Trojan fields with the sword (I set aside those drained of life at the high walls by war, those men that river Simois drowned) have paid throughout the world in unspeakable tortures and penalties for our wickedness, a band of men pitied even by Priam: he knows the sad star of Minerva, the Euboean crags, and the avenger Caphereus. Among those troops, driven to scattered shores, Menelaus, son of Atreus, is in exile all the way to the pillars of Proteus, and Ulysses sees the Etnean Cyclopes.")

While in *Inferno* XXVI Vergil only mentions Ulysses and Diomedes in the context of the ruse of the Trojan horse and theft of the Palladium, both stories with roots in *Aeneid* 2, this other passage links even more clearly Ulysses with Diomedes as exiles from the Trojan War, who have suffered greatly in its aftermath. His point is an important one, relevant to Dante's concerns: even though we won the war, Diomedes says, we have paid a terrible price for that victory, being driven to the ends of the earth. The two characters are linked through their trickery, but they are also tied together through the pain they suffered as exiles.

Moreover, this passage, more than the one Vergil himself mentions, has an afterlife in the commentaries that suggests its importance to Dante. In Guido da Pisa's *I fatti di Enea*, Diomedes explains:

> Lo re Menelao, per la cui moglie nacque quella guerra, tristo e tapino ne va per lo mondo: lo re Ulisse, che 'n tutte le cose fu mio compagno, va errando per mare ed ora è intorno alla montagna di Mongibello. (Rubrica 46)[25]

(King Menelaus, whose wife was the cause of that war, sad and wandering, traveled throughout the world: king Ulysses, who was in every action my companion, wandered around the sea and now is near the mountain of Mongibello.)

Ciampolo di Meo degli Ugurgieri translates the Vergilian passage as:

> Da quella guerra partiti, rimossi a diversa riva, Menelao d'Atreo va fuori
> della patria sua, infino alle Colonne d'Ercule; Ulixe vidde i Ciclopi d'Ethna.[26]

(Having left that war, they dispersed to diverse shores: Menelaus, son of Atreus, went outside his homeland, all the way to the columns of Hercules; Ulysses sees the Cyclopes at Etna.)

Notice that Ulysses progresses from seeing the Etnean Cyclops to wandering across the seas and landing at Etna where he is to this day (*ora* in Guido da Pisa's account). In every version, Ulysses ends in Sicily. This fits with Vergil's own text, which mentions Ulysses in this passage in *Aeneid* 11 as well as in the Achaemenides passage in *Aeneid* 3.613–54, where Ulysses is said to have been last seen on Sicily. Vergil believes that Ulysses passes—or perhaps even, like Aeneas, fails to pass—through the straits of Messina; is washed ashore and can to this day be found "at Etna."

It would seem that Vergil poses the question of *dove* to Ulysses in large part to see if he will volunteer to resolve the debate, a resolution Vergil himself believes to know: the whereabouts of Ulysses is Sicily. In Vergil's understanding, Ulysses never did travel beyond the "inner sea." It seems plausible to suggest that the version we hear in answer to the question Vergil poses, conforms to Vergil's own expectations about where Ulysses traveled. And this is the speech that is introduced by Dante saying "in questa forma lui parlare audivi" ("in this form I heard him speak," *Inf.* XXVI.78).[27]

But the very debate about where Ulysses traveled is overwritten by a debate about how to read.[28] In the *Epistulae Morales* 88.7 of Seneca the Younger we find the question of Ulysses' journey turned to a new end.[29]

In *Epistula* 88.7 Seneca asks:

Quaeris Ulixes ubi erraverit potius quam efficias ne nos semper erremus? Non vacat audire utrum inter Italiam et Siciliam iactatus sit an extra notum nobis orbem.[30]

(Do you ask, "Where did Ulysses stray?" instead of trying to prevent ourselves from going astray at all times? We have no leisure to hear lectures on the question whether he was sea-tossed between Italy and Sicily, or outside the world known to us.)

Vergil asserts that he knew what Dante wanted to ask, yet he poses the question Seneca would argue is precisely the wrong one, the question of "where." The stress on *dove* makes this clear. Rather than clarifying where he went, Ulysses dramatizes the debate itself, offering a series of quotations that blur rather than clarify his itinerary, and suggesting in some spots that he went beyond the straits of Gibraltar and in others that he stayed inside the Mediterranean.

But Seneca goes further in his epistle, as he tells us that even though debating the "where" does little good, the journey of Ulysses nonetheless does raise important questions, questions that have to do with reading and interpretation:

Hoc me doce, quomodo patriam amem, quomodo uxorem, quomodo patrem, quomodo ad haec tam honesta vel naufragus navigem.

(From this show me rather how I am to love my country, how my wife, how my father, and how, even after suffering shipwreck, I am to sail toward these ends, honourable as they are.)[31]

Seneca's point is a hermeneutic one: the questions you ask of a text determine its value. The question Vergil asks Ulysses (and Diomedes) is not the question that should have been asked, since it leads to nothing that is not trivial. Instead, as we have seen, it prevaricates in its very efforts at an answer. Rather, the questions Seneca urges are ones that have to do with bigger issues, issues of honorable ends, of love: of how or why over where.[32] These, according to Seneca, are the benefits of reading, and arguably they are the questions that Dante himself would have asked. For when Vergil silences Dante, Dante indicates what he would like to have asked:

> "S'ei posson dentro da quelle faville
> Parlar," diss' io, "maestro, assai ten priego   65
> e ripriego, che 'l priego vaglia mille,
> che non mi facci de l'attender niego
> fin che la fiamma cornuta qua vegna;
> vedi che del disio ver' lei mi piego!" (*Inf.* XXVI.64–9)

("If they can speak within those sparks," I said,
"I pray you and repray and, master, may
my prayer be worth a thousand pleas, do not

forbid my waiting here until the flame
with horns approaches us; for you can see
how, out of my desire, I bend toward it.")

The repetition of *priego* in the first three lines is enacted by its near-echo in the last word of the passage, *piego*, "I bend." Dante's desire, later picked up by the Vergilian phrase *antica fiamma* is what draws him to Ulysses; presumably his questions, had he been able to ask them, would have been drawn from that source. They would have been questions of ardor.

Desire surfaces as a driving force of reading, but desire is also, of course, associated with Ulysses' sin. As Elena Lombardi points out, however, we must be careful to recognize that it is not the desire itself that constitutes Ulysses' sin, but what he does with that desire.[33] The object that Seneca points to—to return home and love his wife—is not the one Ulysses chooses. Interestingly, it is also not the one Diomedes opts for. Partners in crime, they are also infernal cellmates: according to the versions told in Vergil and Ovid, neither returns home. Both remain in exile, pursuing their lust for adventure, until their deaths.

The point of the passage is not only that wrong questions lead to useless answers, but even the right questions—questions involving honorable motives—can lead you astray.[34] Dante leans toward Ulysses demonstrating passion, the *antica fiamma*; but as any reader of Vergil knows, the ancient flame is what Dido felt for Aeneas: it is a dangerous force. Like Ulysses, and like Aeneas had he stayed in Carthage, Dante at this point would have to choose adventure over family, exile over his fated new home. The choice Ulysses gives his comrades is exactly this: experience life while you can, and that life does not include family and home. But what becomes clear in the later canticles is something quite different. In *Purgatorio* Dante will learn that in that cosmology not only is there, in fact, experience beyond this life, but the choice Seneca points to—and the choice Ulysses forces on his men—is not a true choice. That is, in the later canticles, Dante learns that the journey out is also the return home: exile ends in nostos.[35] As he climbs farther and farther up the mountain of Purgatory he will also approach and eventually enter the Garden of Eden: the journey winds up the mountain in space even as it unwinds in time. But this also means that the choice Seneca poses—ask why, not where; approach Ulysses as a character known for love not experience—is ultimately itself seen to be false, since the doubt that surrounds you can be sustained by a multilevel reading rooted in love. Rather than choosing between two objects, Dante suggests that such a higher reading enables doubt to remain: the straits can be both Gibraltar and Messina.

And, more than that, the mountain can be both Purgatory and Etna.[36] That is, while Etna had been paired throughout the medieval tradition with the transition to death, first as a place like Gehenna, then as a region of redemption, what Dante's version of the Ulysses' tale suggests is that Etna for him was a place of poetry. Turning back to Seneca's description of the mountain, discussed in the last chapter, Etna is "a lofty summit, which rises so far beyond the reach of any missile as to tower high above all fortune." Getting there is a struggle: the path is "steep and rugged," although it is only "the first part [that] has rocks and cliffs and appears impassable." And, as we have seen, Etna in particular is and has always been the proving ground for authors, the one where you demonstrate your talents, both in terms of the virtue you reveal and in the approach you take in writing.[37]

It is worth mentioning at this juncture that not only does Seneca the Younger pair Ulysses with Hercules, but he also says that both pale in comparison to Cato, who will stand as guard to Dante's *Purgatorio*.[38] Through the Senecan intertext we are encouraged to see Purgatory not only as Etna but also as achieved through the good, as opposed to the uninformed, interpretive process.

Inferno XXVI offers an illustration of Dante presenting the challenge offered by Seneca. Where Ulysses goes, literally, is not as important as how we read what he says, and how we learn from his example. Ulysses, in short, is not as important as the poetry about him and the way it is read. If we take his story literally, we enter a trap; if we interpret the higher meaning, as Seneca urges us to do, we see how poetry—any poetry—can illuminate. But this is a lesson for *Purgatorio*, not *Inferno*.

If the point of Ulysses' speech is more about the redemptive power of language than about truth and lies, and if through this speech *Purgatorio* becomes affiliated with the relationship between language and redemption, then *Inferno* XXVI comes to serve as introduction to critical issues developed in the second canticle as it interrogates the powers of language and interpretation.[39] The specific identification of the mountain of Purgatory both here and in *Paradiso* as lying beyond the straits of Gibraltar, would seem to undercut any notion that Sicily is influential to Dante's thinking. However, an examination of the intertexts activated in the description of Purgatory by Ulysses confirms an association between Sicily and Purgatory, which opens the door to a renewed reading of the entire second canticle, based in part on Seneca and so connected to Vergil's and Ovid's use of the island as a location for the enactment of imperial resistance through the interaction of poets. For Ulysses, traveling to the end of the known world, is seen by Vergil to get only as far as the straits of Messina, something Vergil tries his hardest to make clear to Dante without actually calling Ulysses a liar, since Ulysses does not lie: like most of the other inhabitants of the *Inferno*, Ulysses tells what he believes to be the truth; what the Vergilian intertexts make clear is that his perception of the truth is limited by his abilities to interpret. What Dante elucidates, in turn, is that Vergil's own awareness of Ulysses' journey is itself limited by his own pagan blinders.

And the hermeneutic questions are focused on Sicily. The backdrop of Dante's poems is always Italy, much as it was for the ancient poets we started with, yet Italy's place in the world has changed radically by the time Dante writes the *Commedia*. While the western Mediterranean remains critical to trade and transport, it does not hold the same mythical power that it once did.[40] The struggles of the Crusades turn the gaze of the world *Outremer*, and while the church retains tremendous power, Rome has diminished in population and strength.⁴¹ The city-states granted isolated regions limited power, and, for Dante, Italy was united by the ridge of the Apennines, which provided the backbone of his country. Sicily, too, does not retain the power it held even during the first Crusades. Sicily's role in modeling and resisting empire all but drops from view.⁴²

Following a similar trajectory, Sicily does not enter much into discussions of Dante and his works. It does not warrant an entry in the *Dante Encyclopedia*, and it would seem to play a minimal part in Dante's own worldview, although, as we shall see in the next chapter, it is central to the *De vulgari eloquentia*. Yet I would argue that it continues to be important in his cultural imaginary, especially as he tries to sketch out a vision for future empire in the *Commedia*, since Sicily for Dante is linked to narrative accounts of the source of true empire. Precisely because Dante is involved in the work of poets rather than politicians at this stage, his understanding of, use of, and adaptation of the history of Sicily is based more on literary accounts than historical ones, and more on poetic geography than actual landforms. The Sicily that is important to Dante is Sicily as a concept, "Sicily," if you will: the Sicily of Cicero, Vergil, and Ovid, yet overlain with narratives of redemption.

After Dante and Vergil leave Ulysses and head farther down into the pit of Hell, the Sicilian echoes increase. As Diskin Clay has pointed out, the very last line in the canticle, *E quindi uscimmo a riveder le stelle* ("And from there we exited to behold the stars once more"), alludes, strikingly, to a passage from *Metamorphoses* 5, the story Arethusa tells.⁴³ There, escaping from Alpheus by descending to the underworld, Arethusa resurfaces in Sicily where *hic caput attollo desuetaque sidera cerno*. ("Here I lift my head and behold the unfamiliar stars" *Met.* 5.503).

Emerging from the depths, having confronted the ruler of the underworld at its core, Dante is compared to none other than Arethusa who resurfaces from Hell on Sicily, having just seen Proserpina held captive by Hades. In Ovid, as we have seen, Arethusa provides the key for the recovery of Proserpina, as her revelation of Proserpina's whereabouts enables Ceres to find her. Arethusa's appearance at the end of *Inferno* offers something similar: the love Dante experiences in the presence of Ulysses, the reading that love enables, and his tale are what will allow him to move on to *Purgatorio*, where he will find the object of his quest. The expansion of love into the afterlife that Proserpina's abduction offers to Ovid is identified first through the Ulysses canto then corrected and refined in *Purgatorio* proper.

In the end both Ulysses and Vergil are each only partially right; only Dante, as we shall see, can make the dead poetry rise, can understand the true meaning of each of their speeches. Only Dante, guided by the forces of love that function like those Augustine discusses in *De doctrina Christiana* can see that Purgatory should be understood allegorically as Etna, and Etna as Purgatory. The ardor that Seneca urges as the true message of Ulysses' journey is not the goal but the means to a goal: Ulysses remains a figure of *cupiditas* and libido throughout *Inferno*, yet he introduces Dante to the power of ardor, which opens the way to something very different, to an appreciation of love for higher goals in *Purgatorio*. Etna, the very spot in the *Aeneid* where the waves lifted Aeneas up to the heavens and down to the infernal depths, becomes in Dante increasingly associated with the transition to the other world and, within that cosmology, with the place of transition itself, the mountain of Purgatory. Ulysses doesn't see this; Vergil himself doesn't see this; but Dante does, murkily, and through the story of Ulysses in particular and of Sicily in general he offers an exemplum of what he will come to understand in *Purgatorio* as the way that dead poetry, through love, can aid in redemption while it, too, is resurrected.

Joan Ferrante argues that *Inferno* shows traces of present-day Florence, *Paradiso*, ancient Rome, but Purgatory, she says, "is situated on the surface of this earth . . . potentially accessible to the living—Ulysses sailed within sight of it."[44] Yet the strange thing about Purgatory is that it is the one realm in Dante's epic that has any sort of existence on earth: the others are clearly fictions with echoes of the real.[45] What I am suggesting is that the tradition's belief that the location of Purgatory should be understood solely in terms of its description in *Inferno* XXVI and *Paradiso* does both the location and canticle a disservice. I would urge a reading overall that grants to *Purgatorio* the same richness found in the other canticles, just, perhaps, inverted. In other words, we can accept Dante's localization of the mountain on the edge of the known world, yet we have to also grant that mountain an allusive literary depth—a fictional existence—akin to the depth we grant *Inferno* and *Paradiso*. In so doing the literary and poetic resonance of *Purgatorio*—a resonance I argue that is steeped in Sicilian tales—takes on tremendous power, and *Purgatorio*, far from being the most literal of the canticles becomes the most poetic, the most fictional, and thereby the most powerful in Dante's quest to sketch out the future of empire.

Barolini has noted how Ulysses, throughout the *Commedia*, is paired with Dante the pilgrim.[46] I would add that the argument made at the start of the

Ulysses section of *Inferno* XXVI can be brought to bear at this point: Ulysses and Diomedes were the Greeks who allowed for the foundation of Rome, by causing the fall of Troy and forcing or enabling Aeneas to travel west to Italy. This early *felix culpa* argument fits well here: Ulysses' story, as told by Vergil and relayed to us by Dante, offers a "negative variant," to use Barolini's phrase, for Dante himself, one based on the need to interpret correctly and with love. It is perhaps not so much the object of love that changes but its very role: if love becomes the means, it can be paired with impossible objects and can sustain irresolvable conflict.

Read back against this argument, then, the speech of Ulysses takes on a particular importance for the understanding of empire, since empire, according to Dante, is as much about language as it is about government. The greed and aggression that cause Ulysses to end up in *Inferno* is corrected by the good reading of Dante: as we shall see in the next chapter, Dante's affiliation with Ulysses extends beyond *Inferno* and informs our reading of his pilgrim persona in *Purgatorio*. But the difference between the two heroes hinges on their treatment of language. The figure of Ulysses and his intertextual association with Sicily set the scene for what Dante will argue in *Purgatorio* concerning the necessities for good government and the possibilities for empire. Far from serving only a negative function in the *Commedia*, Ulysses is a key source for the typological persona Dante will assume in *Purgatorio*. Moreover, his location on Sicily links him, however loosely, with other Sicilian leaders, especially Frederick II, and suggests that the roots for empire extend back in Sicily's history.

While Dante's portrayal of Sicily is not as obviously derived from Cicero's formulation as the Latin texts are, it nonetheless betrays an awareness of long-term associations between Sicily and empire and develops them in terms of the importance of language and interpretation to the possibilities of empire. Moreover, taking Seneca as a lead, we are encouraged to find in Ulysses not a deceitful Greek but the roots of a model citizen. As we shall see, when Dante begins *Purgatorio* with a call to bring the dead poetry to life, he refers specifically to the case of Ulysses. As corrupt as Ulysses is when approached on a literal level, his story and his intertextual affiliations with Sicily suggest that the seeds of redemption for him and for empire lie, as Seneca suggested, within his story if it is read with love.

7

Purgatorio, Etna, and the Empire of Love

IF A distinction between *Inferno* and *Purgatorio* can be drawn in terms of reading and desire, as we argued in the last chapter, and if the difference between the two variants of the Proserpina myth can be traced in terms of the centrality of negotiation, Dante's *Purgatorio* can be approached as a poem where interpretation and negotiation are skills that are gradually acquired in aid of progress toward an *imperium* of the future. As the central canticle in the *Divina Commedia*, this part of the poem focuses on those who have been saved but cannot immediately enter *Paradiso*. The mountain of Purgatory is composed of seven terraces, after ante-Purgatory, and the penitents find themselves on the terrace that corresponds to their greatest vice, in the process of redeeming themselves from their sin. Dante, however, with Vergil, climbs up the terraces, from bottom to top: having acquired seven letter "P"s on his forehead, he works to have each erased as he progresses from ante-Purgatory to the earthly Paradise found at the top of the mountain.[1] There are, as a result, strong resonances between Dante's progress and the return of Proserpina, especially as recounted in the *Ovide*. Moreover, if we see *Purgatorio* as unfolding in the non-space of Easter Saturday, between the Good Friday of *Inferno* and the Easter of *Paradiso*,[2] the myth of Proserpina, especially in its Ovidian form, offers a means for successfully understanding that time, as it, too, speaks of a descent followed by a gradual and negotiated return.

Dante's version of the negotiation required for Proserpina's return, echoing the one voiced in the *Ovide Moralisé*, is nonetheless different from all others as it entails a process of erasure, or, to use the Hollanders' translation, "unsinning."[3] Even as the extension of love Proserpina's abduction enables in Ovid becomes in Dante's hands the rule of charitable love, so the negotiation for her return, the one that initially creates the cycle of seasons, comes instead to instantiate through poetry a secular form of the spiritual cycle of penitence and salvation.

Dante's evocation of Seneca's letters in *Inferno* XXVI, and the interest he shows there in both interpretation and competition among poets about Etna, constitute a theme that begins *Purgatorio*. Not only does the canticle open, as we shall see, with a reference to Ovid's treatment of Sicily in *Metamorphoses* 5, a story told as part of a poetic competition, but Dante's progress up the mountain is marked by two complementary motivations: a force toward redemption and a force toward clarity through poetic echoing and citation.[4] These two go hand in hand. Whereas Ovid's competition with Vergil, as allegorized in *Metamorphoses* 13, is solely antagonistic—there is a clear winner and loser—for Dante this drive turns from a competition to an accommodating, charitable, and collegial communion among poets, very much along the lines of Seneca's recommendations.

Significantly, this erasure of poetic limits constitutes a decision and a choice: Dante opts to return to the classical stories and myths with their definitions of empire, to uncover the source of his own writing not in his immediate surroundings but in the works of the ancients.[5] As he winds his way up the mountain and back to the Garden, he chooses to return to classical works rather than comment on contemporary ones. In *Purgatorio* he moves away from his political world and into the world of poetry, and in so doing his imperial language is burdened with mentions of Sicily in the ancients rather than Sicily at present.

Sicilian Echoes

Purgatorio begins with an invocation:

> Per correr miglior acque alza le vele
> omai la navicella del mio ingegno,
> che lascia dietro a sé mar sì crudele;
> e canterò di quel secondo regno
> dove l'umano spirito si purga   5
> e di salire al ciel diventa degno.
> Ma qui la morta poesì resurga,
> o sante Muse, poi che vostro sono;
> e qui Calïopè alquanto surga,

seguitando il mio canto con quel suono   10
    di cui le Piche misere sentiro
    lo colpo tal, che disperar perdono.
Dolce color d'orïental zaffiro,
    che s'accoglieva nel sereno aspetto
    del mezzo, puro infino al primo giro,   15
a li occhi miei ricominciò diletto,
    tosto ch'io usci' fuor de l'aura morta
    che m'avea contristati li occhi e 'l petto.
Lo bel pianeto che d'amar conforta
    faceva tutto rider l'orïente,   20
    velando i Pesci ch'erano in sua scorta. (*Purg.* I.1–21)

(To course across more kindly waters now
my talent's little vessel lifts her sails,
leaving behind herself a sea so cruel;

and what I sing will be that second kingdom,
in which the human soul is cleansed of sin,
becoming worthy of ascent to Heaven.

But here, since I am yours, o holy Muses,
may this poem rise again from Hell's dead realm;
and may Calliope rise somewhat here,

accompanying my singing with that music
whose power struck the poor magpies
so forcefully that they despaired of pardon.

The gentle hue of oriental sapphire
in which the sky's serenity was steeped—
its aspect pure as far as the horizon—

brought back my joy in seeing just as soon
as I had left behind the air of death
that had afflicted both my sight and breast.

The lovely planet that is patroness
of love made all the eastern heavens glad,
veiling the Pisces in the train she led.)[6]

The poet-narrator identifies himself as a sailor, cutting through the seas of poetry, leaving behind the cruel landscape of *Inferno* and entering the second realm where *la morta poesì resurga*. Many have noted the echo of the Ulysses canto here, pointing to similarities between Dante and Ulysses.[7] If, as we have argued, the point of the Ulysses canto is to urge a certain kind of reading, triggered by intertexts relating to Sicily, it would seem significant that Dante references him here. Moreover, these lines may well evoke the opening of Claudian's *De Raptu Proserpinae*, whose preface likewise begins with a nautical image.[8] In addition, in these lines, Dante not only invokes the Muses, but focuses specifically on Calliope and her poetic competition in *Metamorphoses* 5.[9] As we have seen, Ovid's story of the Pierides, who become magpies, is told in a complicated way. Nine sisters, children of Pierus and Euippe, challenged the Muses to a competition of voice and artistry. The Muses agreed, and appointed Calliope to tell their tale, and the tale she tells is that of the abduction of Proserpina.[10] Ovid frames Proserpina's abduction with the observation that of the Olympians only Hades has not fallen prey to her powers; as a result, Venus charges Cupid to cause Hades to fall in love. The tale of Proserpina, in Ovid's hands, is initiated, if not explained, by the introduction of love into the afterlife.

When Dante begins his second canticle, then, the one that will bring dead poetry to life (or, in the Hollanders' translation, bring the dead to life through poetry), with an allusion not just to the magpies but also to Calliope and Venus, he clearly intends us to return to Ovid's tale to see why.[11] What we find there informs our reading of *Purgatorio* I, as we learn that the story Calliope tells is in fact about love, and about love conquering the afterlife. But the *Commedia*, overall, is often focused on the intersection of love and the afterlife (or, in the case of *Inferno*, its failure to do so), and *Purgatorio* in particular is about the intermingling of love, the afterlife, and song. The Ovidian intertext is not only well chosen, it strikes all the chords in the opening canto that Dante would have wanted played. For he also is able to suggest, through this, a difference between Ovid's pagan tale—the message of "dead poetry"—and his own: he makes the dead poetry rise by transforming love from the pagan Venus to Christian love: here, in Purgatory, love will indeed enter the afterlife, but the effect will be very different from the effect it has in Ovid. That love enters this part of the afterlife after *Inferno* is no surprise: though we have expected love throughout the *Commedia*, it has been markedly absent from the text up to this point. Yet its introduction in the opening to *Purgatorio* makes a statement about its importance throughout the canticle. Love is what sets this class of the dead apart from those who came before, and it is the force that drives this canticle.

It has been argued that for Dante love makes justice a meaningful category, since out of love we derive free will, which, capable of morality, creates a world governed by just laws (sixth canto of each canticle). Proceeding from love we find the resolution of faction, division, and lawlessness. For Dante, justice is the arrangement of elements according to reason or nature that achieves the good of each constituent part. Through love, the will becomes allied and aligned with reason and is increasingly freed from perverse inclinations.[12] Love is an essential part of good rule and of subsequent *imperium*.

But we must not lose sight of the other aspect of Ovid's tale: that the story Calliope tells takes place on Sicily. That Dante doesn't want us to forget this is first implied by the reference to Sicily that occurs at the end of *Inferno*, as we have seen, a reference carried over, via the mention of Arethusa, to the beginning of *Purgatorio*.[13] The tales of both Arethusa and Proserpina are connected not just by being told in *Metamorphoses* 5 but also by the fact that they draw our attention to Sicily. Through Dante's careful use of *Metamorphoses* 5, both at the start of *Purgatorio* and the end of *Inferno*, and taking into account the other Sicilian texts echoed in the Ulysses canto, the intertextual web of allusions points to an association between Purgatory and Sicily.[14]

As we have seen, in Ovid, *Metamorphoses* 5, Sicily provides the setting for Venus's expansion of empire. In this canticle, Venus's action is set in an allegorized context and corresponds to what becomes perceived as a playing out of *felix culpa*: the abduction of Proserpina establishes the need for the reinstatement of her innocence, even as the fall of Adam leads to the need for Christ. Applied to Venus, one should look not just at love but also at the notion of empire: her assertion of an empire of love that leads to Proserpina's loss creates the need for an empire of love that repairs that loss. Here her action creates the need for a Christian Empire.

Empire, as we have seen, is a tricky thing in Dante's hands. Opposed to the notion of empire in his own world, largely because it has become the space in which church and state are dangerously intertwined, he nonetheless yearns for an *imperium* in the future in which church will be separated from state, in which the ideals of the ancient Roman empire can be revivified.[15] In Dante's own time Henry VII of Luxembourg was such a ruler, but in the *Commedia* the figure he singles out is Frederick II who, though ruling the *regno*, situated himself in Sicily, where he allied himself with the Norman cause, and adopted the notion that the northern rule over the island was a proto-Crusade.[16] Frederick also identified strongly with Augustus: he was buried in a porphyry tomb in the style of emperors, not kings.[17] While Dante places him in *Inferno* X.119 among the heretics, he sings his praises elsewhere as both emperor and humanist.[18] In *Il convivio* (*trattato* IV, cap. 3) (1303–1306), Dante identifies him

(1194–1250) as the last Roman emperor (*Federigo di Soave, ultimo imperadore de li Romani*), and in the *De vulgari eloquentia* he is praised for his cultural interests. Through these passages Dante may well be referring to Frederick's role as heir not just to Augustus, but to the notion of a penitential recovery of the past that becomes associated through the literature with Sicily.[19]

In large part this is because it was on Sicily that Frederick II created, as Dante tells us in the *De vulgari eloquentia*, a court where poetry was written in the mother tongue of the vernacular:

> Siquidem illustres heroes, Fredericus Cesar et benegenitus eius Manfredus, nobilitatem ac rectitudinem sue forme pandentes, donec fortuna permisit, humana secuti sunt, brutalia dedignantes. Propter quod corde nobiles atque gratiarum dotati inherere tantorum principum maiestati conati sunt, ita ut eorum tempore quicquid excellentes animi Latinorum enitebantur primitus in tantorum coronatorum aula prodibat; et quia regale solium erat Sicilia, factum est ut quicquid nostri predecessores vulgariter protulerunt, sicilianum vocetur. . . . laudabilissimum est. (*DVE* 1.xii.4; 1.xii.6)

> (Indeed, those illustrious heroes, the Emperor Frederick and his worthy son Manfred, knew how to reveal the nobility and integrity that were in their hearts; and, as long as fortune allowed, they lived in a manner befitting men, despising the bestial life. On this account, all who were noble of heart and rich in graces strove to attach themselves to the majesty of such worthy princes, so that, in their day, all that the most gifted individuals in Italy brought forth first came to light in the court of these two great monarchs. And since Sicily was the seat of the imperial throne, it came about that whatever our predecessors wrote in the vernacular was called "Sicilian," . . . the most praiseworthy variety of the vernacular.)[20]

Frederick's Sicily was thus the place where the possibility of empire as Dante defines it in *De monarchia* was best realized.[21] As Joan Ferrante summarizes, "man needs the help of his fellows in order to achieve a happy life on earth, government is essential if men are to live together in society, . . . but only . . . an empire can control the greed and aggressions of individual cities and princes."[22] In addition, empire, according to Dante, must be supplemented by a philosophical plan.[23] While in *Monarchia* this plan is best offered by the writings of Aristotle, in the earlier version of *Commedia*, it is offered instead by the poets. It is for this reason that Vergil, rather than Aristotle, serves as Dante's guide.[24] Not only is Frederick II the last Roman Emperor, his career epitomizes what Dante sees as essential for imperial leadership: the ruling of a community of men sustained and defined by the vision of the poets.

Geography of Poetry

Dante's community of poets in *Purgatorio* includes Vergil, Ovid, and Lucan who, in a manner resonant of the passage from Seneca's *Epistle* 79, in which the competition among poets is set on Etna, are linked through a discussion of Sicily.

Early on in *Purgatorio* proper, Dante alludes to a passage from Lucan which discusses the rivers pouring down the Apennines, mountains which, according to the passage in both Dante and Lucan, are cut off by the straits of Messina at Pelorus:

> ché dal principio suo, ov'è sì pregno
>   l'alpestro monte ond'è tronco Peloro,
>   che 'n pochi luoghi passa oltra quel segno (*Purg.* XIV. 31–33)

> for from its source (at which the rugged chain—
> from which Pelorus was cut off—surpasses
> most other places with its mass of mountains)

All editions of *Purgatorio* point us here to Lucan, *De bello civili*:

> umbrosis mediam qua collibus Appenninus
> erigit Italiam, nulloque a vertice tellus
> altius intumuit propiusque accessit Olympo.
> mons inter geminas medius se porrigit undas
> inferni superique maris, collesque coercent   400
> hinc Tyrrhena vado frangentes aequora Pisae,
> illinc Dalmaticis obnoxia fluctibus Ancon . . .

> longior educto qua surgit in aera dorso,
> Gallica rura videt deuexasque excipit Alpes.
> tunc Umbris Marsisque ferax domitusque Sabello   430
> vomere, piniferis amplexus rupibus omnis
> indigenas Latii populos, non deserit ante
> Hesperiam, quam cum Scyllaeis clauditur undis,
> extenditque suas in templa Lacinia rupes,
> longior Italia, donec confinia pontus   435

solveret incumbens terrasque repelleret aequor;
at, postquam gemino tellus elisa profundo est,
extremi colles Siculo cessere Peloro. (Lucan, *De bello civili* II. 396–402;
   428–38)

(where Apennine lifts central Italy
with shady hills; with no other peak does the earth
swell higher or approach Olympus nearer.
Midway between twin waters of the Lower and Upper Seas
the mountain-range extends, on this side bounded
by Pisa's hills which in the shallows break Tyrrhenian seas,
on that side by Ancona exposed to Dalmatian waves ...
Where the mountain rises further on with ridge raised up
into the air, it sees Gallic lands and intercepts declining Alps.
Then, fertile for the Umbrians and Marsians and tamed by Sabine
ploughshare, it embraces with its pine-clad crags
all Latium's native peoples, not abandoning
Hesperia until cut short by Scylla's waves
and stretching its crags to Lacinium's temple,
longer once than Italy, until the sea's attack
destroyed the junction and the water drove back the land;
but, after earth was smothered by twin depths,
its furthest hills became the property of Sicilian Pelorus.)[25]

Lucan's argument, derived from authors such as Vergil and Ovid, is the one we reviewed in the first chapter: because Sicily was originally joined to the mainland of Italy, the Apennines ran straight across from northern Italy to Etna. With change caused by time and floods, however, Sicily was separated from the mainland, and Etna now stands on its own, a fragmented piece of an earlier whole. Here Lucan himself edits the earlier versions: while Vergil emphasizes the original unity that can perhaps be restored through empire, Lucan, writing of civil war, points instead to the rift between the two landmasses and the impossibility of ever bridging the gap. Dante's use of the passage from Lucan reflects awareness of this difference as it occurs in the canto where the Arno and Florence are mentioned as a means to discuss the lack of civil unity and cohesion.[26]

In the earlier *De vulgari eloquentia*, Dante explicitly cites this same Lucan passage, introducing, however, an element not found there, as he focuses on the role of the Apennines in dividing the rivers east and west:

Dicimus ergo primo Latium bipartitum esse in dextrum et sinistrum. Si quis autem querat de linea dividente, breviter respondemus esse iugum Apenini, quod, ceu fistule culmen hinc inde ad diversa stillicidia grundat aquas, ad alterna hinc inde litora per ymbricia longa distillat, ut Lucanus in secundo describit: dextrum quoque latus Tyrenum mare grundatorium habet, levum vero in Adriaticum cadit. (*DVE* I.x.6)

(First of all, then, I state that Latium[27] is divided in two, a left hand and a right hand side. If anyone should ask where the dividing-line is drawn, I reply briefly that it is the range of the Apennines; for just as from the topmost rain-gutter water is carried to the ground dripping down through pipes on each side, these likewise irrigate the whole country through long conduits, on one side and the other, as far as the two opposite shores. All this is described in the second book of Lucan. The drip-tray on the right-hand side is the Tyrrhenian Sea, while the left-hand side drips into the Adriatic.)

Although Dante here identifies Lucan as his source, his emphasis on the division of the rivers leads us instead to another ancient author: Cicero, who, in *De oratore*, refers to the Apennine ridge in a discussion about the origin of oratory:

Haec autem, ut ex Apennino fluminum, sic ex communi sapientium iugo sunt doctrinarum facta divortia, ut philosophi tanquam in superum mare defluerent Graecum quoddam et portuosum, oratores autem in inferum hoc Tuscum et barbarum, scopulosum atque infestum, laberentur, in quo etiam ipse Ulysses errasset.... si his contenti estis atque eis etiam quae dici voluistis a me, ex ingenti quodam oratorem immensoque campo in exiguum sane gyrum compellitis. (*De Oratore* III.19.69–71)[28]

(However the streams of learning flowing from the common watershed of wisdom, as rivers do from the Apennines, divided in two, the philosophers flowing down into the entirely Greek waters of the Eastern Mediterranean with its plentiful supply of harbors, while the orators glided into the rocky and inhospitable Western seas of our outlandish Tuscany, where even Ulysses himself lost his bearings... if you are content with these rules and also the ones you have desired me to state, you are making the orator abandon a vast, immeasurable plain and confine himself to quite a narrow circle.)

Here it is the relationship of the rivers to the mountains that is foregrounded. Cicero, like Dante, is lamenting the loss of unity in the context of rhetoric. The present age, he says, has been corrupted by the separation of eloquence from wisdom: like the rivers flowing east and west off the Apennine ridge, wisdom has flowed east to Greece, pure eloquence west to Rome. But in an earlier age, the two were united. The thrust of his treatise, then, is an effort to return to the source, to the time when the two halves of oratory were one.

In *De vulgari eloquentia* Dante makes a similar argument. Throughout the first book, he tries hard to track down the quintessential quality of the best vernacular, his vernacular, Italian:

> Hoc autem vulgare quod illustre, cardinale, aulicum et curiale ostensum est, dicimus esse illud quod vulgare latium appellatur. Nam sicut quoddam vulgare est invenire quod proprium est Cremone, sic quoddam est invenire quod proprium est Lombardie; et sicut est invenire aliquod quod sit proprium Lombardie, [sic] est invenire aliquod quod totius sinistre Ytalie proprium; et sicut omnia hec est invenire, sic et illud quod totius Ytalie est. Et sicut illud cremonense ac illud lombardum et tertium semilatium dicitur, sic istud, quod totius Ytalie est, latium vulgare vocatur. Hoc enim usi sunt doctores illustres qui lingua vulgari poetati sunt in Ytalia, ut Siculi, Apuli, Tusci, Romandioli, Lombardi et utriusque Marchie viri. (*DVE* I.xix.1)

> (So now we can say that this vernacular, which has been shown to be illustrious, cardinal, aulic, and curial, is the vernacular that is called Italian. For, just as one vernacular can be identified as belonging to Cremona, so can another that belongs to Lombardy; and just as one can be identified that belongs to Lombardy, so can another that belongs to the whole left-hand side of Italy; and just as all these can be identified in this way, so can that which belongs to Italy as a whole. And just as the first is called Cremonese, the second Lombard, and the third half-Latian, so this last, which belongs to all Italy, is called the Latian vernacular.[29] This is the language used by the illustrious authors who have written vernacular poetry in Italy, whether they came from Sicily, Apulia, Tuscany, Romagna, Lombardy, or either of the Marches.)

Even as Dante, in *De vulgari eloquentia*, sends us, via Lucan and Cicero, up the Apennines to the source of language, so he as pilgrim climbs up the mountain of Purgatory to the source of life, the earthly Paradise, at the top. Following the guidance of *De vulgari eloquentia*, we are inclined, I would argue, to see this climb as a hunt for the best vernacular, a hunt, we have been taught, that is like the one Cicero situated on the Apennines, here found on the mountain of Purgatory.[30] As we as readers climb the path of redemption we learn to interpret, which entails acknowledging the changes and modifications of time. It is tempting to posit that language as Occitan: certainly Arnaut's appearance in the later cantos and the use of Occitan in the *terza rima* there suggests the importance of that language in this hunt for the vernacular.[31] But Arnaut appears first in *Purgatorio* XXVI, not at the top of the mountain, and while his language is superior to Latin it is not the essential vernacular we are in search of. Instead, as we have been urged by *De vulgari eloquentia*, what we are searching for is the language that lies at the heart of Italian, the one most closely allied with Latin, which, Dante tells us, is the language of *Sì*, or Sicilian.[32]

A brief clarification of Sicilian is needed in this context. Dante uses the term in two very different ways, as referring to a dialect and as characteristic of the original vernacular poetry that has fallen into disuse. As a dialect, it belongs in the category of provincial tongues, where it sits alongside other disparaged, splintered languages. As the language of the first vernacular poetry in the court of Frederick II, it is an illustrious vernacular.

And this is the language we find, strikingly, as Dante crosses the river Lethe and greets Beatrice face to face:

> Confusione e paura insieme miste
>   mi pinsero un tal "sì" fuor de la bocca,
>   al quale intender fuor mestier le viste. (*Purg.* XXXI.13–15)

> (Confusion mixed with fear compelled a Yes
> out of my mouth, and yet that Yes was such—
> one needed eyes to make out what it was.)

In his own treatise Dante is clear that the contemporary vernaculars are characterized precisely by the word they use for "yes":

> Est igitur super quod gradimur ydioma tractando tripharium, ut superius dictum est: nam alii *oc*, alii *sì*, alii vero dicunt *oïl*. Et quod unum fuerit a principio confusionis (quod prius probandum est) apparet, quia convenimus in vocabulis multis, velut eloquentes doctores ostendunt: que quidem convenientia ipsi confusioni repugnat, que ruit celitus in edificatione Babel. (*DVE* I.ix.2)

> (The language with which I shall be concerned, then, has three parts, as I said above: for some say *oc*, some say *sì*, and others, indeed, say *oïl*. And the fact—which must first of all be proved—that this language was once unitary, at the time of the primal confusion, is clear, because the three parts agree on so many words, as masters of eloquence and learning show. This agreement denies the very confusion that was hurled down from heaven at the time of the building of Babel.)

When Dante crosses the river to join Beatrice, cleansed by the new baptism of Lethe, the language he speaks is the language of *Sì*, of Sicilian, by which he means the quintessential poetic Italian used in the court of Frederick II. He does not mean the modern-day version of Latin, which he terms Latian, though others mistakenly call it Sicilian.[33]

Other passages point to the presence of Sicily here at the top of the mountain.[34] When Beatrice appears in *Purgatorio* XXX, her affect is reminiscent of Ceres when searching for Proserpina:

> "... Per questo visitai l'uscio d'i morti,
>   e a colui che l'ha qua sù condotto,   140
>   li preghi miei, piangendo, furon porti.
> Alto fato di Dio sarebbe rotto,
>   se Letè si passasse e tal vivanda
>   fosse gustata sanza alcuno scotto
> di pentimento che lagrime spanda." (*Purg.* XXX.139–45)

> ("... For this I visited the gateway of
> the dead; to him who guided him above
> my prayers were offered even as I wept.
>
> The deep design of God would have been broken
> if Lethe had been crossed and he had drunk
> such waters but had not discharged the debt
>
> of penitence that's paid when tears are shed.")

Beatrice's tone is hard to justify. Yet glancing first at the end of her speech, we find, perhaps, a way to understand her anger. In the last lines she says that God states that those who pass Lethe must repent of what they have eaten. Broadly speaking, this is the apple of Eden, but as we have seen, the same argument is made in the *Ovide Moralisé*, not about the apple but rather about the seven seeds of the pomegranate Proserpina eats in the underworld.[35] Thinking back on the climb up Purgatory, we have a possible matrix for approaching it: the seven seeds are the seven sins that Dante progresses through. Although he only ate the seeds of the pomegranate metaphorically, he still must repent of what he has "eaten," before he, like Proserpina, can progress. Even as Ceres in her anger is key to the negotiation for Proserpina, so Beatrice here oversees the erasure of Dante's sins. Through this action Proserpina is returned to Sicily. Here, too, the land of recovery resounds with texts about Sicily.

In addition, it is in *Purgatorio* XXX that we hear loudest from Vergil, and not just any Vergilian texts, but precisely those that relate one way or another with Sicily.

> Ma Virgilio n'avea lasciati scemi
>   di sé, Virgilio dolcissimo patre, 50
>   Virgilio a cui per mia salute die'mi;
> né quantunque perdeo l'antica matre,
>   valse a le guance nette di rugiada
>   che, lagrimando, non tornasser atre. (*Purg.* XXX.49–54)

> (But Virgil had deprived us of himself,
> Virgil, the gentlest father, Virgil, he
> to whom I gave my self for my salvation;
>
> and even all our ancient mother lost
> was not enough to keep my cheeks, though washed
> with dew, from darkening again with tears.)

Rachel Jacoff, among others, has noted the evocation of Orpheus here from *Georgics* 4 (via Statius), an evocation made through the triple echo of Vergil's name,[36] but there is another Vergilian allusion, in line 52: *l'antica matre*, referencing the loss of the ancient mother, which the commentaries gloss as referring to Eve. Yet Singleton notes how Latinate and archaizing the phrase *antica matre* is (*matre* instead of *madre*) and the phrase does occur, in its original Latin form, in the prophecy about the journey to Rome, where Anius prophesies to Anchises:[37]

> "Dardanidae duri, quae vos a stirpe parentum
> Prima tulit tellus, eadem vos ubere laeto 95
> Accipiet reduces. Antiquam exquirite matrem.
> Hic domus Aeneae cunctis dominabitur oris
> Et nati natorum et qui nascentur ab illis." (*Aen.* 3.94–98)

> ("Tough Dardans, the same earth that first bore you from parental stock, that same earth will welcome you, led back, in her happy breast. Seek out the ancient mother. Here the house of Aeneas will rule over all shores and sons of sons and those born from them.")

"*Antiquam exquirite matrem*": seek out the ancient mother, first thought by Anchises to be Crete, then learned by Aeneas in a dream to be Italy:

"... non haec litora suasit
Delius aut Cretae iussit considere Apollo.
est locus, Hesperiam Grai cognomine dicunt,
terra antiqua, potens armis atque ubere glaebae;
Oenotri coluere viri; nunc fama minores 165
Italiam dixisse ducis de nomine gentem" (*Aen.* 3.161–66)

("Delian Apollo did not urge these shores, or order you to settle in Crete. There is a place the Greeks call Hesperia, an ancient land, powerful in arms and in the richness of soil; Oenotrian men have cultivated it; now the rumor is that their descendants call the race Italian from the name of their leader.")

If the archaizing of *matre*, and the phrase *antica matre*, in *Purgatorio* XXX refer us to Italy, instead of, or in addition to, Eve as the ancient mother, then the question becomes: in what way is Dante like that ancient mother, Italy? The text offers two clues: the first within the same passage in *Purgatorio* XXX, the other earlier in the canticle when Vergil is referred to as *dolcissimo patre* (*Purg.* XXX.50). For not only is *matre* archaizing, but so, arguably, is *patre*.[38] The ancient mother lost the sweetest father. But the father lost to Italy in the *Aeneid* is Anchises, Aeneas's father who dies on Sicily before the Trojans make it to Rome. As we have seen, in *Aeneid* 5, the Troades, the Trojan women who decide finally to stay on Sicily, *amissum Anchisen flebant*, wept for their lost Anchises.

Moreover, Dante offers a further gloss to this passage:

Di retro a tutti dicean: "Prima fue
   morta la gente a cui il mar s'aperse,
   che vedesse Iordan le rede sue. 135
E quella che l'affanno non sofferse
   fino a la fine col figlio d'Anchise,
   sé stessa a vita sanza gloria offerse." (*Purg.* XVIII.133–38)

(... And I heard those two say

behind all of the rest: "The ones for whom
the sea parted were dead before the Jordan
saw those who had inherited its lands;

and those who did not suffer trials until
the end together with Anchises' son
gave themselves up to life without renown.")

Here Dante urges a comparison between the souls in Purgatory, the journey of the Israelites in the desert, and those left behind on Sicily in the *Aeneid*, Anchises and the Troades. Even as the Israelites who sacrificed themselves led the way to the promised land, so the Troades and Anchises made it possible for the younger Trojans to reach Rome. In addition, both, I would argue, provide a model for Vergil's staying behind in *Purgatorio* XXX: Vergil, like Anchises, and like the Israelites, enables progress through his own refusal to go on.

But if the *antica matre* is Italy and Eve, it is also Beatrice as Ceres who rebukes Dante as a mother does a child. He crosses the river that miraculously erases memory and separation. The Sicily where Dante bid his Anchises, Vergil, farewell is also the land, that *regale solium*, associated with the optimal vernacular of the poets. Marianne Shapiro sums this up: "Out of the unified cultural climate that had been allowed to evolve in Sicily, Dante swiftly draws the image of a quasi-national poetic movement in which not only Sicilians but all Italians who compose participate in virtue of the foundational quality of its linguistic medium ... Dante recognizes the potentially unifying character of the poetry, cultivated not by Sicilians alone but by members of a wide aristocratic culture."[39] For Dante, the river that leads to Beatrice and the erasure of memory is also the mark of another unity, of the political unity of Frederick II and Manfred, who not only brought together "politics and culture, intelligence and magnanimity" but also ruled over the kingdom of Sicily, marked, not divided, by the break at Messina.[40] Dante aims to recover the island through poetry, and create through the earthly Paradise the means to creating that empire *onde Cristo è romano* ("where Christ is a Roman"). In the earthly paradise where past and future converge, the past having enabled the future to emerge as Anchises did for Aeneas and Vergil for Dante, the Sicily of poetry, of unity, will also be found.[41] The recovery of spring, of Eden—even, to pick up from Jacoff's work, Arcadia[42]—the attainment of the earthly paradise with the river that runs through it, is the recovery of the unity of Italy, a unity symbolized for Dante by the language and concept of the kingdom of Sicily.

Sources of Meaning

It is my argument that to invoke Sicily as Vergil leaves is to turn a poetico-political lens on *Purgatorio* as a whole. As in *Inferno* XXVI, the presence of Sicily is evident through intertexts, but also through the treatment of the fundamental qualities of language. The many languages Dante encounters on his journey up Purgatory, from the Latin of the Psalms to the Occitan of Arnaut Daniel and the Italian that runs all the way through, are at first confusing, since they seem randomly distributed over the climb. But the languages, like the terraces, are arranged in an order, and the process of unsinning can be tracked in terms of the languages used.

In *De vulgari eloquentia* Dante suggests that the purest language of Italian is that of its own vernacular poetry, which is at its root Sicilian. Dante claims it as his at the critical point of crossing the river Lethe: he acknowledges the role played by the troubadours and Sicilian School poets, even as he joins their company in search of his own vernacular, which, as he says in *De vulgari eloquentia*, is there in essence in all Italian tongues. But, like the rivers from the Apennines, it is purest at its source. The progress Dante makes up the mountain of Purgatory follows the implicit peregrinations suggested by Cicero to return oratory to its original state at the top of the mountain—before wisdom was divorced from eloquence, before language split into natural and artificial forms. We track the elusive prey of the vernacular and find it finally in the *Sì* he speaks to Beatrice as he crosses Lethe. Strikingly, but perhaps now not surprisingly, in the preceding canto, as he sees Beatrice for the first time, both Dante and his heart, at the top of this mountain, are likened to none other than rivers flowing from the Apennines:

> Sì come neve tra le vive travi 85
>   per lo dosso d'Italia si congela,
>   soffiata e stretta da li venti schiavi,
> poi, liquefatta, in sé stessa trapela
>
> . . .
>
> così fui sanza lagrime e sospiri
>
> . . .
>
> lo gel che m'era intorno al cor ristretto,
>   spirito e acqua fessi, e con angoscia
>   de la bocca e de li occhi uscì del petto. (*Purg.* XXX.85–88; 91; 97–99)

(Even as snow among the sap-filled trees
along the spine of Italy will freeze
when gripped by gusts of the Slavonian winds,
then, as it melts, will trickle through itself—

. . .

Just so was I with neither tears nor sighs

. . .

then did the ice that had restrained my heart
become water and breath; and from my breast
and through my lips and eyes they issued—anguished.)

Dante's allusion to Cicero through his repeated reference to the rivers that flow from the Apennines has a further point to make. The diction of sources and source-hunting prevails in *Purgatorio* as Dante seeks for the best language because, as he says in *De vulgari eloquentia*, not all poets have the right to use the most illustrious vernacular, the best language suited to the best thinking.[43] This language, he suggests, is the language of *Sì*, which is the word he speaks to Beatrice at the top of the mountain of Purgatory, where it becomes identified as the language of love, and of a love that is even purer than the one sung by Arnaut. Whereas for Cicero rhetoric was the ennobling force of Roman culture, for Dante, the ennobling force is that of love, and the point of *Purgatorio* in general is that love can reach the underworld through prayer, even as song can resurrect dead poetry through love.[44] But the story entails a break as well—Venus's love can reach the underworld only on account of Proserpina. What *Purgatorio* shows us again and again is that Christian love, *caritas*, which, adapted, becomes love in Dante's poetry, is indeed capable of repairing a fall such as this. Where oratory, when comprising a combination of wisdom and eloquence, can reunite society for Cicero, love, the language of the true poets, is the force which, for Dante, repairs the breaks of the past and creates community, a community that undergirds the notion of *imperium*.[45]

In the end, the rifts of the past are not to be erased but rather mended by love as represented in Italian vernacular poetry. The confusion of language caused by the destruction of the tower of Babel, which Dante mentions repeatedly in *De vulgari eloquentia*, is repaired by the ability of everyone at the top of Purgatory, the mountain that is also a tower, to understand multiple tongues. In a secular version of Pentecost, Arnaut's Occitan is understood by everyone around him. The argument, found in *De vulgari eloquentia*, that all Italian shares an essential source (see, e.g., 1.ix.2; 1.xvi.6) is here expanded to suggest that all who speak a language of love can communicate with each other. Climbing the mountain of Purgatory addresses the linguistic chaos created by the destruction of Babel, even as wisdom and eloquence are rejoined in the Apennine myth of Cicero. In just the one word, "*sì*," the sources converge—of love, of language, of vision. Dante speaks the language of "Sicily," of unity, of before both the fall and Proserpina's abduction, as he faces Beatrice across the river that will soon erase all memory of division.

The Mountain of Purgatory

To return one final time to Seneca, it seems plausible to suggest that Purgatory, that mountain that clearly encourages competition between Dante and the preceding poets, especially Vergil, Ovid, and Lucan, and calls up passages about Sicily, is none other than Etna. As we have seen, in *Epistle* 79, Seneca writes:

> Praeterea condicio optima est ultimi: parata verba invenit, quae aliter instructa novam faciem habent. Nec illis manus inicit tamquam alienis; sunt enim publica.... Aut ego te non novi aut Aetna tibi salivam movet; iam cupis grande aliquid et par prioribus scribere. Plus enim sperare modestia tibi tua non permittit, quae tanta in te est ut videaris mihi retracturus ingenii tui vires, si vincendi periculum sit: tanta tibi priorum reverentia est.[46]

> (Furthermore, the best situation falls to the last; he finds prepared words which, when arranged differently show a new face. He does no violence to those [words] of others. For they are public property.... Either I don't know you or Etna makes your mouth water. You have been wanting to write something in the grand style and equal to your forebears. Your modesty does not allow you to hope for more, which is such a great factor for you that you seem to me to be about to rein in the force of your natural talent, if there should be any risk of outstripping others, so great is your reverence for the earlier writers.)

Poets compete throughout the canticle. The reference to Ovid's story of Proserpina at the start of *Purgatorio* lays the groundwork for the climb up the mountain, the erasure of the seven sins, and the appearance of Beatrice at the top. Beyond that, the emphasis on Venus enables Dante to weave in the notion of *felix culpa*, which insists that, without the shortsightedness of the earlier texts, the current one would have little to argue. Most of all, however, the Ovid text insists on the importance of Ceres in the story, and of her conversation with Jupiter and, as such, offers both an implicit goal for the climb up the mountain, and an explanation for the attitude Beatrice strikes when Dante arrives.

It is my argument that for Dante Purgatory is Sicily, or, at least, the idea of Sicily where poetry and justice unite, where "poets are the only fit guides to contemporary society... The words of poets speak to men across time and even across the boundaries of language. Dante moves toward one language in *Purgatorio*, as he is moving towards a unified people under the empire, and he does it through the poets."[47] While language may be transcended in *Paradiso*—through music, through symbol—in *Purgatorio* it is all there is. Sicily, whose language, unlike its rivers, is not divided at Messina from the Italian peninsula, is the land of unity—of politics and poetry. Its relationship to the mainland provides the model for what will become, in *Paradiso*, *legato con amore* ("bound with love," *Par*. XXXIII.86).

In *Purgatorio* XXVII, "in the hour ... when Cytherea [Venus], who seems always burning with the fire of love, first shone on the mountain from the east ... before the splendors which precede the dawn ... the shades of night fled on every side," Vergil speaks to Dante for the last time:

> ... "Il temporal foco e l'etterno
> veduto hai, figlio; e se' venuto in parte
> dov' io per me più oltre non discerno.
> Tratto t'ho qui con ingegno e con arte;   130
> lo tuo piacere omai prendi per duce;
> fuor se' de l'erte vie, fuor se' de l'arte.
> Vedi lo sol che 'n fronte ti riluce;
> vedi l'erbette, i fiori e li arbuscelli
> che qui la terra sol da sé produce.   135
> Mentre che vegnan lieti li occhi belli
> che, lagrimando, a te venir mi fenno,
> seder ti puoi e puoi andar tra elli.
> Non aspettar mio dir più né mio cenno;
> libero, dritto e sano è tuo arbitrio,   140
> e fallo fora non fare a suo senno:
> per ch'io te sovra te corono e mitrio." (*Purg.* XXVII. 127–42)

("My son, you've seen the temporary fire
and the eternal fire; you have reached
the place past which my powers cannot see.

I've brought you here through intellect and art;
from now on, let your pleasure be your guide;
you're past the steep and past the narrow paths.

Look at the sun that shines upon your brow;
look at the grasses, flowers, and the shrubs
born here, spontaneously, of the earth.

Among them, you can rest or walk until
the coming of the glad and lovely eyes—
those eyes that, weeping, sent me to your side.

Await no further word or sign from me:
your will is free, erect, and whole—to act
against that will would be to err: therefore

I crown and miter you over yourself.")

Vergil leaves Dante and, as he does, dubs him monarch, or emperor, and bishop. The strange thing about *Purgatorio*, made clear here, is that it is the canticle that walks a fine line between the temporal and the eternal: souls here are in motion much the way they are in life. This fact is particularly striking here at the top of the mountain, as Dante enters the earthly paradise, a land he calls up in *Monarchia* (III.xvi.7–8):

> (7) Duos igitur fines providentia illa inenarrabilis homini proposuit intendendos: beatitudinem scilicet huius vite, que in operatione proprie virtutis consistit et per terrestrem paradisum figuratur; et beatitudinem vite ecterne, qui consistit in fruitione divini aspectus ad quam propria virtus ascendere non potest, nisi lumine divino adiuta, que per paradisum celestem intelligi datur.
> (8) Ad has quidem beatitudines, velut ad diversas conclusiones, per diversa media venire oportet. Nam ad primam per phylosophica documenta venimus, dummodo illa sequamur secundum virtutes morales et intellectuales operando; ad secundam vero per documenta spiritualia que humanam rationem transcendunt, dummodo illa sequamur secundum virtutes theologicas operando, fidem spem scilicet et karitatem.
>
> ((7) Ineffable providence has thus set before us two goals to aim at: i.e., happiness in this life, which consists in the exercise of our own powers and is figured in the earthly paradise; and happiness in the eternal life, which consists in the enjoyment of the vision of God (to which our own powers cannot raise us except with the help of God's light) and which is signified by the heavenly paradise.
> (8) Now these two kinds of happiness must be reached by different means, as representing different ends. For we attain the first through the teachings of philosophy, provided that we follow them putting into practice the moral and intellectual virtues; whereas we attain the second through spiritual teachings which transcend human reason, provided that we follow them putting into practice the theological virtues, i.e., faith, hope and charity.)[48]

But Dante presents this slightly differently at the top of Purgatory as he heads into the earthly paradise: he has not reached this garden through the teachings of philosophy alone, but rather through the deployment of the poetic word, and that poetic word is different from the eternal one: the poetic proceeds out of love, *amar*. The poetic word, unlike the spiritual, is not beyond reason; justified by temporal love, it still does not become eternal.

Augustine's treatise on language, *De doctrina Christiana,* as well as his *Confessions,* suggest that language moves toward music, silence, epiphany, a truth beyond words.[49] Dante's does not. For him the truth of poetry never leaves the sensible realm: instead, it leads to increased sensuality, beauty, music, vision. If anything, through the richness of the poetry, language becomes more prominent and important as the garden is explored via a poetry in time that does not aspire to the eternal. *Purgatorio* is marked by a progressive unfolding through poetic vision, not prophetic declamation.[50]

In *Paradiso,* Barolini argues, "the pilgrim must move from unity to difference, and so the rapt ecstasy of his thanks to God is fragmented by the splendor of Beatrice's smile, which divides his attention, diversifying his unified mind, and causing it to move from one thing to many."[51] In *Purgatorio,* when the pilgrim first sees Beatrice again after her death, the emphasis is on a unity that comes from love, a unity that echoes the end of discord argued for in *Monarchia.* Progress up the mountain of *Purgatorio* is a process of erasure. But it is also a training in the power of the temporal through an exploration of the vision love provides through poetry.[52] Our ability to discern the temporal from the eternal increases as we climb toward the "citadel of simplicity," and even as we add on layer after layer, terrace after terrace, so the mountain also gets narrower and narrower until it reaches its focus, its point in the earthly paradise, where "the root of mankind was innocent" where "it's always spring, and every fruit" grows. It is, I think significant that at this point Dante says:

> Io mi rivolsi 'n dietro allora tutto 145
> a' miei poeti, e vidi che con riso
> udito avëan l'ultimo costrutto (*Purg.* XXVIII.145–47)

("Then I turned round completely, and I faced / my poets; I could see that they had heard / with smiles this final corollary spoken.")

It is the poets, specifically the Latin poets, but here also the vernacular ones he has just encountered, who usher Dante into the earthly paradise, where Dante sees Beatrice again and becomes literally one with the lush landscape in the last words of the canticle:

> Io ritornai da la santissima onda
> rifatto sì come piante novelle
> rinovellate di novella fronda
> puro e disposto a salire a le stelle. (*Purg.* XXXIII.142–45)

(From that most holy wave I now returned / to Beatrice; remade, as new trees are / renewed when they bring forth new boughs, I was / pure and prepared to climb unto the stars.)

The beauty of the earthly garden, which we learn of through poetry—courtly poetry in particular, as Olivia Holmes has argued—is denser and richer than any landscape before it, yet its truths are simple and clear.[53] The earthly paradise is a paradise of words and echoes, specifically vernacular words and rhymes, the stuff of the *De vulgari eloquentia*, words arranged temporally in meter following the rules of the poetic game. The words of this canticle bear the burden of philosophy, but do so in more clearly marked temporal means; what they refrain from doing is crossing the line into the eternal: these words are not the Word.[54] And the poet—Dante, not Vergil—is ultimately the one to discern that difference and to promulgate through language an empire ordered by temporal love—*amar*, not *caritas*—that Venus introduces into the afterlife at the start of *Purgatorio*.

As we have seen, Venus is mentioned in *Purgatorio* XXVII in a setting that reminds us of Ovid's Proserpina:

> Ne l'ora, credo, che de l'orïente
>   prima raggiò nel monte Citerea,   95
>   che di foco d'amor par sempre ardente,
> giovane e bella in sogno mi parea
>   donna vedere andar per una landa
>   cogliendo fiori; . . . (*Purg.* XXVII.94–9)

(It was the hour, I think, when Cytherea,
who always seems aflame with fires of love,
first shines upon the mountains from the east,

that, in my dream, I seemed to see a woman
both young and fair; along a plain she gathered
flowers . . .)

This passage in many ways prepares us for the very next canto, where Dante greets Matelda[55] near the top of the mountain of Purgatory with

> ". . . Tu mi fai rimembrar dove e qual era
>   Proserpina nel tempo che perdette   50
>   la madre lei, ed ella primavera." (*Purg.* XXVIII.49–51)

("... You have reminded me of where and what—
just when her mother was deprived of her
and she deprived of spring—Proserpina was.")[56]

as we find ourselves in that very moment Cicero identifies, that moment both before Proserpina was abducted and after she was returned.[57] Most of Dante's commentators identify the location of Proserpina's abduction as Mt. Etna, and Benvenuto da Imola goes so far as to make the comparison between Etna and Purgatory explicit: *nam Proserpina pulcerrima inventa est in prato florido, colligens diversa genera florum, juxta montem qui ex summitate emittit ignem apud lacum lucidissimum; ita Mathildis talis per omnia inventa est in monte purgatorii propinqua igni et rivo purissimo, colligens flores etc.* ("as the most beautiful Proserpina was found in a floral meadow, gathering different types of flowers on the mountain that emits fire from its summit near the clearest lake, so the same can be said of Matelda, found on the mountain of Purgatory near to fire and the purest stream, gathering flowers, etc.").[58] As we unwind time in our climb up Purgatory, from the present moment back to the garden of Eden in the earthly paradise, we return to exactly that spot Cicero hoped to recover throughout the Verrine orations: the moment before Proserpina was abducted, when Sicily in its role as first overseas province created empire. But it is also a moment in the future. And when we realize that *Purgatorio* begins with a strong allusion to *Metamorphoses* 5 through mention of the muses, the magpies, and Venus, we have to recognize that Dante is casting the canticle as a response to Ovid (which is itself a response to Cicero), and to Ovid's statement about the need for empire to be extended into the afterlife through love. The recovery of Proserpina provides an opportunity for discussion of purgation and redemption in the context of the new empire, where language is shown to be an instrument of redemption, and the empire created and brought about through language is one that extends love into the afterlife through the poetic word.[59] Irène Rosier-Catach concurs:

> Dante's plan is not to return to the original state, to a paradise definitively lost, to the initial unity of the Hebrew language.... If Babel is a divine intervention, everything that follows relating to political, social, and linguistic organization ... is the result of human competence, with all the positive and negative consequences that that entails, due essentially to the infinite variability and instability of man. For if *confusio* is divine, *variatio* is human, and thus the *reductio ad unum* which, thanks to reason, art, and poetry, could remedy the situation, ought to be human as well. [Dante's] personal

Pentecost is not a miracle but a work of man, and it has for its object not the restitution of the universal church, but unity of another type, at once linguistic, literary, and political.[60]

The nature of this empire may be different from that of Cicero, Vergil, or Ovid, but Sicily and the recovery of Proserpina still provide the geographic and mythic bases for analyzing the key work that empire accomplishes. The climb up the mountain erases the effects of sin, and the success of the future empire, *onde Cristo è romano* ("where Christ is a Roman"), is characterized by the return and redemption of Proserpina.

Dante's use of Sicily owes much to Vergil, though finally the poetic use and significance of the island differ. For Vergil the tension between unity and separation proffers a language of Augustan empire. For Dante that empire is marked by unity: the water at the straits of Messina, like the river that went out of Eden, identifies it as the kingdom of Sicily where the river joins rather than separates. The earthly Paradise is modeled on the memory of Sicily under Frederick II and the dream of a future empire that will restore that cultural ideal.

For Ovid, Ulysses is the winner of the competition and Achilles' shield; for Dante, winning and losing are replaced by harmony and collegiality as the poets compete in order to improve. Turning away from internal struggle and competition to imperial expansion that will cleanse the poetic soul, Dante suggests that empire is undergirded by an inclusive drive toward a reading based in love, where the goal is to learn to interpret as a way of establishing community.[61] Through Seneca and Ovid, Sicily enters Dante's vocabulary as setting for poetic competition and the need for interpretive reading. Through Dante's mingling of Seneca's drive with an Augustinian understanding of *caritas*, that style becomes, at the start of *Purgatorio*, fused with the power of love in the afterlife, though in Dante's hands that love is a poetic, secular one. By extending love into the afterlife, as Venus accomplishes in *Metamorphoses* 5, Dante suggests that the true empire *sine fine* will be one where love in the form of charitable reading and interpretation expands to include all poets, even as it, paradoxically, reduces the message to a clarity and simplicity accessible to all.

Conclusion

CICERO'S IDENTIFICATION of Sicily as the province that defined empire marked it as a location—even *the* location—for Latin discussions of empire. Had Cicero not explained the origins of empire in Western mythological terms—invoking as he does the story of Proserpina—Sicily might not have entered the literature so closely allied with questioning the nature of empire. History, of course, helped: it would be hard to think of another landmass of such limited scope that has been inhabited by as many cultures. But the argument of this book has been that largely because of Cicero's identification of the island as the location of Proserpina's abduction and potential return, Sicily began to inhabit a space apart from the everyday. That this made it strikingly similar to the place occupied by the literary only encouraged poets from Vergil to Dante to turn to it as the setting for discussions of empire. In a sense, thanks to Cicero, Sicily itself became the first imperial text, which then opened itself up to interpretation and reworking by writers who followed along after. It is through the geography of Sicily that Vergil chooses to explicate his understanding of the dream of empire, and it is on Sicily that Vergil questions the protocols of that very dream. Through allusions to Sicily, Dante shows the reader how to interpret and, in so doing, speaks to the future empire in which poets will lead. Along the way, accounts of Sicily draw us back to the question of empire on the one hand and poetry on the other.

In the Latin literary tradition, to which Dante responds, Sicily is unique in its identification with the intersection of poetry and empire. In the era considered here, when empire was a defining political cause, Sicily's very existence offered an opportunity for poets to write about what mattered most because Sicily, as the first overseas Roman province, was also a land in need of recovery. The poetics of Sicily entails a mirroring of the dynamics and strategies of the political, refracted through myth and legend. The doubleness cuts both ways: King Arthur no more lived on Sicily than Ulysses sailed through the straits of Messina or Dante and Vergil climbed Etna. But in each case, the evocation of Sicily brings to bear a tradition in which the most familiar details are imbued with a complexity and ambiguity that characterize the literary, while the literary, in turn, is charged with a political purpose. Ovid is never more pointed in his critique of empire than in the story of Proserpina; nor is he ever more engaged in poetic competition with Vergil than at the same spot in the *Metamorphoses*.

It is perhaps a lucky fluke that Cicero's Verrine orations were in circulation in the north of France at the time leading up to the first Crusade, since they enabled the association between Sicily and the new Christian empire to assume a familiar cast. Or perhaps that section of the *Verrines* associated with penitence and renewal became of interest in the universities of the north because it resonated with the burgeoning effort to understand empire, particularly as it might develop from the rifts of civil strife. The fact that the message taken from Cicero's text diverges from what Ovid or Vergil saw there speaks to the strength of the *Verrines* as foundation text. It also opens the door for Dante to talk about future empire through the myth of Proserpina and the redemptive power of love, a tale ultimately of poetic resistance. The cycle of seasons becomes a cycle of sin and redemption.

And yet, perhaps key to all these discussions is the role of the past. If we take the Proserpina myth as one that translates the epic journey into a temporal one, as we have seen especially with Ovid but also, differently, with Dante, where the recovery of Proserpina is also to some extent the recovery of the world before she was abducted, we can understand the role Sicily plays as the land threatened most by empire. In medieval texts Sicily becomes identified with the passage to the future through redemption but also with the recovery of a past, be it the *imperium* of Augustus in Dante's hands or the recovery of the Holy Sepulchre in Jerusalem. There the return of Proserpina renegotiates the relationship between the present and the past based on an interest in redeeming that past in the future, but always with the awareness of the violence that has led to that point. It offers a version of empire that through compromise neither ignores nor glorifies what preceded empire but, instead, turns to the past in the spirit of renegotiation. In the end, Sicily helps create empire by its resistance to it, while Proserpina stands as the embodiment both of the pre-imperial world and of the promise of a renegotiation that acknowledges her story in its entirety.

NOTES

Introduction: Negotiating Empire

1. The location of Proserpina's abduction changes over time, as we shall see. For the most part, Roman authors place the abduction on Sicily, but see Propertius 3.22.1–4. Discussion of the variety of locations can be found in Claudian, *Le Rapt de Proserpine*, ed. Charlet, xxxv–xxxvi.

2. For an excellent overview of the myth of Proserpina throughout Western literary history, see Brehm.

3. See Foley; Richardson, *Homeric Hymn to Demeter*.

4. See Richardson, *Homeric Hymn to Demeter*, 76–77; Hinds, 53.

5. The word *repeto*, not a common verb, also occurs twice in the context of the abduction of Proserpina in Ovid, *Met.* 5, at lines 464 and 473, in slightly different forms. Both uses refer to Ceres' knowledge that Proserpina is in Hades.

6. Here see also Nancy Worman, whose focus on the "intersection of figurative space and real place" (5) I found useful.

7. Hinds, *Metamorphosis*, especially part two.

8. It is what Giovanni Salmeri calls "the emblematic province."

9. Thomas Biggs has argued persuasively for the role of Sicily in the origins of Latin letters. The place of Sicily in Vergil's poetic scheme is also hinted at in the *Eclogues*, especially at the start of the fourth: "*Sicelides Musae, paulo maiora canamus.*"

10. Here I would disagree with Le Goff, *La naissance du Purgatoire*, 280–81, who argues that Mt. Etna falls away from the cultural imagination as a setting for Purgatory. In the minds of those whose understanding of Purgatory is derived at least in part from Cicero's version of the Proserpina tale, Etna remains central.

11. See Mallette, *Kingdom of Sicily*; Akbari and Mallette, *Sea of Languages*; Granara, *Narrating Muslim Sicily*.

12. But here see Denis Feeney, *Beyond Greek*, especially 123–25, for further discussion of the role of Sicily in the development of Latin literature.

13. Barchiesi, "Colonial Readings," 152. See the introduction to the same volume where the editors (Asper and Rimell) argue that "spaces of all kinds . . . are seen to be both complicit in and produced by those dynamic forces" (1).

14. Hinds, *Metamorphosis*, passim; Quint, *Epic and Empire*: "Epic draws an equation between power and narrative. It tells of a power able to end the indeterminacy of war and to emerge victorious, showing that the struggle had all along been leading up to its victory and thus imposing upon it a narrative teleology—the teleology that epic identifies with the very idea of

narrative. Power, moreover, is defined by its capacity to maintain itself across time, and it therefore requires narrative to represent itself. In this sense, narrative, like ideology, is itself empowering. The epic victors both project their present power prophetically into the future and trace its legitimating origins back into the past. The first of these narrative procedures in some sense depends on and is implied by the second" (45). See also his *Virgil's Double Cross*, especially chaps. 1 and 2, which provide discussion of the complex interaction between poetry and empire.

15. Wolfson, *Borderlines*, 1–2.

Chapter 1. The Straits of Messina: Geography and Empire

1. Most thoughtful here is Joy Connolly, *The State of Speech: Rhetoric and Political Thought in Ancient Rome*. See also my *Rhetorics of Reason and Desire: Vergil, Augustine, and the Troubadours*, chap. 1.

2. Cicero, *Orationes, Verr.* 2.3.6.12–15.

3. Strabo, *Geographica* 6.2.7.

4. Ennius, *Annales*, fr. 8.16 as attested by Servius, ad *Aen.* 1.281, 12.841. Further ancient discussions of Sicily include Livy, *Ab urbe condita*, books 21–30; Julius Caesar, *Bellum Civile*, passim.

5. Galinsky, *Aeneas, Sicily and Rome*, 173–75.

6. Diod. Sic., *Library of History*, 5.2.3 (marriage of Proserpina and Pluto); Diod. Sic. 5.2.3–3.1 (home of goddesses). Diodorus is also the first to place the rape of Persephone on Sicily, 5.3.

7. Diod. Sic. 4.77.9–78.5.

8. Strabo 6.2.4–5 (the story of Arethusa also plays a prominent role in Ovid, *Met.* 5.572–641, as we shall discuss in subsequent chapters).

9. Callim. *Aetia* 2.12–80.

10. Diod. Sic. 4.23.1–24.6.

11. See Holloway, *The Archaeology of Ancient Sicily*. Also see Burgersdijk et al., eds., *Sicily and the Sea*, esp. chap. 4.

12. Badian, *"provincia / province,"* OCD, 1228–30. See also Harris, *War and Imperialism in Republican Rome*; Lintott, *Imperium Romanum*.

13. The argument is perhaps even subtler, in that Cicero argues that it is the Greeks on Sicily who are more Romans than the Romans. In this he paves the way for the kind of argument Ovid will make in the *Metamorphoses*, where the Greek precursors to Roman thought are presented as proto-Romans. See also Frazel, *The Rhetoric of Cicero's "In Verrem,"* and Steel, *Cicero, Rhetoric, and Empire*; Prag, *Sicilia nutrix plebis Romanae: Rhetoric, Law, and Taxation in Cicero's Verrines*, and Prag, "Sicily and Sardinia-Corsica: The First Provinces."

14. Cicero, *Orationes*, vol. 3.

15. Quintilian, *Institutio Oratoria*, ed. Michael Winterbottom, vol. 1, with minor orthographical changes. Bibliography on Quintilian, though extensive, tends to focus on rhetoric and education, but now see Peirano Garrison, who characterizes the *Institutio* as "a grand literary and cultural project that spans several genres" (103). For further on Quintilian's relationship to Cicero, see Vasaly, *Representations*.

16. Härter, *Digressionen*, chap. 1.

17. For further on the poetic in Quintilian, see Peirano Garrison, *Persuasion, Rhetoric and Roman Poetry*, chap. 3.

18. Ward, "Reading and Interpretation."

19. The geography of Sicily was long believed to support these ancient myths in what amounts to a form of geomythology. It is only recently, with the increased understanding of tectonic plates, that we have learned that Sicily, in fact, was originally farther away from Italy and is now encroaching on the mainland.

20. Translation from *Library of History, Volume 3: Books 4.59–8*, trans. Oldfather, 87.

21. The most exciting reading of the *Verrines* to date is that of Miles, *Art as Plunder*, esp. chap 2. See also Dubouloz and Pittia, eds., *La Sicile de Cicéron*, and Frazel, *Rhetoric*, esp. chap. 4.

22. Cheyfitz, *The Poetics of Imperialism*, 112. See also Todorov, *The Conquest of America*.

23. Cheyfitz, 107.

24. For a useful overview of Sicily's mention in all of Vergil's works, see Aricò, "La Sicilia nell'opera di Virgilio," 65–87.

25. Moreover, Servius draws Sicily into discussion of the *Aeneid* from the start. Glossing "Italiam . . . venit" (*Aen.* 1.2), he explains that the name derives from that of the Sicilian Italus: . . . *rex Siculorum profectus de Sicilia venit ad loca quae sunt iuxta Tiberim*, an argument returned to later in the epic.

26. Useful overviews of *Aen.* 3 include Putnam, *Virgil's Aeneid*, 50–72; Hexter, "Imitating Troy," in *Reading Vergil's Aeneid*, chap. 3; Horsfall, *Virgil*, Aeneid 3.

27. See, e.g., Diod. Sic. 4.85.3; Mela 2.115; Pliny, *Nat. Hist.* 3.8.86–7.

28. This advice is mentioned again in *Aen.* 3.558–69.

29. Apollonius Rhodius, *Argonautica*, 404–7.

30. Neither the trip of the Argonauts nor that of Odysseus is situated geographically. Nonetheless, Jason and Odysseus both pass by Scylla and Charybdis through straits which Apollonius later identifies with the straits of Messina, and he identifies Thrinacia as Sicily.

31. This aspect of the *Aeneid* is seen most readily with Actium, which as key to Octavian's success is also a stop on Aeneas's journey (*Aen.* 3.279–89), but other stops along the way have also been identified as key to Augustus's imperial program and the events that preceded it. See here Barchiesi, "Colonial Readings," and Giusti. See also Horsfall, "Aeneas the Colonist."

32. So O'Hara, *True Names*, 148, who suggests the discussion of Sicilian cities in Callimachus, *Aet.* 2, fr. 43, as source of these names. See also Geymonat, "Callimachus," 329.

33. For further on the importance of the maritime to the developing Roman Empire, see Leigh.

34. Hadas, *Sextus Pompey*, 77.

35. In this context it is certainly worth noting that Octavian's fleet had come from the Adriatic, and so should have been able to go back the same way. See Hadas, *Sextus*, 75. It is unclear exactly where Octavian departed from, but it is specifically stated that he circumnavigated the island. See Pensabene, who explains the route as *evitando lo stretto più per un atto di sfida che per sicuressa* ("avoiding the straits more as an act of defiance than for reasons of safety," 46).

36. As we will see repeatedly, the straits pose almost insurmountable difficulties to sailors coming from the south. The combination of winds and tides make northward passage by oar or sail extremely treacherous.

37. See Horsfall, *Commentary*, on *Aen.* 3.412, 413.

38. Most helpful here are Wilson, *Sicily under the Roman Empire*; Finley, *Ancient Sicily*; Christopher Smith and John Serrati, eds., *Sicily from Aeneas to Augustus*. See also Pfuntner, *Urbanism*.

39. Powell and Welch, eds., *Sextus Pompeius*; Stone, "Sextus Pompey." See also Prag, "Sicily and the Punic Wars," in *Sicily and the Sea*.

40. See Senatore, esp. 111–27; Pensabene.

41. Brunt and Moore, *Res Gestae*, 25.

42. Velleius Paterculus, *The Caesarian and Augustan Narrative (2.41–93)*, 31–32.

43. See Finley, *Ancient Sicily*, chap. 12, esp. 150–53.

44. Powell and Welch, *Sextus*, xi.

45. On this passage in Velleius, see Woodman, *Velleius*, 220–25. See also Lobur.

46. Text from Woodman, 39–40.

47. Dio Cassius, *Roman History*, ed. and trans. Earnest Cary, Loeb Classical Library 82, 492–95.

48. Quint, *Epic and Empire*, chap.1. It is interesting to note here Quint's discussion of Sicily in the second chapter, 54–55. See also Barchiesi, "Colonial Readings," for a nuanced discussion of the role of Actium in the *Aeneid*.

49. Syed, *Vergil's* Aeneid *and the Roman Self*, 178.

50. Feeney, "*Tenui . . . latens discrimine*."

51. It is conceivable, in fact, that at the time Vergil was writing the *Aeneid*, the presence of Sextus was felt more strongly than is now apparent. Octavian attributed his victory at Naulochus to Apollo, with whom he identified, but also to Diana. The temple to Apollo he built after Actium on the Palatine is directly across the Circus Maximus from the temple to Diana on the Aventine rebuilt in 33 (see Richardson, *A New Topographical Dictionary*, 108–9, "Diana, Aedes," for pre-Augustan history). This temple is mentioned by Livy (1.45.1–7) and appears on a fragment of the Marble Plan (*Forma Urbis Romae*, pl. 23; Almeida, pl. 15). But the echoing between the Aventine and Palatine, alluded to in the story of Cacus in *Aeneid* 8, suggests a prominence the Aventine fails to retain in the official histories. See Coarelli, "Il tempio di Diana 'in circo Flaminio.'"

52. Powell and Welch, *Sextus Pompeius*, xv. Yet even in the *Aeneid* we find traces of Sextus and the battle of Naulochus. In what is perhaps the most propagandistic version of the battle of Actium and Octavian's defeat of Antony we find a reference to the victory over Sextus in Agrippa's beaked headgear (*rostrata*: 8.684). As Gransden notes, "the unique honour of a corona navalis or rostrata . . . was awarded to Agrippa after his defeat of Pompey at Naulochus . . . [in] 36 B.C." (*Aeneid* 8: Cambridge Greek and Latin Classics, 177).

53. See Kellum, "Sculptural Programs and Propaganda," 169–76.

54. Welch, "Both Sides of the Coin," *Sextus Pompeius*, 14. See also Powell, "'An Island Amid the Flame'" in the same volume.

55. Text and translation from Brunt and Moore, *Res Gestae*.

56. *Res Gestae*, 19. But here see Gowing, *The Triumviral Narratives*.

57. This identification is reflected in a carnelian intaglio in Boston (MFA, inv. 27.733), dated a few years before Actium, which shows Octavian likened to Neptune as he rides in a chariot led by hippocamps over the enemy, whom Zanker identifies as "either Sextus Pompey or Antony," 97. See also Zarrow, "Sicily and the Coinage of Octavian and Sextus Pompey," 123–35.

58. Zanker, *Power of Images*, 40–41. The denarius of Sextus Pompey is in the Niggeler collection, no. 1010 (Giard 13): see Zanker, 372. The denarius with Octavian in a similar pose exists in a number of locations, including the Medagliere at the Capitoline Museum (RIC I, 2, 256 [inv. n. 1909]). The image Zanker includes is a cast of a coin whose whereabouts are unknown (Zanker, 41, 372).

59. Note Anton Powell's observation in "Peopling of the Underworld," that Sextus is from Vergil's underworld (92–4).

60. It is also possible to argue, as Syme almost does, that Lepidus merges with Sextus at the end of the Sicilian campaign. After Sextus flees in defeat, Lepidus rises as enemy, whom Octavian defeats. In this, Sextus becomes, in essence, a triumvir, thus completing the triangulation of this era. Syme, *Roman Revolution*, chap. 13.

61. On the cultural erasure of Sextus that also asserts his presence, see Gowers, "Dangerous Sailing," 446–49.

62. Sicily's association with the bridge between civil war and empire continues in the literature. In the second book of Lucan's *Bellum civile*, as Pompey prepares to encounter Caesar, Lucan breaks away to a discussion of the Apennines, which formerly connected Sicily to Italy, but does no longer (2.432–9), as we will see in detail in chap. 7. The rift empire sutures is caused, Lucan reiterates, by civil war. (That Lucan draws on geography to discuss politics is made clear by his discussion of Crassus in the first simile in book one [1.99–104]: "nam sola futuri / Crassus erat belli medius mora. qualiter undas / qui secat et geminum gracilis mare separat Isthmos / nec patitur conferre fretum, si terra recedat, / Ionium Aegaeo frangat mare, sic … Crassus" (the only check / to future war was Crassus in between. Just as the slender / Isthmus, which cuts the waves and separates twin seas / and stops the waters meeting, if its land receded, / would smash Ionian Sea against Aegean: such was Crassus). Sicily's relationship to the mainland of Italy is clearly seen in geographic terms that recall those of Vergil.

63. Hawkes, *Shakespeare in the Present*, 31.

64. Hawkes, *Shakespeare in the Present*, 36.

65. Hawkes, *Shakespeare in the Present*, 32.

66. On Proserpina in the *Verrines*, see Romano, "Cicerone e il ratto di Proserpina," 191–201.

Chapter 2. Drepanum and the Limits of the *Aeneid*

1. The previous two visits to Sicily are both in *Aeneid* 3:569–691 and 707–15.

2. Here see the insightful remarks by Nelis, *Vergil's* Aeneid *and the* Argonautica, 193.

3. Vergil, *Opera*, ed. Mynors. I have used this text, with minor orthographical changes, throughout. Translations are my own.

4. Line 39 is ambiguous. Richard Thomas, in his Cambridge edition of the *Georgics*, 75, notes that *veniat* can be taken as hortatory or jussive. He takes it as hortatory, pairing the first two lines: Hell does not want you as king, nor should you want to rule there. My reading takes the verb as jussive, placing the emphasis on *dira* and *repetita*: if Octavian were to rule the underworld, that would be ominous, since it would cause Proserpina, sought again, this time by Octavian, to remain in Hades. All commentaries agree that the passage suggests that Proserpina will not return to earth, but few see the importance of the mention of her mother, Ceres, who will reinstate the cycle of seasons only if her daughter returns to earth, which will not happen if Octavian extends his empire into the underworld. See also Fratantuono, "*Nondum Proserpina abstulerat*," who traces a link between Proserpina and Eurydice, both of whom remain in the underworld, and Aeneas and Orpheus, who suggest they might care to stay; see especially 431.

5. See Nelis and Nelis-Clément.

6. Servius, ad *Aeneid* 2.714, offers Proserpina's abandonment as one possible explanation for *deserta*; *Schol. Ver.* and R. D. Williams follow suit. Horsfall takes exception to this reading: *Virgil, Aeneid 2*, 505. But see Casali's commentary, 318: *"potrebbe forse richiamare anche la perdita di Proserpina da parte della madre Cerere . . . specialmente se fosse nel vero Servio a vedere nell'*antiqua cupressus *un riferimento al dolore della dea per la perdita della figlia; si anticerebbe, quindi, l' 'abbandono' di Creusa. . . . L'appuntamento di deserta Creusa con Enea è al tempio di* deserta Ceres" (318); ("it could perhaps also recall the loss of Proserpina on the part of her mother Ceres . . . especially if Servius were right to see in *antiqua cupressus* a reference to the sorrow of the goddess for the loss of her daughter; one would thus anticipate the abandonment of Creusa. . . . The appointment of *deserta Creusa* with Aeneas is at the temple of *deserta Ceres*.") Fratantuono makes a similar point, "*Nondum Proserpina abstulerat*" (433). See also Fratantuono, "*Tumulum antiquae Cereris*," 456–72.

7. This echo is reinforced in the last lines of *Aen.* 2, where Creusa reappears briefly to Aeneas, only to disappear for good. The scene, as many have observed, is modeled on that of Eurydice retreating from Orpheus in the fourth *Georgic* following the law of Proserpina (*Geo.* 4.487) that stipulates that Orpheus must not look back at his wife who follows behind until they reach the upper air. That Creusa evanesces in the same manner as Eurydice suggests that Proserpina's law still exists: not only is Proserpina still in the underworld, but her law, which attempts to set limits, still needs to be invoked.

8. Rauk, "Macrobius, Cornutus, and the Cutting of Dido's Lock," 345–54. See Fratantuono's persuasive analysis of this act in "*Nondum Proserpina abstulerat.*"

9. Note the mentions of Proserpina in the underworld at *Aen.* 6.138, *Iunoni infernae*, and by name at *Aen.* 6.142, 251, and 402. See the comment of Servius on *Aen.* 6.273, who remarks that Vergil, in the presence of Proserpina and Orcus, or Hades, alludes to Cicero's *Verrines* 2.4.50. See also Mendolia, "Servius, ad *Aen.* VI. 136," 253–66. Vergil, too, was thinking of Proserpina in the underworld in the context of Cicero's plea for her to return.

10. The prominence of Ceres' shrine in the *Verrines* may well influence our reading here. In both texts, loss is the dominant theme; in both as well there is hope for restitution, although that hope is somewhat clouded by the end of the *Aeneid*.

11. Nugent, "Vergil's Voice of the Women," 255–92; Jeffrey Ulrich, "*Vox omnibus una*," 139–60.

12. As Ann Vasaly has argued, "it seems clear that in this elaborate and poetic account, [Cicero] . . . wished them to read in the story an allegory for Verres' rape of Sicily itself." Vasaly, *Representations*, 124.

13. See commentary and bibliography on the boat race in *Virgil*, Aeneid 5, eds. Frantantuono and Smith, 213–340.

14. It is tempting to suggest that Vergil's use of digression here—the opening boat race fits Quintilian's definition of *egressio*—may have influenced the later rhetorician's choice of examples from Sicily. Further links between digression and Sicily can be found in the works of Silius Italicus; see Marks.

15. Here see most usefully the bibliography cited by Nelis, 217n121.

16. For further resonance between the straits of Messina and the *meta* of the race, see Putnam, *Poetry of the* Aeneid, 213–14.

17. See Feldherr, "Ships of State," 245–65, and literature cited there. While it is true that the boat race looks both ahead (to the circus in Rome) and back (to book 23 of the *Iliad*), the fact that it is introduced via a simile emphasizes, to my mind at least, its literariness.

18. Nelis, chap. 5, esp. 215.

19. Although, as Philip Hardie points out, there is the intermediary of both *Od.* 13.81–3 and *Aen.* 4.463–4. See Hardie, "Ships and Ship-Names," 163–71.

20. Putnam, *Poetry of the Aeneid*, chap. 2.

21. Feldherr, "Ships of State," 265.

22. Putnam rightly argues this: the verbal echoes are strong. See his *Poetry*, 77.

23. Hardie, "Ships and Ship-Names," 165–67. See also Leigh, 265–80.

24. While Vergil is not inclined toward allegory for the most part, for questions of cosmology, there is ample precedent. See Feeney, *Gods in Epic*, 129–87 (chap. 4); Hardie, *Virgil's* Aeneid, chap. 2.

25. Text and translation from *De rerum natura*, ed. Bailey, I: 213.

26. Bailey, in *De rerum natura*, II: 723.

27. I owe this observation to Denis Feeney.

28. While Feldherr observes a link between the setting of the boat race and the three realms of sea, earth, and air (251), he does not link these elements to Empedocles nor does he suggest a connection between them and the boat names.

29. Bailey, *De rerum natura*, I:213, 217.

30. There is debate about the exact name of the helmsman; some texts read Gyges, while others read Gyas. The two major branches of Horatian manuscripts read *gigas*.

31. Hardie, "Ships and Ship-Names," 165.

32. Clausen, *A Commentary on Virgil*, Eclogues, 204–5.

33. For further on the *Ciris*, see Gorman, "Vergilian Models," 35–48.

34. *Aen.* 1.135.

35. Cf. Feldherr's very different analysis of the boats, their names, and their actions during the race, "Ships of State," 245–65.

36. For an early, and slightly different, version of this argument, see my "Meta-Textuality," 69–81.

37. Farrell, *Latin Language and Latin Culture*, 43–51, esp. 43–45.

38. In this Vergil is most likely commenting as well on Lucretius, *DRN* 1.823–7.

39. The order here is sometimes debated. Given the relative weight of each element, some later writers switch Hera and Aidoneus, aligning the first with the aether, the second with earth. See K. Scarlett Kingsley and Richard Parry, "Empedocles," *The Stanford Encyclopedia of Philosophy* (Summer 2020 Edition), edited by Edward N. Zalta, https://plato.stanford.edu/archives/sum2020/entries/empedocles/.

40. So Kingsley, *Ancient Philosophy*, chap. 22. On Ovid's adaptation of these four elements in the *Metamorphoses* see Moser, "Ovide lecteur d'Empédocle," 80–96, who demonstrates the care with which Ovid read Empedocles, especially in his identification of Nestis with both water and air (on which, further, see Picot, "La brillance de Nestis," 75–100). On the identification between Proserpina and Nestis, see Portale, "Le 'nymphai' e l'acqua in Sicilia," 169–91; moreover, the prize cloak Cloanthus receives is embroidered with the abduction of Ganymede. Linked in the iconography (see, e.g., Eustathius ad *Iliad* 1180.14), the tales of Proserpina and Ganymede share many traits (see Cosentino, *Animals in Greek and Roman Religion and Myth*, 189–212). In particular, both tell of a boundary that is crossed as a beautiful mortal is taken, against their will, to live with an Olympian. As with the earlier examples of Proserpina's absence from the *Aeneid*, here again we find a tale that alludes to her predicament without fully

discussing it, suggesting perhaps further that the poem unfolds in the period before her return. She is absent from the time of the poem and the *Aeneid* refuses to discuss her plight directly, while frequently pointing toward the problems her absence creates.

41. Fratantuono and Smith, *Virgil*, Aeneid 5, 290–96.

42. Nelis, *Vergil's* Aeneid, chap. 5, esp. 214.

43. Apollonius Rhodius, *Argonautica*, 400, with minor emendations.

44. *Aeneia nutrix: hanc alii Aeneae, alii Creusae, alii Ascanii nutricem volunt. lectum tamen est in philologis in hoc loco classem Troianorum casu concrematam, unde Caieta dicta est*, ἀπὸ τοῦ καίειν. ("Aeneas's nurse: some see her as nurse to Aeneas, some to Creusa, some to Ascanius. In this passage, nevertheless, it is taken etymologically: since her ship was burned in the fall of Troy, she is called Caieta from 'to burn.' ")

45. See the compatible reading of empire in Rimell, *The Closure of Space*.

46. On the games overall, see Putnam, "Game and Reality," *The Poetry of the* Aeneid, 64–104; Z. Pavlovskis, "*Aeneid V*," 193–205, esp. 200; S. Bertram, "The Generation Gap," 9–12; J. Glazewski, "The Function of Vergil's Funeral Games." See also Fratantuono and Smith, *Virgil*, Aeneid 5; Anderson and Dix, "Vergil at the Races," 3–21. For a reading of the games in the context of *Romanitas*, see Syed, 207.

47. So, too, Feldherr: "The rest of the poem, this reading would suggest, remains within the frame imposed by the spectacle of the games. The problematic ending of the funeral games thus focuses attention precisely on the relationship between Vergil's text and the public spectacle it describes, and makes this issue crucial to the interpretation not only of the book but of the whole poem as well . . . Since the validity of such spectacles depends upon their all-inclusiveness, Vergil's narrative calls into question the political implications of the games simply by revealing their limit" (265).

48. See Sallust, *Histories*, book 2, col.2, frag. 8, 124–25.

49. Here see Ulrich, "Vox omnibus una," 156–57n40.

50. Putnam, *Virgil's Epic Designs*, 160–62.

51. For an illuminating study of Juno's role in the *Aeneid*, see Farrell, *Juno's Aeneid*, especially 1–40, 48–56.

52. See Tarrant, ed., *Virgil*, Aeneid Book XII, ad Aen. 12.951–2.

53. For further commentary on the importance of Venus to the role of Sicily in the epic, see Barchiesi, "Mobilità e religione nell'*Eneide*," especially 26–30.

54. Biggs, "*Primus Romanorum*," 350–67.

Chapter 3. Venus's Other Son: Cupid and Ovid's Empire of Poetry

1. Feldherr, *Playing Gods*, 349.

2. Ginsberg, "Ovid's *Metamorphoses*," 222–31, at 227.

3. Poggio Bracciolini is credited with initiating the *literaria res publica*, for which he was thanked by Francesco Barbaro in a letter in 1417.

4. Here see Tarrant, Ovid, *Metamorphoses*, 1.2.

5. Text, with minor orthographical changes, from Tarrant, *Metamorphoses*. All translations are my own except where indicated.

6. Hinds, *Metamorphosis*, 121.

7. Conte, *Latin Literature*, 350.
8. O'Hara, *Inconsistency in Roman Epic*, 122.
9. Barchiesi, "Endgames," 195.
10. Hinds, *Metamorphosis*, 27–28, 30. See also Sampson, "Callimachean Tradition," 83–103.
11. For an overview of the connection of the Proserpina myth to Sicily, see Mazzara, "Persephone."
12. Johnson, "Constructions of Venus," 125–49, at 146.
13. Habinek, *The Politics of Latin Literature*, 156, who argues along similar lines for Ovid's exile poetry.
14. Hinds, *Metamorphosis*, 109, who identifies the rape with the expansion of Venus's empire.
15. Conte, *Latin Literature*, 342, argues against the notion of Ovid as political opponent, seeing instead a poetry that corresponds to the tastes and drives of his world.
16. Feldherr, *Playing Gods*, 343.
17. *Amores*, ed. J. C. McKeown, with minor orthographical changes.
18. Hinds, *Allusion and Intertext*, 109–110.
19. Volk, *The Poetics of Latin Didactic*, 162–64.
20. Davis, *Ovid and Augustus*, 73–78.
21. Papaioannou, *Epic Succession*, 11.
22. Johnson, "Constructions of Venus," 128.
23. Johnson, "Constructions of Venus," 136–38.
24. *Verr.*, 2.2.2.5–6.
25. *Verr.*, 2.2.3.7–9.
26. *Verr.*, 2.2.1.2.
27. *Verr.*, 2.2.1.3.
28. Much has been written recently about Ovid as a superb reader of Vergil. See, e.g., Martelli, *Ovid's Revisions*; Boyd, "'When Ovid Reads Vergil . . . ,'" 123–30. On Ovid's adaptation of the *Homeric Hymns*, see also Barchiesi, "Venus' Masterplot," *Ovidian Transformations*, 112–26.
29. Ginsberg, "Ovid's *Metamorphoses*," 222–23.
30. On the various locations associated with the abduction, see Richardson, *Homeric Hymn to Demeter*, 149–50. See the succinct summary of Greek and Hellenistic antecedents in Ovidio, *Metamorfosi*, vol. 3, 191–94.
31. Putnam, *Poetry of the* Aeneid, 67–68.
32. Putnam, *Poetry of the* Aeneid, 91. In a dream, Anchises encourages his son to establish a colony on Sicily. Although both parties descend from Trojan origins and have endured the same hardships of flight, the ones who remain are distinct, because they decide not to endure to the fulfillment of their destiny in Rome.
33. In *Fasti* 4.467–80, though, Ovid does rehearse a similar tour of the edge of the island, drawn in part from *Aeneid* 3.689–707, which in turn relies on Callimachus *Aitia* 11. fr.43, ed. Pfeiffer. See O'Hara, "Callimachean Influences," 369–400.
34. Hinds, *Metamorphosis*, 133–34. On Ovidian intertextuality more generally, see Barchiesi, *Speaking Volumes*.
35. It seems likely that the rape imagery here is derived from that of Cicero.
36. Johnson, "Constructions of Venus," 139. See also *Ovid before Exile*, 63–71.
37. Zissos, "The Rape of Proserpina," especially 97–98.

38. While Arethusa is first mentioned in line 409, she does not feature prominently until lines 487–508, when she informs Ceres of Proserpina's abduction into the underworld. The story of her own arrival upon Sicily, promised for after the resolution of the current conflict, is fulfilled in lines 572–641.

39. Note also that Ovid's version of the abduction is the first to involve Etna. As Leroux notes, this opens the door for Claudian's version, discussed in the next chapter. Leroux, "L'Etna dans les récits," 33–55, especially 34.

40. Johnson, "Constructions of Venus," 138.

41. Cicero, *Verr.* 2.2.4.111.

42. Hinds, *Metamorphosis*, 38, where he references E. J. Kenney, who argues that "setting and subject would be apprehended in a moment by a public who needed to read no further than *haud procul Hennaeis* . . . before recalling one of the most famous ecphrases in Roman literature, Cicero, *Verrines*, 2.2.4.106–7."

43. Segal, *Landscape in Ovid's Metamorphoses*, 54.

44. Hinds, *Metamorphosis*, 60–61.

45. Fränkel, *Ovid: A Poet Between Two Worlds*, 75.

46. Johnson, "Constructions of Venus," 126–27.

47. On the significance of Venus to Ovid's adaptation of the Greek past, especially that of the *Homeric Hymns*, see Barchiesi, "Venus' Masterplot," 112–26.

48. Anderson, review of Brooks Otis, *AJP* 89 (1968), 93–104, esp. 102–3.

49. *Aen.* 3.692–6.

50. *Metamorphoses* 5.372.

51. Zissos, "Rape of Proserpina," 103.

52. Solodow, *World of Ovid's Metamorphoses*, 138–39.

53. Further on Ovid's complex narratology is found in Barchiesi, "Narrative Technique and Narratology." See also Papaioannou, *Epic Succession*, 43.

54. Papaioannou, *Epic Succession*, 1.

55. On the debate between Ajax and Ulysses, see Casanova-Robin, "D'Homère à Ovide." For background, see Ovidio, *Metamorfosi*, 6:213–71.

56. Many have commented on the parallels. See, e.g., Pavlock, *The Image of the Poet*, especially 12; Hardie, "Warring Words."

57. The competition is in many ways comparable to the ads that once ran on TV (and will presumably continue to run on YouTube: https://www.youtube.com/watch?v=0eEG5LVXdK0; accessed 14 November 2021) over the superiority of Mac to PC. Vergil (PC) as Ajax is portrayed as bloated and slow; Ovid (Mac) as Ulysses, wily and clever.

58. Solodow, *World of Ovid's Metamorphoses*, 143.

59. Perhaps the mention of Ceres in *Metamorphoses* 13.639 is meant to take our minds back to the events of *Metamorphoses* 5.

60. Hinds, *Allusion and Intertext*, 109.

61. Ellsworth, "Ovid's 'Odyssey,' " 334–35.

62. Wilkinson, *Ovid Recalled*, 235.

63. Ahl, *Metaformations*, 64.

64. Anderson, "Multiple Change."

65. Balsley, "Truthseeking and Truthmaking," 65.

66. Cicero, *Verr.*, 1.1.4.12; *Verr.*, 2.2.5.13; *Verr.*, 2.2.6.17.

67. Barchiesi, "Endgames," 194.

68. Barchiesi, "Endgames," 195–96.

69. Including, of course, those poets who preceded him. The sentiment here is a reworking of that expressed by Horace, *Carmina* 3.30.

70. See the arguments made here in chaps. 1–2.

71. Hinds, *Allusion and Intertext*, 55. See also Ovid, *Am.* 2.9.19 and Cic. *De Orat.* 3.165.

72. For a complementary reading of the end of the poem, see Gladhill, "Gods, Caesars and Fate."

73. While the six months remain constant in the *Metamorphoses* and *Fasti*, the number of pomegranate seeds varies. In *Met.* 5 it is seven, in *Fasti* 4, three, and Proserpina must return to the underworld for twice that many months.

74. For the importance of poetic memory to the *Metamorphoses* see Miller, "Ovidian Allusion."

Chapter 4. Claudian, Etna, and the Loss of Proserpina

1. Van Peteghem, *Italian Readers*; Peter of Eboli, *Liber ad Honorem Augusti*; and Sampieri, "La cultura letteraria." See also the poems anthologized in *I Poeti della Scuola Siciliana*. Granara's work on the poetry of Ibn Hamis, though, articulates a view of Sicily focused on loss and abandonment.

2. The six authors in the *Liber Catonianus* typically include: Claudian, Cato (*Disticha Catonis*), Theodulus (*Eclogae*), Avianus (Aesopic fables), Maximianus (elegies), and Statius's *Achilleid*.

3. Marginalization of the *Verrines* is discussed in *The Rhetoric of Cicero in Its Medieval and Early Renaissance Commentary Tradition*, ed. Cox and Ward, chaps. 2 and 3, and Reeve, "Medieval Tradition."

4. Claudian's text is riddled with problems, from the circumstances of its creation to the form it took in its reception. For good overviews of the poem see Claudian, *De Raptu Proserpinae*, ed. J. B. Hall, 64–111; *De Raptu Proserpinae*, ed. and trans. Gruzelier (Oxford: Oxford Univ. Press, 1993), xvii–xxxvi. See also Hinds, "Claudianism in the *De Raptu Proserpinae*," 169–92.

5. The rich field of Ovid's influence on late antique poetry is starting to get the attention it deserves. See Fielding, *Transformations of Ovid in Late Antiquity* and *Ovid in Late Antiquity*, ed. Consoloni. Here also see the fourth-century author Firmicus Maternus, whose version of the Proserpina myth in *De Errore Profanarum Religionum* is drawn largely from Ovid, although he ends her tale before she returns, arguing that she is not abducted but drowned. See Quacquarelli.

6. For an overview of the availability of *DRP* between 400 and 1200 see Chance, *Medieval Mythography*, 1:591–92n6. She notes its presence in Charlemagne's library (clearly indicated as three books, as Charlet remarks, xlviii). In this context it is worth noting that the third-century Roman sarcophagus that contained Charlemagne's corpse (before it was transferred after his canonization) depicts the abduction of Proserpina but not the return. It is part of the Cathedral Treasury at Aachen. See also McKitterick, *History and Memory*, 154; Curtius, *European Literature and the Latin Middle Ages*, 48–57; and Pavarani, "Claudian and the *Metamorphoses*," in *Ovid in Late Antiquity*, 119–39.

7. Copeland, "The Curricular Classics in the Middle Ages," in *The Oxford History of Classical Reception in English Literature*, 1: 21–33. For a comparable view of how Dido's story is adapted by and for the medieval classroom, see Woods, *Weeping for Dido*.

8. The reason for choosing these texts remains a mystery, though it has been suggested that all six communicate elements of *Romanitas*. See Copeland, 27–28, and Willoughby, "The Transmission and Circulation of Classical Literature: Libraries and Florilegia," in *The Oxford History of Classical Reception in English Literature*, 95–120, esp. 97 and 103. See also Gillespie, "From the Twelfth Century to c. 1450," in *Cambridge History of Literary Criticism*, 2: 145–236. On one branch of Claudian's influence, see Duffey, "The Proserpinean Metamyth: Claudian's *De raptu Proserpinae* and Alan of Lille's *Anticlaudianus*," *Florilegium* V (1983): 105–39.

9. Cameron's *Claudian: Poetry and Propaganda* remains essential to understanding the poet's audience, purpose and methods. See especially chaps. 9 and 10. Now see also Coombe, *Claudian the Poet*. See Ware; Duc.

10. Text, with minor orthographical changes, from Fantham, *Fasti, Book IV*, 69–70.

11. Gruzelier notes Claudian's decision to set the scene on Etna rather than at Enna, and comments on the change from Cicero and Ovid, among others. No explanation is offered for the change; the manuscript tradition is "largely in favour of Aetna," 111. She does note the mention of Lake Pergus (2.112), which is presumably merely carried over from Ovid's description in *Met.* 5.386. Here see the detailed defense of reading Etna in Hall, ad 1.122. Here see also Moro, "Il vulcano degli dei," 171–226.

12. Text and translation, slightly adapted, from Gruzelier, 12–13.

13. Gruzelier, 12–15.

14. Note that even in the *Pervigilium Veneris* (49–52) Etna is noted for its flowers. Here see Poddi, "L'invidia di Ibla," 113–37.

15. Hinds, "Return to Enna." For further on the timing of the move, see my "Reading against the Grain." See also R. Jakobi, "Zur Frühen Wirkungsgeschichte von Claudians *De Raptu Proserpinae*."

16. Geoffrey of Vitry's twelfth-century commentary on Claudian confirms these two factors, both in text and marginalia: *The Commentary of Geoffrey of Vitry on Claudian, "De Raptu Proserpinae,"* esp. 45, 104 (*Aethnae quae ita bene erat disposita prout habitum est*), 110, and 113, and *Pluto per Aethnam ascendebat ad nostrum hemisperium*. For further on the relocation, see Cameron, *Last Pagans*; Hall; Ware.

17. Hyginus, *Fabulae*, ed. P. K. Marshall, esp. *Fabula* CXLVI.

18. Kulcsár, *Mythographi*, II: 185; edited and repunctuated following Pepin, *The Vatican Mythographers*, 145. The dating is complicated, but these myths appear to have been collected in the seventh century. As Jane Chance argues, the text was written probably during the Carolingian period, but no earlier than Isidore and no later than the tenth century. See *Medieval Mythography*, vol. 1: 300–346, esp. 300.

19. See Bresson, "*Tex a Grecis dicitur*." See also Burnett; Elliott and Elder; Zorzetti and Berlioz. Note *DRP* ad 1.122, ed. Hall, who also cites Lactantius Placidus, *Proserpinam circa cacumen Aetnae flores legentem*.

20. Georg H. Bode, ed., *Scriptores rerum mythicarum Latini tres Romae nuper reperti*, 1: 197–98. Pepin, *Vatican Mythographers*, 264.

21. On the richness of Enna as a space in Cicero that hovers between oratory and myth or fiction, see Baldo.

22. See Gowers, "The Road to Sicily," for further on Seneca's letter and especially the perplexing identification of Lucilius.

23. See Williams (*Pietro Bembo on Etna*), who draws connections between Vergil's depictions of the mountain here and the one embodied by Atlas in *Aeneid* 4: "But these points of contact between Etna in *Aeneid* 3 and Atlas and *Fama* in Book 4 are further complicated by Virgil's simultaneous engagement with Lucretius: the latter's portrayal of *religio* in *De rerum natura* 1 has important affinities with Virgil's *Fama*, and his deployment of Etna in connection with the Gigantomachy theme also provides a counterpoise for Virgil's experimentation with the same idea" (38).

24. Seneca, *Epistulae Morales*, 79.5–10, ed. L. D. Reynolds, 255.

25. For further on the *Dialogues* in the context of the development of Purgatory, see Moreira, *Heaven's Purge*, 81–112.

26. Gregory the Great, *Dialogi*, ed. De Vogüé and Antin, 199. See Le Goff, *La naissance du Purgatoire*, 130; Purcell, *Corrupting Sea*; Boesch Gajano. On Gregory see, most usefully, the edited collection, *A Companion to Gregory the Great*, ed. Bronwen Neil and Matthew dal Santo.

27. Iohanni Campulu de Missina, *Libru de lu dialagu di Sanctu Gregoriu*, 161. The dialogues had a robust afterlife throughout the Middle Ages in Sicily. See Barcellona, "Percorsi di un testo 'fortunato,'" 33–57.

28. As Le Goff notes (*La naissance du Purgatoire*, 192), it is in a twelfth-century Anglo-Norman translation of Gregory's dialogues that the noun *purgatorie* first appears (*Dialogue* 4.40). See *Li Dialoge Gregoire lo Pape*, ed. W. Foerster, 254. In the edition of *Les Dialogues de Grégoire le Grand traduits par Angier*, it appears in line 18393 (p. 603).

29. Etienne de Bourbon, *Tractatus de diversis materiis predicabilibus*, 153.

30. Honess, *From Florence to the Heavenly City*, 89–90; 94.

31. Le Goff, *La naissance du Purgatoire*, 280–81.

32. Although there appears not to be a strictly linguistic basis for associating Enna, or Henna, and Gehenna through an arabicization, there is the tantalizing possibility of what would amount to a folk etymology between the two based on the complex back-and-forth of the multiple languages that coexisted on Sicily during the time. Henna becomes arabicized from Castrum Hennae or Ienna to *Qasr Yanan* which is then re-romanicized as *Castrogiovanni*, a name it retains until well into the twentieth century. See Lanzafame, "Linguistic Contaminations in Sicily," esp. 114–16. See also Agius, "Who Spoke Siculo-Arabic?" in *Incontro italiano di Linguistica Camito-semitica (Afroasiatica)*, 25–33; Michele Amari, *Storia dei mussulmani in Sicilia*, vol. 1; Caracausi, *Arabismi medievali di Sicilia*; and Pellegrini, *Terminologia geografica araba in Sicilia*, 137, who lists *ghimeni* as "terreno improduttivo, anche le erbe che vi crescono sopra" ("unproductive land, as well as the plants that grow above").

33. *The Etymologies of Isidore of Seville*, ed. and trans., Barney et al., 298.

34. Ribémont has identified several other mentions of Etna as Gehenna, most notably in a sermon of Julian of Vézélay. See "Le volcan médiéval," in *Mythologies de l'Etna*, 65–76.

35. *La conquesta di Sichilia fatta per li Normandi*, 89. This fourteenth-century text by Simone da Lentini appears to have been intended, at least at first, as a translation of the Latin works of Goffredo Malaterra.

36. Amico, *Lexicon Topographicum Siculum*, 1: 208. "Cluverius" is Philipp Cluver, Polish geographer (1580–1622).

37. Amico, *Lexicon*, 1.223.

38. The Hereford *mappa mundi* belongs to Hereford Cathedral. It measures 1.58 × 1.33 m (5 ft. 2 in. × 4 ft. 4 in.).

39. Kupfer, *Art and Optics in the Hereford Map*. See also Westrem.

40. This is still the case. See Mercatanti, "Etna and the Perception of Volcanic Risk."

41. *Fabularius*, ed. van de Loo, p. 160. See also Guy of Bazoches (Wright, *Geographical Lore*, 221–22), who, in a letter to his nephews as he is on his way to the Holy Land, describes Etna as both fiery and snowy. He places the abduction on Etna specifically and associates the volcanic island near Etna as Aeolus's home. See Langlois, *La Connaissance de la nature et du monde au Moyen Âge*, and Wattenbach, "Aus den Briefen des Guido von Bazoches," esp. 106–8.

42. Goffredo Malaterra, book 2, section 30, *Ruggero I e Roberto Il Guiscardo*, trans. Lo Curto, 134. It is worth noting that Goffredo also refers to a legend that suggests that Etna is a passageway to either heaven or hell (*Angelicam pennam capiet hic, ille gehennam*; book 3, section 16), *Ruggero I e Roberto il Guiscardo*, 214.

43. PL 144, col. 0936A–0936B.

44. Peter of Blois (c. 1130–1211), *Epistola* 46, PL 207 cols. 133B–134B; 137A–137B.

45. For a thorough history of Etna's eruptions during the period discussed here, complete with textual sources and illustrations, see Guidoboni et al., *L'Etna nella storia*, 57–175. A bit technical, but still fascinating, is Tanguy et al., "Mount Etna Eruptions of the Last 2,750 Years." See also Thomaidis et al., "A Message from the 'Underground Forge of the Gods'"; Chester et al., *Mount Etna*; and Chester et al., "Human Response to Etna Volcano During the Classical Period," 179–88.

46. Ugo Falcando, *La Historia o liber de regno sicilie* (Rome: Forzani, 1897), 164, 175. Translation is that of Loud and Wiedemann, *The History of the Tyrants of Sicily, by 'Hugo Falcandus,'* with some modification. Hugo, or pseudo-Hugo, more precisely, drew on many classical texts, including Cicero's *Verrines*, whom he quotes.

47. A comparable later story involving a miracle of Saint Agatha that saved fish parched by an eruption of Mt. Etna is told by Roger Howden (1148–1201) in his *Chronicles*.

48. Hyginus, *Fabulae*, 132.

49. It is possible that the mention of Deucalion in Sicily derives ultimately from Nonnos, *Dionysiaca*, book 6, where Sicily is specifically mentioned in the context of the flood. See Nonnos, *Dionysiaca*, 6.155–295.

50. *Historiarum libri XII*, ed. Allen, 1.1.25: 51. It should be noted that the location of the mountain is disputed in the sources: some cite the location as *Sicilia*, others as *Socile*. The passage quotes from Josephus, *Antiquities* 3.1.6: "Nay Nicolaus of Damascus, in his ninety sixth Book, hath a particular relation about them: where he speaks thus: 'There is a great mountain in Armenia, over Minyas, called Baris: upon which it is reported that many who fled at the time of the deluge were saved: and that one who was carried in an Ark, came on shore upon the top of it; and that the remains of the timber were a great while preserved: this might be the man about whom Moses, the Legislator of the Jews, wrote.'" Note that Josephus does not mention Sicily. *Ovide Moralisé*, in the commentary on the story of Deucalion, includes reference to Noah.

51. Gervase of Tilbury, *Otia Imperialia*, ed. and trans., Banks and Binns, 338–41. The division of Sicily from the mainland is replicated in medieval texts by the irruption of stories about imperial figures and terrestrial paradises. The best examples of this can be found in descriptions of Alexander the Great in the *Li Fet des Romains* and *I Fatti di Cesare*; and in the address to Otto in the *Otia Imperialia*, in which Gervase discourses on the nature of ruling an empire. While the separation of the island from the mainland becomes strikingly minimized during this time,

the narrative of division remains important. Through Ovid, the Etna / Messina complex becomes a textual site for enabling the discussion of empire, a fact that leads to the development of a subgenre of narratives that introduce discussions not of lost paradise but of terrestrial paradise: places on earth that either remain perfect despite surrounding corruptions or become perfect again through redemption.

52. Gervase of Tilbury, *Otia Imperialia*, 334–37. The *Otia* was translated numerous times. From the French: "Il y a en Cecille mont Ethna, que on appelle communement Gibel.... Les gens du pays comptent que le roy Arthus a esté veu en nostre temps es desers de mon Gibel"; ("There is in Sicily Mount Etna, that is known locally as Gibel.... The locals report that in our day King Arthur has been seen in an uninhabited region of Mont Gibel [Mt. Etna]." Jean d'Antioche / Jean de Vignay, App. V. *Les Traductions Francaises des "Otia Imperialia,"* ed. Pignatelli and Gerner, 426–27. Similar stories exist in the German tradition. See Otto of Freising (c. 1143–45), *Chronica sive historia de duabus civitatibus*, Book V, chap. 3, line 14, where Theodoric rides to his death in Etna. This is seen as a correction of Gregory the Great, who puts Theodoric in a volcano on the Aeolian or Liparian islands. See Aurell, *La Légende du Roi Arthur: 550–1250*. See also Williams, "King Arthur in History and Legend," esp. 85–86. Williams mentions that in the thirteenth-century Arthurian romance, *Floriant et Florete*, "Arthur was destined to be brought [to Etna], evidently to be healed of his wounds by his sister Morgain. The connection of Morgan le Fay with Sicily probably accounts for the name Fata Morgana for the mirage of Messina" (86).

53. See Picone, "Giullari d'Italia." See also Graf, "Artu nell'Etna" and Paris, "La Sicile dans la littérature française du Moyen Age."

54. For further on adaptation of Ovid's myths in the Middle Ages, see Hays, "The Mythographic Tradition after Ovid," 129–43.

55. Gruzelier, 70–71.

56. It is perhaps for this reason as well that the myth of Proserpina does not play a part in the early vernacular literature of Sicily.

57. Gregorius Turonensis, *Liber in gloria martyrum*, 38.

58. Hays, "Tales out of School," 22–47. Helm, ed., *Fabii Planciadis Fulgentii V.C. Opera*, rev. J. Preaux; and Whitbread, *Fulgentius the Mythographer*.

59. Fo has suggested that Claudian may have originally intended to write a fourth book that would, presumably, have told of the return, but did not, either due to historic circumstances or the poet's death. See "Osservazioni su alcune questioni relative al *De raptu Proserpinae* di Claudiano."

60. Marjorie Curry Woods, "The Classics and After."

Chapter 5. The Redemption of Proserpina

1. Richard of Devizes, *Chronicon*, 18–20.

2. Goffredo Malaterra, *Ruggero I e Roberto Il Guiscardo*, 90.

3. Peter of Eboli, *Liber ad Honorem Augusti*, eds. Kölzer and Stähli, 134. The image depicts the arrival of Constanza of Sicily at Messina and her reception by her husband Tancred (f. 120r). For an English translation, see Hood.

4. On the history of Etna's eruptions see now the comprehensive *L'Etna nella Storia*, eds. Guidoboni et al. As these texts demonstrate, there was a cluster of eruptions in the late twelfth

century (142–56). See also Hyde, "The Volcanic History of Etna"; Tanguy, "Les Éruptions historiques de l'Etna"; and, more generally, Sigursson, *Melting the Earth*.

5. The most graphic version of this can be seen at https://www.windy.com/37.846/15.265?37.350,15.265,8,m:eIfagAB (accessed 29 October 2021), which shows the wind patterns over hours, days, and weeks around the globe. Focusing on the straits we see clearly that the winds from the north and east always predominate, making passage south easy, passage north virtually impossible. When the movement of the tides (which vary with the hour) is added to this, the difference becomes substantial.

6. See, for instance, Ibn Jubayr, *The Travels of Ibn Jubayr*, summarized in Guidoboni, 149–50. Many of the Arabic descriptions of the straits and Etna emphasize their violence. A generous sampling of medieval Arabic descriptions of Sicily, especially focused on Etna, is offered in Guidoboni et al., eds., *L'Etna nella Storia*, 128–50. The descriptions include stock phrases, suggesting, as noted, that "solo pochi autori arabi che scrissero della Sicilia visitarono realmente l'isola e videro di persona i suoi vulcani" (129).

7. The history of the discovery of the Vatican palimpsest of the orations is beyond the scope of this argument, though it is a fabulous story. See Sandys, "The Vatican Palimpsest"; Peterson, "The Vatican Codex of Cicero's *Verrines*." Lazzeretti has noted that in the part describing Proserpina, Cicero employs the superlative more often than elsewhere: *M. Tulli Ciceronis, In C. Verrem actionis secundae liber quartus (De signis)* (318).

8. Reynolds, *Texts and Transmission*, 71. For a full history of the *Verrines* in the Middle Ages and humanistic texts, see Reeve, "Medieval Tradition." Text and notes here are invaluable, especially Peterson, "The MSS. of the *Verrines*." See particularly the discussion of excerpts from the *Verrines* identified in the *Florilegium Angelicum*, which Reeve notes was "compiled in 12th-century France and indeed probably about 1160 in Champagne ... They number 18 and all come from II 4–5" (31).

9. Williams, "The Cathedral School of Rheims": "contemporaneously with Herimann other masters were teaching there. The most celebrated of these was Bruno" (665).

10. *Epist*. 65: *Briefe Meinhards von Bamberg: Briefsammlungen Der Zeit Heinrichs IV*. Monumenta Germaniae Historica 113.23.

11. Riley-Smith, *The First Crusade and the Idea of Crusading*, 21–22. See also Runciman, *The First Crusade*, chap. 2; Powell, *The Crusades, the Kingdom of Sicily and the Mediterranean*; Erdmann, *The Origin of the Idea of Crusade*, 355–71; Mayer, *The Crusades*; Rubenstein, *Armies of Heaven*, chap. 1; Asbridge, *The First Crusade*, chap. 10.

12. Hagenmeyer, ed., *Historia Hierosolymitana* (Heidelberg, 1913), 135, 137–38. Also found in Bongars, *Gesta Dei per Francos*, 513–18. A useful comparison of the extant versions of Urban's sermon is provided by Munro, "The Speech of Pope Urban II at Clermont." Of the massive bibliography on the literature of the Crusades, I have found the work of Marcus Bull and John Tolan particularly insightful.

13. *Recueil des Historiens des Croisades* (Occidentaux) 3.728–9.

14. Sweetenham, *Robert the Monk's History*, 81.

15. William of Tyre, *Chronicon*, 131–32; *History of Deeds Done beyond the Sea*, translated and annotated by Babcock and Krey (NY: Columbia Univ. Press, 1976), 89–90. See also Edbury and Rowe, *William of Tyre*; Nicholson and Edgington, *Deeds Done beyond the Sea*; Issa, *La Version latine et l'adaptation française*. Now see also Yolles, *Making the East Latin*, who notes that while

"the crusades are not typically associated with intellectual pursuit, ... the crusader settlers responded to their new environment in increasingly sophisticated ways while maintaining ties with their European homelands" (4–5).

16. Examples of the Norman invasion as a proto-Crusade include: Orderic Vitalis, *Hist. Ecclesiastica*; *Canso d'Antioca*, lines 385–91; Anna Comnena, *Alexiad*. See also d'Onofrio, ed., *I Normanni: popolo d'Europa 1030–1200*, and Borsook, *Messages in Mosaic*, xxii.

17. Sweetenham, *Robert the Monk's History*, 81. Note the reference here to the fact that the language points to an attained paradise, more purgatorial than Edenic.

18. Wright, *Geographical Lore of the Time of the Crusades*.

19. Although at quite a remove, it is interesting to note that *Moby Dick* relates "that still more wonderful story of the Arethusa fountain near Syracuse (whose waters were believed to have come from the Holy Land by an underground passage)." See Melville, *Moby Dick*, 263.

20. Useful overviews of Ovid's reception and manuscript tradition in the high Middle Ages can be found in Boyd, ed., *Brill's Companion to Ovid*, chaps. 13 (Hexter) and 14 (Richmond).

21. Canon 21 of the Fourth Lateran Council (1215) requires all faithful to confess their sins at least once a year. The second Council of Lyon, in 1274, defined the doctrine of Purgatory, saying "If those who are truly repentant die in charity before they have done sufficient penance for their sins of omission and commission, their souls are cleansed after death in purgatorial or cleansing punishments ... The suffrages of the faithful on earth can be of great help in relieving these punishments, as, for instance, the Sacrifice of the Mass, prayers, almsgiving, and other religious deeds which, in the manner of the Church, the faithful are accustomed to offer for others of the faithful." Tanner, ed. and trans., *Decrees of the Ecumenical Councils*, vol. 1; Murray "Counselling in Medieval Confession" in Biller and Minnis, eds., *Handling Sin*.

22. Text from *Appendix Ovidiana*, 108. Dronke ("A Note on Pamphilius," 230) dated the poem to about 1080, although no extant manuscripts earlier than the thirteenth century survive.

23. Gura, "A Critical Edition and Study of Arnulf of Orléans' Philological Commentary to Ovid's *Metamorphoses*" (Diss: The Ohio Univ., 2010). http://rave.ohiolink.edu/etdc/view?acc_num=osu1274904386; accessed 22 November 2021.

24. John of Garland, *Integumenta Ovidii*, ed. Ghisalberti, 57. A useful overview of twelfth-century interpreters of Ovid can be found at Engelbrecht, "Fulco, Arnulf, and William: Twelfth-Century Views on Ovid in Orléans," *Journal of Medieval Latin* 18 (2008): 52–73.

25. Here see the edition of Ghisalberti, *Giovanni del Virgilio Espositore delle* Metamorfosi, 64–65. See also Baker et al., *Traire De Latin et Espondre* and Van Peteghem, "The Vernacular Roots of Dante's Reading of Ovid in the *Commedia*," *Italian Studies* 73 (2018): 223–39.

26. *Ovide Moralisé*, ed. C. de Boer, n.s., vol. 21, 260.

27. *Ovide Moralisé*, 283.

28. I am grateful to Frank T. Coulson, David T. Gura, Gerlinde Huber-Rebenich, and Beatrice Wyss for their insight into these other glosses. See *Commentaire vulgate des Métamorphoses d'Ovide*, eds. Coulson and Martina, esp. 746–75, 772. This text, which dates to the mid-thirteenth century, makes it clear that, although delayed by the eating of the pomegranate seeds, Proserpina does return. Also see Ghisalberti, "Giovanni del Virgilio espositore delle *Metamorfosi*," *Giornale dantesco* 34 (1933): 1–110; Coulson, "The Vulgate Commentary on Ovid's *Metamorphoses*," *Mediaevalia* 13 (1987), 29–61; Coulson, "Ovid's Transformation in Medieval France, c. 1100–c.1350," *Metamorphosis: The Changing Face of Ovid in Medieval and Early Modern Europe*, ed. Keith and

Rupp, (Toronto: Univ. of Toronto Press, 2007), 33–60; Coulson, "Ovid's *Metamorphoses* in the School Tradition of France, 1180–1400: Texts, Manuscript Traditions, Manuscript Settings," *Ovid in the Middle Ages*, ed. Clark, Coulson, and McKinley, 48–82. See also Wallis and Wisnovsky, *Medieval Textual Cultures*, and Knox, "Commenting on Ovid," *A Companion to Ovid*, 327–40.

29. Earlier work that does address the treatment of Proserpina includes Anton, *Der Raub der Proserpina*, which begins with an analysis of the story in the *Ovide*.

30. Possamaï-Pérez, "L'Ovide moralisé du XIVe siècle: Mort ou renaissance des *Métamorphoses* d'Ovide ? *Acta Universitatis Lodziensis. Folia Litteraria Romanica* 9 (2014): 7–15; García, "Les sources de l'*Ovide moralisé*, livre I: Types et traitement," *Le Moyen Age* 124 (2018): 307–36. Baker et al., eds., *Ovide moralisé. Livre I*; Jung, "Ovide, texte, translateur et gloses dans les manuscrits de l'*Ovide moralisé*," *The Medieval Opus: Imitation, Rewriting, and Transmission in the French Tradition*, 75–98; Jung, "Aspects de l'*Ovide Moralisé*," *Ovidius redivivus*, 149–72, esp. 166, where he notes, "Le langage métaphorique des fables d'Ovide a dû constituer une sorte de révélation pour notre auteur, car il y a retrouvé des images et des métaphores qui lui étaient familières à travers la tradition chrétienne." See also Tilliette, "L'Écriture et sa métaphore: remarques sur l'*Ovide Moralisé*," *Ensi firent li ancessor* II: 543–58; Possamaï-Pérez, *L'Ovide moralisé*; Cavagna et al., "La Tradition manuscrite de l'Ovide Moralisé: Prolégomènes à une nouvelle edition," *Romania* 132 (2014): 176–213. Now also see Hult, "Ovide Moralisé: Anonymat et autorisé," in *Ovidius explanatus*, 141–53.

31. The anomalous nature of this passage is not unique. See Copeland, *Rhetoric, Hermeneutics, and Translation in the Middle Ages* (Cambridge, UK: Cambridge Univ. Press, 1995), 108–11; Copeland points out that the author of the *Ovide moralisé* often seems more interested in his own work than Ovid's.

32. For the late antique roots for these texts, see Moreira, *Heaven's Purge*, 3–13.

33. Here see above all Mallette, *Kingdom of Sicily* and *European Modernity and the Arab Mediterranean*, as well as her *Sea of Languages*, co-edited with Akbari. See also Takayama, *Sicily and the Mediterranean in the Middle Ages*; Granara, *Narrating Muslim Sicily*; *Ibn Hamis*.

34. This turn back to the Latin tradition is not unique to literature. See Kassler-Taub, who, in her 2017 Harvard dissertation, "At the Threshold of the Mediterranean," makes a parallel argument about the influence of mainland architectural models in early modern Sicily.

Chapter 6. *Quando n'apparve una montagna*: Purgatory and the Voyage of Ulysses

1. I will refer to the location as Purgatory or Mt. Purgatory, the canticle as *Purgatorio*.

2. Helpful here is Carletti, "Impero, stati particolari e identità nazionale in Dante," in *Il Pensiero Politico* 36 (2003): 293–307. See also Ardizzone, ed., *Dante as Political Theorist*. For a useful overview, see Davis, "Dante and the Empire," in *The Cambridge Companion to Dante*, 257–69. For the relationship between Dante's understanding of empire and that of Vergil, see Kallendorf, "Virgil, Dante and Empire," *Vergilius* 34 (1988): 44–69.

3. See Tuzzo, "Further Discussion on the 'Two Suns Theory,'" *History Research* 5 (2015): 98–108.

4. Here see most usefully Reeves, "Dante and the Prophetic View of History," in *The World of Dante*, 44–60.

5. Such an approach is of course clearly spelled out in Dante's letter to Cangrande (*Epist.* XIII), whose authorship remains disputed. The notion that multivalent reading guides the progress of the text more in *Purgatorio* than *Inferno* is shown by many, including Franke, *Dante's Interpretive Journey*.

6. The variants of the Proserpina myth that end before her return never deny the possibility that someday she will leave the underworld.

7. Dante's references to Sicily are catalogued by Vigo. Much has been written on charting the afterlife in Dante and preceding texts. Now see Gee, *Mapping the Afterlife*.

8. Text is taken from the edition of Petrocchi; the translation is that of Mandelbaum. Both can be found at https://digitaldante.columbia.edu/, accessed 30 April 2021.

9. There is debate about how to translate this line. I have emended the Mandelbaum translation here, since I believe the thrust of the Italian is more general than his translation ("may this poem rise again from Hell's dead realm") suggests. See Hollander and Hollander, *Purgatorio*, 15, for further discussion of this line.

10. The bibliography is massive: over 1200 references to this canto alone appear in the *Bibliografia Dantesca Internazionale*. For a useful and insightful approach to these arguments, see Barolini, *Dante Encyclopedia*, "Ulysses." See also her *Undivine Comedy*, chap. 3. Glenn Most has written on Ulysses' Greekness, concluding that Ulysses was "Dante's evil twin" and pointing to parallels between Ulysses in the *Inferno* and Dante in *Purgatorio*. See his "Dante's Greeks," *Arion* 13 (2006): 15–48. See also Cassell, "'Ulisseana'; Seriacopi, 155–91; Boitani, "Ulysses and the Three Traditions" in *Dante and the Greeks*, 265–71; Pihas, "Dante's Ulysses: Stoic and Scholastic Models of the Literary Reader's Curiosity and *Inferno* 26," *Dante Studies* 121(2003): 1–24; Forti, "Ulisse dal *nostos* al *folle volo*: Fonti classiche e tradizione medievale in *Inf.* XXVI," *Nuova Rivista di Letteratura Italiana* 9 (2006): 9–24; Basile, "Tragedia di Dante, tragedia di Ulisse: Lettura di *Inferno* XXVI," *Rivista di Studi Danteschi* 5 (2005): 225–52 (see revised version in Enrico Malato and Andrea Mazzucchi, eds., *Canto XXVI: Tragedia di Dante, tragedia di Ulisse, Lectura Dantis Romana: Cento canti per cento anni* [Roma: Salerno, 2013], 1.2, 823–50). See Sasso, *Ulisse e il desiderio: Il canto XXVI dell' "Inferno"* (Roma: Viella, 2011), esp. 245–64. See again Boitani, *The Shadow of Ulysses: Figures of a Myth*; Cerri, *Dante e Ulisse*, 87–134; Corti, *Percorsi dell'invenzione*, 113–45; Freccero, *Dante: The Poetics of Conversion*, 15–24; 136–51; Nardi, "La tragedia d'Ulisse" in *Dante e la cultura medievale*, 125–34; Padoan, *Il pio Enea, l'empio Ulisse*, 170–204; Pagliaro, "Ulisse" in *Ulisse*, 371–432; Fubini, *Il peccato di Ulisse*, 1–76.

11. See Barolini, "*Inferno* 26: The Epic Hero." *Commento Baroliniano*, Digital Dante https://digitaldante.columbia.edu/dante/divine-comedy/inferno/inferno-26/. Accessed 30 April 2021.

12. Text of Reynolds, *Epistulae Morales*.

13. It is conceivable that the mountain that looms in *Inf.* 1 is in fact the mountain of Purgatory. In line 138 of the Ulysses canto there is the suggestive echo, "e percosse del legno *il primo canto*." The meaning of course is entirely other, but the echo sends us back, on some level, to this opening canto where the new Ulysses is escaping, figuratively, from the very shipwreck that killed him and his men in canto 26. See MacDonald, "The Path through the Woods. An alternative interpretation of Dante's *selva oscura*," *Percorsi Danteschi*, 53–61. See also Freccero, "Dante's Prologue Scene," in *Dante: The Critical Complex*, vol. 7, 63–87.

14. So Barolini, "*Inferno* 26: The Epic Hero."

15. Seneca asks similar questions in *De brevitate vitae* 13.2–3: "*Graecorum iste morbus fuit quaerere, quem numerum Ulixes remigum habuisset, prior scripta esset Ilias an Odyssia, praeterea an eiusdem essent auctoris, alia deinceps huius notae, quae sive contineas, nihil tacitam conscientiam iuvant sive proferas, non doctior videaris sed molestior. Ecce Romanos quoque invasit inane studium supervacua discendi.*" ("It was once a foible confined to the Greeks to inquire into what number of rowers Ulysses had, whether the *Iliad* or the *Odyssey* was written first, whether moreover they belong to the same author, and various other matters of this stamp, which, if you keep them to yourself, in no way pleasure your secret soul, and, if you publish them, make you seem more of a bore than a scholar. But now this vain passion for learning useless things has assailed the Romans also"). Text and translation from Seneca, *Moral Essays, Volume II*, 326–29.

16. Aulus Gellius, *Attic Nights*, vol. 3, 42–45.

17. It should be noted here that Guido da Pisa, translating *Aen.* 5.715, renders *senes* as *vecchi*.

18. Lagomarsini, *Aeneis*, 267. For further on vernacular translations of the *Aeneid*, see the introduction to this volume, "Contesto storico e culturale," 4–26. See also Comparetti, *Vergil in the Middle Ages*, 239–377.

19. For further discussion of Ugurgieri's citation of Dante, see Lagomarsini, *Aeneis*, Introduction, 8, and chap. 6.

20. For further on the importance of these translations, see Cornish, *Vernacular Translation*, esp. chap. 1, and Parodi.

21. The text is that of Griffin, *Historia Destructionis Troiae*, 10; the translation is by Mary Meek, *Historia Destructionis Troiae*, 8. It is perhaps significant that Guido is the only Sicilian author Dante mentions in *DVE*.

22. Griffin, 113–14; Meek, 110–11, slightly edited.

23. Pliny, *Historia Naturalis*, 3.86–7.

24. Richard of Devizes, *Chronicon*, 16.

25. Guido da Pisa, *I fatti di Enea*, 82. This tradition continues: a sixteenth-century Italian translation in the Biblioteca Nazionale Centrale in Florence (Magl.VII.386, f.12v) reads:

> D'Atrea il minor figlio Menelao
> Cacciato fino agl'ultimi confini
> Del mondo inculturato et perregrino
> Errando va nel regno di Protheo
> Vidde in Etna per forza i gran cyclopi
> E fu di lor prigion l'astuto Ulisse

> (The younger son of Atreus, Menelaus, hunted to the very edge of the uncivilized world alone and exiled, wandering in the kingdom of Proteus, saw at Etna, by chance, the huge Cyclopes, in whose prison the wise Ulysses was.)

26. Lagomarsini, *Aeneis*, 450.

27. Courtney Wells has pointed out to me the significance of the fact that Dante begins his response in Latin, with the verb *audivi*.

28. It is tempting to suggest that Dante has Ovid's Ulysses in mind from *Met.* 13 where, as we have seen, Ulysses serves as an avatar of the poet and wins precisely because of his use of language. M. Picone has pointed to this echo, focusing on the role of *ingenium* in each.

29. For further on Dante's interest in Seneca, see Black, "Classical Antiquity," in *Dante in Context*, 297–318. See also Pasquini, "Presenze di Seneca in Dante," in *Seneca nella coscienza dell'Europa*, 111–36; and Fenzi, "Dante e Seneca," in *I classici di Dante*, 177–213. See also Durling, "'Io son venuto': Seneca, Plato and the Microcosm," *Dante Studies* 9 (1975): 95–130; reprinted in Dante, ed. Harold Bloom (New York: Chelsea House, 1986), 113–31; also in *Dante: The Critical Complex, Vol. 1: The Poet's Life and the Invention of Poetry*, ed. Richard Lansing (New York & London: Routledge, 2003), 349–83.

30. Text from Reynolds, *Ad Lucilium Epistulae Morales*. See Gower, "The Road to Sicily." The first commentator to note this echo was Giuseppe Vandelli. Seneca was of particular interest to Dante because of his apocryphal correspondence with St. Paul; in the fourteenth letter from Paul to Seneca the "graces of rhetoric" are praised. Moreover, the vision of Paul, influenced by writings about Eden, also would appear to influence descriptions of heavens on earth, since part of what Paul sees is the glory promised in heaven. Bibliography on Seneca and Ulysses includes Reynolds, *The Medieval Tradition of Seneca's Letters*; Meeks and Fitzgerald, *The Writings of St. Paul*; Mayer, "Seneca Redivivus," in *The Cambridge Companion to Seneca*, 277–88. See also Enrico Fenzi, "Seneca e Dante: da Alessandro Magno a Ulisse," *Studi sul canone letterario del Trecento per Michelangelo Picone*, ed. Bartuschat, Rossi, and Crivelli, 67–78; Colish, "Acting against Conscience," in *Dante and the Greeks*, 83–104. See also Rossi, "Dante in un commento trecentesco alle 'Epistole' di Seneca," in *Il ritorno dei classici nell'Umanesimo*, 513–30. See also G. Mezzadroli, *Seneca in Dante*.

31. *Epistula* 88.7.

32. Fenzi, "Seneca e Dante," 67–78.

33. Lombardi, "26. The Poetics of Trespassing," *Vertical Readings in Dante's Comedy*, vol. 3, 71–88. See also Brownlee, "Language and Desire in *Par*. XXVI," *Lectura Dantis* 6 (1990): 46–59.

34. For further on the moral dimension of the Ulysses passage, see Gambale.

35. It is interesting to note how this parallels Aeneas's journey, as discussed in chapter 1.

36. For a different, and disputed, approach to the location of the mountain of Purgatory, see Benini, *Origine, Sito, Forma e Dimensioni del Monte del Purgatorio e dell'Inferno Dantesco*.

37. For further on Dante and Seneca in the context of the Ulysses passage see Barbieri, "Ulisse," *Dante: Rivista internazionale di studi su Dante Alighieri* 8 (2011): 43–67.

38. In his essay on the steadiness of the wise man (*De Constantia* 2.2), Seneca says that the ancient (Greek) world offered up two examples of the wise man: Ulysses and Hercules. Both were wise because they were unconquered by struggles. It is perhaps relevant that Tacitus, too, associates Hercules with Ulysses in *Germania*, chap. 3, where they appear one right after the other. Seneca and Cato are discussed by Berra, *Catone custode della penitenza*, in *Peccato, penitenza e santità nella* Commedia, 125–36.

39. An in-depth and useful analysis of Dante's hermeneutics throughout the *Commedia* is supplied by Baur, *Dante's Hermeneutics of Salvation*. Particularly useful is chapter 5, "The Hermeneutics of Conversion," with its emphasis on using language to escape the bonds of humanity.

40. Norwich, *The Middle Sea: A History of the Mediterranean*, chaps. 6–10. Perhaps more to the point, Brunetto Latini provides a verbal *mappa mundi* that would be familiar to Dante. See the description of Ulysses in Brunetto Latini, *Tesoretto*, and bibliography mentioned in Kupfer, *Art and Optics in the Hereford Map*.

41. Morreale and Paul, eds., *The French of Outremer.*

42. For a broad view of the literary context at this time, see *Dante and the Greeks,* ed. Jan M. Ziolkowski, Introduction.

43. Clay, "The Metamorphosis of Ovid in Dante's *Divine Comedy,*" *A Handbook to the Reception of Ovid,* 174–86 at 181.

44. Ferrante, *The Political Vision of the* Divine Comedy, 198.

45. For further on this, see Hollander, *Purgatorio* (New York: Doubleday, 2003), xx.

46. Barolini, "Dante, Teacher of His Reader," in *Approaches to Teaching Dante's* Divine Comedy, 36–44.

Chapter 7. *Purgatorio,* Etna, and the Empire of Love

1. A useful overview of the canticle is provided by Hollander, "Introduction," *Purgatorio,* xv–xxii. His recommendations for the central notions of Purgatory include works of Rajna, *La materia e la forma della "Divina Commedia,"* 1998 [1874]) and Morgan, *Dante and the Medieval Other World.*

2. The timing of *Purgatorio* is debated. Hollander in *Purgatorio,* xxi–xxii, argues that it takes place on Easter Sunday; others that the three canticles span Easter weekend, with *Purgatorio* bridging between *Inferno* and *Paradiso,* much as Easter Saturday carries us from Good Friday to Easter Sunday; or, as Benini, Easter week, 1117–29.

3. Hollander and Hollander, *Purgatorio,* 257. They translate *lo monte che salendo altrui dismala* as "the mountain that unsins us as we climb" (*Purg.* XIII.3).

4. The importance of redemption, discussed in chapter 5, remains critical for Dante. As Dameron argues, in early fourteenth-century Florence, "men and women were considered fallen and deeply imperfect creatures who repeatedly sinned and disobeyed God, inheriting the stain of original sin. Salvation was possible only through the reception of God's healing grace, made accessible through the sacraments, which were administered by the clergy.... The sacrament of penance was necessary for the remission of all sins committed since baptism. The faithful were supposed to confess to a priest a least once a year (as stipulated by the Fourth Lateran Council)." "Church and Orthodoxy" in *Dante in Context,* 85–86.

5. Key here is the work of Mallette, especially *Kingdom of Sicily,* 56: "The attenuation of Arabic as a language of culture in general and of poetry in particular made the consolidation of Latin letters and the generation of a Romance poetic culture possible and even necessary."

6. As in the previous chapter, the text is that of Petrocchi; the translation is that of Allen Mandelbaum. Both can be found at https://digitaldante.columbia.edu/, accessed 30 April 2021.

7. See Barolini, "*Purgatorio* 1: The Sapphire Sea." *Commento Baroliniano,* Digital Dante, https://digitaldante.columbia.edu/dante/divine-comedy/purgatorio/purgatorio-1/. See also Most, "Dante's Greeks," 15–48.

8. "Inventa secuit primus qui nave profundum / et rudibus remis sollicitavit aquas..." (*DRP* 1.1–2).

9. Dante will return to this passage in *Par.* VIII.67–70.

10. See Levenstein, "Resurrecting Ovid's Pierides: Dante's Invocation to Calliope in '*Purgatorio*' 1.7–2," *Dante Studies* 126 (2008): 1–19. See also Mercuri, "Ovidio e Dante: le *Metamorfosi*

come ipotesto della *Commedia*," *Dante: Rivista internazionale di studi su Dante Alighieri* 6 (2009): 21–37.

11. Dante also mentions magpies and their connection to *Met.* 5 in *DVE* I.ii.7.

12. See especially Honess, "Divided City, Slavish Italy, Universal Empire," *Vertical Readings in Dante's* Comedy, 1: 119–42. Accessed 20 May 2021.

13. Mallette, *Kingdom of Sicily*, chap. 4, notes that Dante includes Sicilians across all canticles of the *Commedia*.

14. We will return to this point later in this chapter, but it is worth noting at the start that all of the Dante commentators who mention *Met.* 5 in the context of *Purgatorio* assert nonetheless that Proserpina is abducted from Mt. Etna. It is also assumed that Proserpina will return to earth on a regular basis. See the Dartmouth Dante Project, "Proserpina," https://dante.dartmouth.edu, where the location of the abduction is identified variously as, e.g., *giunta a Messina* (Jacopo della Lana) and *non longe ab Ethena* (Pietro Alighieri). In most commentaries as well Proserpina is likened to the moon because of her periodic appearance.

15. For further on empire in Dante, see Caferro, "Empire, Italy, and Florence," *Dante in Context*, 9–29. I am also indebted to conversations with James Hankins and Eric Nelson, whose political science course, "Dante in Contexts" (History 2113, Harvard Univ., spring 2015) clarified many of these points for me.

16. For the importance of Frederick II to Dante's understanding of Sicily, see Mallette, *Kingdom of Sicily*: "During Frederick's reign, for the first time since the collapse of the Roman Empire, Sicily came to be seen and ruled as an extension of the European mainland" (50). See also Donald Matthew, *The Norman Kingdom of Sicily* (Cambridge, UK: Cambridge Univ. Press, 1992), 336: "Frederick saw himself as the renovator of the Norman kingdom and the Roman imperial ideal."

17. Borsook, *Messages in Mosaic*, 73. See also Tronzo, ed., *Intellectual Life at the Court of Frederick II Hohenstaufen*, and Antonelli, "La corte 'italiana' di Federico II e la letteratura europea," in *Federico II e le nuove culture*, 319–45.

18. For Dante's complex treatment of Frederick II, see Mallette, *Kingdom of Sicily*, 65–68; Dragonetti, "Dante and Frederick II," *Exemplaria* 1 (1989): 1–15.

19. Useful in approaching Frederick II is Abulafia, *Frederick II: A Medieval Emperor*. See also Kantorowicz, *Frederick II: 1194–1250*, but on this, note the caveat by Lerner, *Ernst Kantorowicz: A Life*, 101–16.

20. *De vulgari eloquentia*, ed. and trans. Botterill (Cambridge, UK: Cambridge Univ. Press, 1996). Here see the useful bibliography by Rosier-Catach, "Tour de Babel," 184n2, as well as her edition and French translation of the text. Mengaldo, chap. 1, provides an excellent overview.

21. While the poets fostered by Frederick II turned to their Roman forebears, especially Ovid, as Van Peteghem has shown in *Italian Readers*, their interest focused on love, not empire or politics. Ovid's love poems provide the most influence, and the myths from the *Metamorphoses* that recur are centered on love. Proserpina does not appear.

22. See Ferrante, *The Political Vision of the* Divine Comedy, 44.

23. Here see Costa, "The Will of the Emperor and Freedom in the Empire," in *Dante as Political Theorist*, 98–112. See also the introduction to the fine translation by Prue Shaw.

24. See Barolini, *Dante's Poets: Textuality and Truth in the* Comedy, Introduction.

25. Lucan, *De bello civili*, book 2; translation is that of Susanna Braund.

26. In this terrace of Envy, rivalry among warring factions in Italy is foregrounded.

27. I revise Botterill's text here to reflect the Latin.

28. Cicero, *On the Orator: Book 3*, 56–57.

29. As in the preceding quotation from *DVE* I here also revise Botterill's translation to reflect the Latin.

30. The language of the hunt is specifically invoked in *DVE*: see, e.g., I.xi.1, xv.1, xvi.1–2.

31. That Dante believed that the contemporary vernacular poetry originated in the south of France is made clear in *De vulgari eloquentia* I.x.2.

32. See, in particular, *DVE* I.xii.2–6. So also Mallette, *Kingdom of Sicily*, 68–69. She argues that Sicilians were not translators but originators, according to Dante.

33. "Sicilianum vocatur." On this distinction between Sicilian as a dialect and Sicilian as an illustrious poetic tool, see Wells, "Pensemus qualiter viri prehonorati a propria divertentur" (*DVE* I, xiv, 5): els textos occitans d'un cercle de poetes toscans," *Mot so razo* 18, 2019: 23–40 and "In lingua est diversitas," 473–505, esp. 492–97. See also Mengaldo, 292. As Barolini has argued persuasively, Dante's aim in both *DVE* and the *Commedia* is not to assert the power of the vernacular per se but rather to argue for the preeminence of his own particular vernacular. See *Dante's Poets*, 179.

34. Mallette, *Kingdom of Sicily*, 102–4, notes that the first Italianate literary movement emerged in Sicily, a borderland rather than a heartland. This is due to Frederick II, in part, but also to Sicily's centrality culturally and the fact that it offered a "monolinguistic template upon an environment characterized by plurilingualism" (104).

35. We have seen the influence of vernacular translations of Ovid in the preceding chapter. For further, see Van Peteghem, "The Vernacular Roots of Dante's Reading of Ovid in the *Commedia*," *Italian Studies* 73 (2018): 223–39.

36. Jacoff, "Intertextualities in Arcadia: *Purgatorio* 30.49–51," *The Poetry of Allusion*, 131–44. See also Putnam, "Virgil's *Inferno*" in the same volume, 94–112.

37. Hollander, "Le opere di Virgilio nella *Commedia* di Dante," *Dante e la "Bella Scola" della poesia*, 247–343.

38. Cf. *Par.* XXVI.92, where *padre antico* refers to Adam. An early version of this argument appears in Spence, "Straits."

39. Marianne Shapiro, *De Vulgari Eloquentia: Dante's Book of Exile* (Lincoln: Univ. of Nebraska Press, 1990), 96–97.

40. The *Enciclopedia Dantesca* (s.v. "Sicilia") echoes this: "*la Sicilia federiciana non solo è centro di un'unità linguistico-poetica, per cui tutto ciò che di poetico veniva allora creato in Italia era detto 'siciliano', ma centro altresì di unità politica, in virtù dei due principi, Federico e Manfredi, che avevano saputo far convergere, in armoniosa sintesi, politica e cultura, intelligenza e magnanimità*" (5: 221) ("Sicily under Frederick II is not only the center of a linguistic-poetic unity, through which everything poetic created in Italy became known as Sicilian, but also a different kind of center of political unity, by virtue of the two princes, Frederick and Manfred, who had the wisdom to make converge, in a harmonious synthesis, poltiics and culture, intelligence and generosity").

41. Curiously there is precious little connecting Proserpina to Eve at this stage, though the two will become linked later, most notably in Milton, *Paradise Lost*, Bk. 4. See also the work of Milton's near-contemporary in the 1689 *Metamorfoseo d'Ovidio* (Houghton MS Eng 1087) which compares the two (fable 72). This manuscript combines a well-known sixteenth-century version of Ovid's tales by Gabriele Simeoni, which does not mention Eve, with later anonymous commentary that does.

42. Jacoff, "Intertextualities," esp. 139–40.
43. This is the main argument of the second book; see, e.g., *DVE* II.1.5.
44. Wetherbee, *The Ancient Flame*, 98–99.
45. On the importance of community to *Purgatorio*, see Ferrante, *The Political Vision*, chap. 4.
46. Seneca, *Epistulae Morales*, 79.6–7, ed. Reynolds, 255.
47. Ferrante, *Political Vision*, 239, 373.
48. *De Monarchia*, ed. and trans. Shaw, 144–47.
49. Augustine, *De doctrina Christiana*, esp. 1.13. See also, *Confessions*, 9.10.24, ed. and trans. Carolyn J.-B. Hammond, 49: *Et dum loquimur et inhiamus illi, attingimus eam modice toto ictu cordis. et suspiravimus et reliquimus ibi religatas primitias spiritus et remeavimus ad strepitum oris nostri, ubi verbum et incipitur et finitur* ("While we spoke, we also gazed upon wisdom with longing; we reached out and touched it as best we could, with every beat of our heart. Then we sighed and left behind us, where they belonged, those firstfruits of the Spirit. We returned to the clamor of our usual kind of speech, in which words have both beginnings and endings").
50. Marchesi characterizes Dante's complicated relationship with Augustine as "a constant reference point for his reflections, whether ... wilfully silenced ... or ... confidently recuperated" (*Dante and Augustine*, ix).
51. Barolini, *Undivine Comedy*, 212.
52. Love and songs of love have a penitential aspect as well. The songs of love that constitute the bulk of *Purgatorio* are also songs of penitents. Moreover, the stories Dante borrows from Ovid to bridge the two canticles—those of Arethusa and Proserpina—are tales of penitence and pilgrimage; Arethusa in Ovid describes herself as a *peregrina*. The language of pilgrimage resonates throughout *Purgatorio* and adds a further element to Dante's argument. The efforts of the penitents as well as the reader are not only to interpret well but to effect penitential action through these efforts. See here Kay, *Dante's Lyric Redemption*, 69–79. See also Regn, "Mythopoiesis, Cosmogony and Authorship in Dante's *Commedia*: Virgil's 'Perhaps' in *Inf.* XXXIV, 106–26," *Germanisch-Romanische Monatsschrift* 63 (2013), 313–28.
53. Holmes, "Dante's Choice and Romance Narratives of Two Beloveds," *Dante Studies* 121, (2003), 109–47. See also her *Dante's Two Beloveds*, 68–98.
54. For further on the transitional elements of these higher cantos, Chiarenza, "The Imageless Vision and Dante's *Paradise*," *Dante Studies* 90 (1972), 77–91, who insists on the importance of poetic imagery throughout the *Commedia*. See also Cornish, "Losing the Meridian: from *Purgatorio* to *Paradiso*," in *Reading Dante's Stars*, 79–92. Freccero, *Dante: The Poetics of Conversion*.
55. The identity of Matelda is disputed. See Lansing, *Dante Encyclopedia*, 600–602, for a thorough discussion of the character. In addition to "real life" characters who may have inspired her, though "it may be that Matelda, like Beatrice, is a person from Dante's private biography and also that the poet transforms Matelda, as he does Beatrice, into a larger allegorical symbol" (602). Among those possible identifications are "human happiness prior to original sin," and the "political ideal of a functional Roman empire" (601). This last supports a possible connection to Proserpina.
56. Fazio degli Uberti (1305 or 1309 to after 1367), a follower of Dante, asserts that this plain is on Etna. See his *Dittamondo* 3.14.1–3; 25–27: *lungo la marina / andavam per le parti di Peloro / in fin che fummo lá dov'è Messina ... Nel prato fummo, dove fior da fiore / Proserpina scegliea, quando Pluto / subitamente ne la trasse fore* ("We went along the coast through the region of Pelorus until we were where Messina is ... We were in the meadow where Proserpina chose the

best flowers when Pluto suddenly dragged her away," I:223). See Hawkins in "Watching Matelda," who notes how Dante's description of Proserpina focuses more on opportunity than place, the when rather than the where of *Inferno*.

57. Brown, "Proserpina, Matelda, and the Pilgrim," 33–48; Buratti, "La primavera di Dante: Percorsi intertestuali da Proserpina a Matelda," 53–123; Carrai, "Matelda, Proserpina e Flora (per *Purgatorio* XXVIII)," 49–64; Carrai, *Dante e l'antico*, 99–117. Useful as well are Ciavorella, "*Purgatorio* XXVIII: Matelda," 3–37; Pasquini, "Il canto XXVIII del *Purgatorio*," in *Gli ultimi canti del "Purgatorio,"* 121–33; Sasso, "Matelda nel suo contesto: considerazioni e ipotesi," in *La Cultura: Rivista di filosofia, letteratura e storia*, 363–442. See also his "*Forti cose a pensar mettere in versi*," 279–382.

58. Benvenuto da Imola (1375–80), *Commentary on* Purgatorio, 28.49–51, Dartmouth Dante Project, https://dante.dartmouth.edu.

59. Exciting recent work on the role of language in Dante includes that of Rosier-Catach. See above all *Le pouvoir des mots au Moyen-Âge*. Brépols, 2014. https://doi.org/10.1484/M .BHCMA-EB.6.09070802050003050501040108; Rosier-Catach (avec la collaboration de Tuedi Imbach), "La tour de Babel dans la philosophie du langage de Dante," in Von Moos, ed. *Zwischen Babel und Pfingsten*, 183–204. See also Fortuna et al., *Dante's Plurilingualism: Authority, Knowledge, Subjectivity*; Tavoni, *Qualche idea su Dante*, chap. 2.

60. Rosier-Catach, "La Tour de Babel": "*Le projet de Dante n'est pas de revenir à l'état original, au paradis définitivement perdu, à l'unité première de l'idiome hébraïque.... Si Babel est une intervention divine, tout ce qui suit, quant à l'organisation politique, sociale et linguistique ... sont du ressort du beneplacitum humain (I, ix, 6), avec toutes les conséquences positives et négatives que cela entraîne, dues essentiellement à l'infinie variabilité et instabilité humaine. Or si la confusio est divine, la variatio est humaine, et humaine devra donc être la reductio ad unum qui, grâce à la raison, l'art et la poésie, pourra y remedier ... [S]a Pentecôte à lui n'est pas un miracle, mais ... une oeuvre de l'homme, et qu'elle n'a pas pour objet le rassemblement de l'Eglise universelle, mais une unité d'un autre ordre, à la fois linguistique, littéraire, et politique*" (197).

61. Scott sums up the mission of *Purgatorio* as announcing "the imminent arrival of a messenger from God on the political plane . . . who shall set the Christian fleet on its proper course toward the harbor of temporal safety." See *Dante's Political Purgatory*, 212.

BIBLIOGRAPHY

Manuscript Sources

Cicero. *M. T. Ciceronis orationes in Verrem.* Paris: Bibliothèque nationale de France, MS lat. 7776.
Messer Gabriello Symeoni his Metamorfoseo d'Ovidio abbreviaro. English't. Cambridge, MA: Houghton, MS Eng. 1087.

Primary Sources

"On the Crafty Messenger." In *Appendix Ovidiana: Latin Poems Ascribed to Ovid in the Middle Ages.* Edited and translated by Ralph Hexter, Laura Pfuntner, and Justin Haynes, 106–33. Dumbarton Oaks Medieval Library 62. Cambridge, MA: Harvard University Press, 2020.
Apollonius of Rhodes. *Argonautica.* Edited and translated by William H. Race. Loeb Classical Library 1. Cambridge, MA: Harvard University Press, 2009.
Appian. *Roman History, Volume V: Civil Wars, Books 3–4.* Edited and translated by Brian McGing. Loeb Classical Library 543. Cambridge, MA: Harvard University Press, 2020.
Arnold of Lübeck. *Chronica Slavorum c. 1172–1209.* Edited by Johann M. Lappenberg. Monumenta Germaniae Historica, Scriptores Rerum Germanicarum 14. Hanover: Hahn, 1868.
Augustine. *Confessions.* Edited and translated by Carolyn J.-B. Hammond. Loeb Classical Library 27. Cambridge, MA: Harvard University Press, 2014.
Augustine. *De doctrina Christiana.* Edited and translated by R.P.H. Green. Oxford: Clarendon Press, 1995.
Aulus Gellius. *Attic Nights.* Edited and translated by J. C. Rolfe. Loeb Classical Library 212. Cambridge, MA: Harvard University Press, 2014.
Bede. *De Natura Rerum.* Patrologia Latina 90. Edited by J.-P. Migne. Paris, 1850.
Benevenuti de Rambaldis de Imola [Benvenuto da Imola]. *Comentum super Dantis Aldigherij Comoediam.* Edited by William Warren Vernon. Florence: G. Barbèra, 1887.
Bongars, Jacques. *Gesta Dei per Francos.* Edited and translated by Oliver J. Thatcher and Edgar Holmes McNeal. In *A Source Book for Medieval History,* 513–18. New York: Scribners, 1905.
Brunetto Latini. *Tesoretto.* Edited and translated by Julia Bolton Holloway. Garland Library of Medieval Literature 2. New York: Garland, 1981.
Callimachus. *Aetia.* In *Callimachus: vol. 1, Fragmenta,* edited by Rudolf Pfeiffer. Oxford: Clarendon Press, 1949.

The Chronicle of the Reigns of Henry II and Richard I A.D. 1169–1192 (Gesta regis Henrici secondi Benedicti abbatis). 2 vols. Edited by William Stubbs. London: Longmans, 1867.

Cicero. *On the Orator: Book 3. On Fate. Stoic Paradoxes. Divisions of Oratory.* Translated by H. Rackham. Loeb Classical Library 349. Cambridge, MA: Harvard University Press, 1942.

Cicero. *Orationes.* Second edition. 5 vols. Edited by William Peterson. Oxford: Oxford University Press, 1917; online, 2017.

Claudian. *De Raptu Proserpinae.* Edited and translated by Claire Gruzelier. Oxford: Oxford University Press, 1993.

Claudian. *De Raptu Proserpinae.* Edited by J. B. Hall. Cambridge Classical Texts and Commentaries 11. Cambridge, UK: Cambridge University Press, 1969.

Commentaire vulgate des Métamorphoses d'Ovide. Edited by Frank T. Coulson and Piero Andrea Martina. Paris: Classiques Garnier, 2021.

Conrad of Muri. [Conradus de Mure]. *Fabularius.* Edited by T. van de Loo. Corpus Christianorum, Continuatio Mediaevalis 210. Turnhout: Brepols, 2006.

Dante. *De vulgari eloquentia.* Edited and translated by Steven Botterill. Cambridge, UK: Cambridge University Press, 1996.

Dante. *Epistola* XIII [Epistola a Cangrande]. Edited by Arsenio Frugoni and Giorgio Brugnoli. In *Dante Alighieri, Opere minori,* vol. 2. Edited by Pier Vincenzo Mengaldo et al. Milan and Naples: Ricciardi, 1979.

Dante. *La* Commedia *secondo l'antica vulgata.* 4 vols. Edited by Giorgio Petrocchi. Milan: Mondadori, 1966–67.

Dante. *Monarchia.* Edited and translated by Prue Shaw. Cambridge, UK: Cambridge University Press, 1995.

Dante. *The Divine Comedy: A Verse Translation.* Translated by Allen Mandelbaum. Berkeley: University of California Press, 1980–84.

Decrees of the Ecumenical Councils, vol. 1: Nicaea to Lateran V. Edited and translated by Norman B. Tanner. Washington, DC: Georgetown University Press, 1990.

Dio Cassius. *Roman History, Volume 5: Books 46–50.* Edited and translated by Earnest Cary and Herbert B. Foster. Loeb Classical Library 82. Cambridge, MA: Harvard University Press, 1917.

Diodorus Siculus. *Library of History, Volume 3: Books 4.59–8.* Translated by C. H. Oldfather. Loeb Classical Library 340. Cambridge, MA: Harvard University Press, 1939.

Fazio degli Uberti. *Il Dittamondo e le Rime.* Edited by Giuseppe Corsi. Bari: Laterza, 1952.

Firmicus Maternus, Julius. *De errore profanarum religionum.* Turnhout: Brepols, 2010.

Freculf of Lisieux [Freculphus]. *Opera omnia.* 2 vols. Edited by Michael I. Allen. Corpus Christianorum, Continuatio Mediaevalis 169, 169A. Turnhout: Brepols, 2002.

Fulcher of Chartres. *Historia Hierosolymitana.* Edited by H. Hagenmeyer. Heidelberg: Universitätsverlag Winter, 1913.

Fulgentius, Fabius Planciades. *Opera.* Edited by R. Helm, revised by J. Preaux. Stuttgart: Teubner, 1970.

Geoffrey Malaterra. *Ruggero I e Roberto Il Guiscardo.* Translated by Vito Lo Curto. Cassino: Ciolfi, 2002.

Geoffrey of Vitry. *Commentary on Claudian,* De Raptu Proserpinae. Edited by A. K. Clarke and P. M. Giles. Mittellateinische Studien und Texte 7. Leiden: Brill, 1973.

Gervase of Tilbury. *Otia Imperialia: Recreation for an Emperor*. Edited and Translated by S. E. Banks and J. W. Binns. Oxford: Clarendon Press, 2002.

Goethe, Johann Wolfgang von. *Italian Journey <1786–1788>*. Translated by W. H. Auden and Elizabeth Mayer. New York: North Point Press, 1982.

Gregory of Tours [Gregorius Turonensis]. *Liber in gloria martyrum*. Edited by Bruno Krusch. Monumenta Germaniae Historica, Scriptores Rerum Merovingiarum 1.2. Hanover, 1885; repr. 1969.

Gregory the Great. *Dialogi*. Edited by Adalbert De Vogüé and Paul Antin. Sources Chrétiennes 265. Paris: Cerf, 1978–80.

Gregory the Great. *Li Dialoge*. Edited by W. Foerster. Paris: Champion, 1876.

Gregory the Great. *Les Dialogues de Grégoire le Grand traduits par Angier*. Edited by Renato Orengo. Paris: Société des anciens textes français, 2013.

Guido delle Colonne. *Historia destructionis Troiae*. Edited by Nathaniel Edward Griffin. Mediaeval Academy of America Publications 26. Cambridge, MA: The Mediaeval Academy of America, 1936.

Guido of Pisa. [Guido da Pisa]. *I fatti di Enea*. Edited by Francesco Fòffano. Florence: Sansoni, 1957.

Homeric Hymn to Demeter. Edited by N. J. Richardson. Oxford: Oxford University Press, 1974.

"Hugo Falcandus." *La Historia o liber de regno Sicilie*. Rome: Forzani, 1897.

Hyginus. *Fabulae*. Edited by P. K. Marshall. Munich: Saur, 2002.

Hyginus. *Miti del mondo classico*. Edited by Fabio Gasti. Santarcangelo di Romano: Rusconi, 2017.

Ibn Jubayr. *The Travels of Ibn Jubayr*. Edited by Robert Irwin and Ronald Broadhurst. London: Tauris, 2019.

Iohanni Campulu de Missina. *Libru de lu dialagu di Sanctu Gregoriu*. Edited by Salvatore Santangelo. Scuola Tipografica "Boccone del Povero." Accademia di scienze, lettere e belle arti di Palermo. Palermo, 1933.

Isidore of Seville. *De natura rerum*. (*Traité de la nature*.) Edited and translated by Jacques Fontaine. Bibliothèque de l'École des Hautes Études Hispaniques 28. Bordeaux: Féret, 1960.

Isidore of Seville. *The Etymologies*. Translated with introduction and notes by Stephen A. Barney, W. J. Lewis, J. A. Beach, and Oliver Berghof. Cambridge, UK: Cambridge University Press, 2006.

Jean of Antioche and Jean of Vignay. *Les traductions françaises des* Otia Imperialia *de Gervais de Tilbury par Jean d'Antioche et Jean de Vignay*. Edited by Cinzia Pignatelli and Dominique Gerner. Publications romanes et françaises 237. Geneva: Droz, 2006.

John of Garland. *Integumenta Ovidii*. Edited by Fausto Ghisalberti. Messina: Principato, 1933.

Lucan. *De bello civili: Book II*. Edited by E. Fantham. Cambridge, UK: Cambridge University Press, 1992.

Lucan. *De bello civili*. Translated by Susanna Braund. Oxford: Clarendon Press, 1992.

Lucretius. *De rerum natura*. 3 vols. Edited by Cyril Bailey. Oxford: Oxford University Press, 1947.

Meinhard of Bramberg. "Epistle 65." In *Briefsammlungen der Zeit Heinrichs IV*, edited by Carl Erdmann and Norbert Fickermann, 112–13. Monumenta Germaniae Historica, Briefe d. dt. Kaiserzeit 5. Weimar, 1950.

Melville, Herman. *Moby Dick*. New York: Modern Library, 1992.

Mythographi Vaticani I et II. Edited by P. Kulcsár. Corpus Christianorum, Series Latina 91C. Turnholt: Brepols, 1987.
Nonnos of Panopolis. *Dionysiaca*. 3 vols. Translated by W.H.D. Rouse. Loeb Classical Library 344, 354, 356. Cambridge, MA: Harvard University Press, 1940.
Otto of Freising. *Chronica sive historia de duabus civitatibus*. Edited by Adolf Hofmeister. Monumenta Germaniae Historica, Scriptores Rerum Germanicarum 45. Hanover and Leipzig, 1912.
Ovid. *Amores, Volumes I–II*. Edited by J. C. McKeown. ARCA 20, 22. Liverpool: Francis Cairns, 1987.
Ovid. *Fasti, Book IV*. Edited by Elaine Fantham. Cambridge Greek and Latin Classics. Cambridge, UK: Cambridge University Press, 1998.
Ovid. *Metamorphoses*. Edited by Richard J. Tarrant. Oxford: Oxford University Press, 2004.
Ovide moralisé. Edited by C. de Boer. Verhandelingen der köninklijke Nederlandse Akademie van Wetenschappen, New Series 21. Amsterdam: Johannes Müller, 1920.
Ovide moralisé. Livre I. Edited by Craig Baker, Marianne Besseyre, Mattia Cavagna, Stefania Cerrito, Olivier Collet, Massimiliano Gaggero, Yan Greub, Jean-Baptiste Guillaumin, Marylène Possamaï-Pérez, Véronique Rouchon Mouilleron, Irene Salvo, Thomas Städtler, and Richard Trachsler. Paris: Société des anciens textes français, 2018.
Peter Damian. "Vita Sancti Odilonis." In Patrologia Latina 144. Edited by J.-P. Migne. Paris, 1867.
Peter of Blois. *Opera omnia*. Patrologia Latina 207. Edited by J.-P. Migne. Paris, 1855.
Peter of Eboli. [Pietro da Eboli]. *Book in Honor of Augustus (Liber ad Honorem Augusti)*. Translated by Gwenyth Hood. Tempe: ACMRS, 2012.
Peter of Eboli. *Liber ad Honorem Augusti sive de rebus Siculis. Codex 120 II der Burgerbibliothek Bern: einer Bilderchronik der Stauferzeit*. Edited by Theo Kölzer and Marlis Stähli. Sigmaringen: Thorbecke, 1994.
Peter of Eboli. *Liber ad Honorem Augusti*. Edited by Francesco De Rosa. Cassino: Ciolfi, 2000.
Peter Tudebode. *Historia de Hierosolymitano itinere*. Translated with introduction and notes by John Hugh Hill and Laurita L. Hill. Paris: Librairie Orientaliste Paul Geuthner, 1977.
Poeti della Scuola Siciliana. 3 vols. Milan: Mondadori. 2008.
Quintilian. *Institutionis Oratoriae libri duodecim*. Edited by Michael Winterbottom. Oxford: Oxford University Press, 1970.
Recueil des Historiens des Croisades (Occidentaux). 5 vols. Paris: Imprimérie Royale, 1844–95.
Res Gestae Divi Augusti: The Achievements of the Divine Augustus. Edited and translated by P. A. Brunt and J. M. Moore. London: Oxford University Press, 1967.
Richard of Devizes. *Chronicon de rebus gestis Ricardi Primi regis Angliae*. Edited by Joseph Stevenson. London: Bohn, 1838; repr. Vaduz: Kraus Reprint, 1964.
Robert the Monk's History of the First Crusade: Historia Iherosolimitana. Edited by Carol Sweetenham. Aldershot, UK: Ashgate, 2005.
Sallust. *Fragments of the Histories. Letters to Caesar*. Edited and translated by John T. Ramsey. Loeb Classical Library 522. Cambridge, MA: Harvard University Press, 2015.
Scriptores rerum mythicarum latini tres Romae nuper reperti. 2 vols. Edited by Georg H. Bode. Celle, 1834; repr. Hildesheim: Georg Olms Verlagsbuchhandlung, 1968.
Seneca. *Moral Essays*. 2 vols. Translated by John W. Basore. Loeb Classical Library 214, 254. Cambridge, MA: Harvard University Press, 1928–32.
Seneca. *Ad Lucilium Epistulae Morales*. Edited by L. D. Reynolds. Oxford: Oxford Classical Texts, 1965.

Simone da Lentini. *La conquesta di Sichilia fatta per li Normandi*. Edited by Giuseppe Rossi Taibbi. Florence: Olschki, 1954.
Stephen of Bourbon. [Etienne de Bourbon]. *Tractatus de diversis materiis predicabilibus*. Edited by J. Berlioz and Jean-Luc Eichenlaub. Corpus Christianorum, Continuatio Mediaevalis 124. Turnhout: Brepols, 2002.
Velleius Paterculus. *The Caesarian and Augustan Narrative (2.41–93)*. Edited by A. J. Woodman. Cambridge, UK: Cambridge University Press, 1983.
Virgil. *Aeneid Book XII*. Edited by Richard Tarrant. Cambridge, UK: Cambridge University Press, 2012.
Virgil. *Aeneis: volgarizzamento senese trecentesco di Ciampolo di Meo Ugurgieri*. Edited by Claudio Lagomarsini. Pisa: Edizioni della Normale, 2018.
Virgil. *Georgics*. 2 vols. Edited by Richard Thomas. Cambridge, UK: Cambridge University Press, 1988.
Virgil. *Opera*. Edited by R.A.B. Mynors. 2 vols. Oxford: Oxford University Press, 1969.
William of Tyre. *Chronicon*. Edited by R.B.C. Huygens. Corpus Christianorum, Continuatio Mediaevalis, 63, 63A. Turnhout: Brepols, 1986.
William of Tyre. *History of Deeds Done beyond the Sea*. Translated and annotated by Emily Atwater Babcock and A. C. Krey. New York: Columbia University Press, 1943; repr., Octagon Books, 1976.

Secondary Sources

Abulafia, David. *Frederick II: A Medieval Emperor*. London: Penguin, 1988.
Agius, Dionisius A. "Who Spoke Siculo-Arabic?" In *Incontro italiano di Linguistica Camito-semitica (Afroasiatica)*, edited by Marco Moriggi, 25–33. Soveria Mannelli: Rubbettino, 2007.
Ahl, Frederick. *Metaformations: Soundplay and Wordplay in Ovid and Other Classical Poets*. Ithaca, NY: Cornell University Press, 1985.
Akbari, Suzanne Conklin, and Karla Mallette, eds. *A Sea of Languages: Rethinking the Arabic Role in Medieval Literary History*. University of Toronto Press, 2013.
Amari, Michele. *Storia dei musulmani in Sicilia*, vol. 1. Catania: Romeo Prampolini, 1933–39.
Amico, Vito. *Dizionario topografico della Sicilia*. 2 vols. Edited and translated by G. Dimarzo. Palermo, 1855–56.
Amico, Vito. *Lexicon Topographicum Siculum, in quo Siciliæ Urbes, Opida, cum vetusta, tum extantia, Montes, Flumina, Portus, adjacentes Insulæ, ac singula Loca describuntur, illustrantur*. 3 vols. Palermo, 1757.
Anderson, Carl A., and T. Keith Dix. "Vergil at the Races: the Contest of Ships in Book 5 of the *Aeneid*." *Vergilius* 59 (2013): 3–21.
Anderson, William S. "Multiple Change in the *Metamorphoses*." *Transactions of the American Philological Association* 94 (1963): 1–27.
Anderson, William S. "Review: *Ovid as an Epic Poet* by Brooks Otis." *American Journal of Philology* 89, no. 1 (1968): 93–104.
Anton, Hans Hubert. *Der Raub der Proserpina: literarische Traditionen eines erotischen Sinnbildes und mythischen Symbols*. Heidelberger Forsch. 11. Heidelberg: Universitätsverlag Winter, 1967.
Antonelli, Roberto. "La corte 'italiana' di Federico II e la letteratura europea." In *Federico II e le nuove culture, Atti del XXXI Convegno storico internazionale*, 319–45. Spoleto: Centro Italiano di studi sull'alto medioevo, 1995.

Ardizzone, Maria Luisa, ed. *Dante as Political Theorist: Reading* Monarchia. Cambridge, UK: Cambridge Scholars, 2018.

Aricò, Giuseppe. "La Sicilia nell'opera di Virgilio." In *Sicilia terra del mito: atti del convegno nazionale di studi*, Palermo 13–14 November 2004, edited by G. Nuzzo, 65–87. Palermo, 2005.

Asbridge, Thomas. *The First Crusade: A New History*. Oxford: Oxford University Press, 2004.

Aurell, Martin. *La Légende du Roi Arthur: 550–1250*. Paris: Perrin, 2007; online 2018.

Badian, Ernst. "*provincia*/province." In *Oxford Classical Dictionary*, 4th edition, edited by Simon Hornblower, Antony Spawforth, and Esther Eidinow, 1228–30. Oxford: Oxford University Press, 2012.

Baker, Craig, Mattia Cavagna, and Elisa Guadagnini, with the collaboration of Pauline Otzenberge. *Traire de Latin et Espondre: études sur la réception médiévale d'Ovide*, Rencontres 477. Paris: Classiques Garnier, 2021.

Baldo, G. "Enna: un paesaggio del mito tra storia e religio (Cicerone, *Verr.* 2, 4, 105–15)." In *Sicilia e Magna Grecia: spazio reale e spazio immaginario nella letteratura greca e latina*, edited by Guido Avezzù and Emilio Pianezzola, 17–57. Padua: Imprimitur, 1999.

Balsley, K. "Truthseeking and Truthmaking in Ovid's *Metamorphoses* 1.163–245." *Law and Literature* 23 (2011): 48–70.

Barbieri, Aroldo. "Ulisse: un eroe della conoscenza e una palinodia di Dante?" *Dante: Rivista internazionale di studi su Dante Alighieri* 8 (2011): 43–67.

Barcellona, Rossana. "Percorsi di un testo 'fortunato': I *Dialogi* di Gregorio Magno nella Sicilia medievale (secoli XII–XIV)." *Reti Medievali Rivista* 14 (2013): 33–57.

Barchiesi, Alessandro. "Endgames: Ovid's *Metamorphoses* 15 and *Fasti* 6." *Classical Closure: Reading the End in Greek and Latin Literature*, edited by Deborah H. Roberts, Francis M. Dunn, and Don Fowler, 181–208. Princeton: Princeton University Press, 1997.

Barchiesi, Alessandro. "Narrative Technique and Narratology in the *Metamorphoses*." In *The Cambridge Companion to Ovid*, edited by Philip R. Hardie, 180–99. Cambridge, UK: Cambridge University Press, 2002.

Barchiesi, Alessandro. "Venus' Masterplot: Ovid and the Homeric Hymns." In *Ovidian Transformations: Essays on the Metamorphoses and Its Reception*, edited by Philip Hardie, Alessandro Barchiesi, and Stephen Hinds, 112–26. Cambridge Philological Society Supplement 23. Cambridge, UK: Cambridge Philological Society, 1999.

Barchiesi, Alessandro. *Speaking Volumes: Narrative and Intertext in Ovid and Other Latin Poets*. London: Duckworth, 2001.

Barchiesi, Alessandro. "Colonial Readings in Virgilian Geopoetics: The Trojans at Buthrotum." In *Imagining Empire*, edited by Victoria Rimell and Markus Asper, 151–65. Heidelberg: Universitätsverlag Winter, 2017.

Barchiesi, Alessandro. "Mobilità e religione nell'*Eneide*: diaspora, culto, spazio, identità locali." In *Texte als Medium und Reflexion von Religion im römischen Reich*, edited by Dorothee Elm von der Osten et al., 13–30. Munich: Steiner, 2006.

Barolini, Teodolinda. "Dante, Teacher of His Reader." In *Approaches to Teaching Dante's Divine Comedy*, edited by Christopher Kleinhenz and Kristina Olson, 36–44. Second edition. New York: Modern Language Association of America, 2020.

Barolini, Teodolinda. "*Inferno* 26: The Epic Hero." *Commento Baroliniano*, Digital Dante. New York: Columbia University Libraries, 2018.

Barolini, Teodolinda. "*Purgatorio* 1: The Sapphire Sea." *Commento Baroliniano*, Digital Dante. New York: Columbia University Libraries, 2014.

Barolini, Teodolinda. *Dante's Poets: Textuality and Truth in the* Comedy. Princeton: Princeton University Press, 1984; online 2014.

Barolini, Teodolinda. *Undivine Comedy: Detheologizing Dante*. Princeton: Princeton University Press, 1992.

Basile, Bruno. "Tragedia di Dante, tragedia di Ulisse: lettura di *Inferno* XXVI." Revised version. In *Canto XXVI: Tragedia di Dante, tragedia di Ulisse, Lectura Dantis Romana: Cento canti per cento anni*, edited by Enrico Malato and Andrea Mazzucchi, 1.2, 823–50. Rome: Salerno, 2013.

Baur, Christine O'Connell. *Dante's Hermeneutics of Salvation: Passages to Freedom in the Divine Comedy*. Toronto: University of Toronto Press, 2007.

Benini, Rodolfo. *Origine, Sito, Forma e Dimensioni del Monte del Purgatorio e dell'Inferno Dantesco*. [Rome:] Rendiconti della Reale Accademie dei Lincei, Serie 5, vol. 25, Fasc. 11, 1916.

Bériou, Nicole, Jean-Patrice Boudet, and Irène Rosier-Catach. *Le pouvoir des mots au Moyen-Âge*. Turnhout: Brépols, 2014.

Berra, Claudia. "Catone custode della penitenza." In *Peccato, penitenza e santità nella Commedia*, edited by Marco Ballarini, Giuseppe Frasso, and Francesco Spera, 125–36. Rome: Bulzoni, 2016.

Bertram, Stephen. "The Generation Gap and *Aeneid* 5." *Vergilius* 17 (1971): 9–12.

Biggs, Thomas. "*Primus Romanorum*: Origin Stories, Fictions of Primacy, and the First Punic War." *Classical Philology* 112, no. 3 (2017): 350–67.

Black, Robert. "Classical Antiquity." In *Dante in Context*, edited by Zygmunt G. Barański and Lino Pertile, 297–318. Cambridge, UK: Cambridge University Press, 2015.

Boesch Gajano, S. "Agiografia e geografia nei Dialoghi di Gregorio Magno." In *Storia della Sicilia e tradizione agiografica nella tarda antichità. Atti del Convegno di Studi (Catania, 20–22 maggio 1986)*, edited by S. Pricoco, 209–20. Catania, 1988.

Boitani, Piero. "Ulysses and the Three Traditions." In *Dante and the Greeks*, edited by Jan M. Ziolkowski, 265–71. Washington, DC: Dumbarton Oaks, 2014.

Boitani, Piero. *The Shadow of Ulysses: Figures of a Myth*. Translated by Anita Weston. Oxford: Oxford University Press, 1994.

Borsook, Eve. *Messages in Mosaic: The Royal Programmes of Norman Sicily, 1130–1187*. Oxford: Oxford University Press, 1990.

Boyd, Barbara Weiden. "'When Ovid Reads Vergil . . .': A Response and Some Observations." *Vergilius* 48 (2002): 123–30.

Brehm, Christiane. "Der Raub der Proserpina: Studien zur Ikonographie und Ikonologie eines Ovidmythos von der Antike bis zur frühen Neuzeit." Diss., Westfälischen Wilhelms-Universität zu Münster, 1996.

Bresson, Gisèle. "*Tex a Grecis dicitur*: les epithètes divines dans le traité du troisième Mythographe du Vatican (ou Pseudo-Albrecht)." *Polymnia* 6 (2021): 65–95.

Brown, Jr., Emerson. "Proserpina, Matelda, and the Pilgrim." *Dante Studies* 89 (1971): 33–48.

Brownlee, Kevin. "Language and Desire in *Paradiso* XXVI." *Lectura Dantis* 6 (1990): 46–59.

Buratti, Giacomo. "La primavera di Dante: percorsi intertestuali da Proserpina a Matelda." *Linguistica e Letteratura* 38 (2013): 53–123.

Burgersdijk, Diederik, Richard Calis, Jorrit Kelder, Alexandra Sofroniew, Sebastiano Tusa and René van Beek, eds. *Sicily and the Sea*. Zwolle: W-Books, 2015.

Burnett, Charles S. F. "A Note on the Origins of the Third Vatican Mythographer." *Journal of the Warburg and Courtauld Institutes* 44 (1981): 160–66.

Caferro, William. "Empire, Italy, and Florence." In *Dante in Context*, edited by Zygmunt G. Barański and Lino Pertile, 9–29. Cambridge, UK: Cambridge University Press, 2015.

Cameron, Alan. *Claudian: Poetry and Propaganda at the Court of Honorius*. Oxford: Clarendon Press, 1970.

Cameron, Alan. *The Last Pagans of Rome*. Oxford: Oxford University Press, 2011.

Caracausi, Girolamo. *Arabismi medievali di Sicilia*. Palermo: Centro di studi filologici e linguistici siciliani, 1983.

Carletti, Gabriele. "Impero, stati particolari e identità nazionale in Dante." *Il Pensiero Politico: Rivista di Storia delle Idee Politiche e Sociali* 36 (2003): 293–307.

Carrai, Stefano. "Matelda, Proserpina e Flora (per *Purgatorio* XXVIII)." *L'Alighieri: Rassegna dantesca* 48, no. 30 (2007): 49–64.

Carrai, Stefano. *Dante e l'antico. L'emulazione dei classici nella* Commedia. Florence: Edizioni del Galluzzo per la Fondazione Ezio Franceschini, 2012.

Casali, Sergio. *Virgilio* Eneide 2: *Introduzione, traduzione e commento*. Pisa: Edizione della Normale, 2017.

Casanova-Robin, Hélène. "D'Homère à Ovide: le discours d'Ulysse dans l' 'armorum iudicium' (*Métamorphoses* XIII): rhétorique et spécularité." *Gaia* 7 (2003): 411–23.

Cassell, Anthony K. " 'Ulisseana': A Bibliography of Dante's Ulysses to 1981." *Italian Culture* 3 (1981): 23–45.

Cavadini, John C., ed. *Gregory the Great: A Symposium*. Notre Dame: University of Notre Dame Press, 2001.

Cavagna, Mattia, Massimiliano Gaggero and Yan Greub. "La Tradition manuscrite de l'Ovide Moralisé: Prolégomènes à une nouvelle edition." *Romania* 132 (2014): 176–213.

Cerri, Giovanni. *Dante e Ulisse: un'esegesi medioevale delle testimonianze antiche*. In *L'antico e la sua eredità: Atti del Colloquio Internazionale di Studi in onore di Antonio Garzya, Napoli 20–21 settembre 2002*, edited by Ugo Criscuolo, 87–134. Naples: D'Auria, 2004.

Chance, Jane. *Medieval Mythography*, vol. 1. Gainesville: University Press of Florida, 1994.

Charlet, Jean-Louis, ed. *Le Rapt de Proserpine*. Paris: Les Belles Lettres, 1999.

Chester, D. K., A. M. Duncan, J. E. Guest, and C.R.J. Kilburn. *Mount Etna*. Dordrecht: Springer Netherlands, 1985.

Chester, D. K., A. M. Duncan, J. E. Guest, P. A. Johnston, and J.J.L. Smolenaars. "Human Response to Etna Volcano During the Classical Period." *Geological Society Special Publication* 171 (2000): 179–88. https://doi.org/10.1144/GSL.SP.2000.171.01.14.

Cheyfitz, Eric. *The Poetics of Imperialism*. Philadelphia: University of Pennsylvania Press, 1991.

Chiarenza, Marguerite Mills. "The Imageless Vision and Dante's *Paradise*." *Dante Studies* 90 (1972): 77–91.

Ciavorella, Giuseppe. "*Purgatorio* XXVIII: Matelda," *Critica Letteraria* 39 CL.1 (2011): 3–37.

Clausen, Wendell. *A Commentary on Virgil, Eclogues*. Oxford: Oxford University Press, 1994.

Clay, Diskin. "The Metamorphosis of Ovid in Dante's *Divine Comedy*." In *A Handbook to the Reception of Ovid*, edited by John F. Miller and Carole E. Newlands, 174–86. Chichester, UK: John Wiley & Sons, 2014.

Coarelli, Filippo. "Il tempio di Diana 'in circo Flaminio' e alcuni problemi connessi." *Dialoghi di Archeologia* 2 (1968): 191–209.

Colish, Marcia L. "Acting against Conscience: Dante and the Aristotelian, Stoic, and Christian Traditions." In *Dante and the Greeks*, edited by Jan M. Ziolkowski, 83–104. Washington, DC: Dumbarton Oaks Research Library and Collection, 2014.

Comparetti, D. *Vergil in the Middle Ages*. Translated E.F.M. Benecke. Princeton: Princeton University Press, 1997.

Connolly, Joy. *The State of Speech: Rhetoric and Political Thought in Ancient Rome*. Princeton: Princeton University Press, 2007.

Consolino, Franca Ela, ed. *Ovid in Late Antiquity*. Studi e Testi Tardoantichi, 16. Turnhout: Brepols, 2018.

Conte, Gian Biagio. *Latin Literature: A History*. Translated by Joseph B. Solodow. Baltimore: Johns Hopkins University Press, 1994.

Coombe, Clare. *Claudian the Poet*. Cambridge, UK: Cambridge University Press, 2018.

Copeland, Rita. "The Curricular Classics in the Middle Ages." In *The Oxford History of Classical Reception in English Literature*, vol. 1, edited by R. Copeland, 21–33. Oxford: Oxford University Press, 2016.

Copeland, Rita. *Rhetoric, Hermeneutics, and Translation in the Middle Ages*. Cambridge, UK: Cambridge University Press, 1995.

Cornish, Alison. *Reading Dante's Stars*. New Haven: Yale University Press, 2000.

Cornish, Alison. *Vernacular Translation in Dante's Italy: Illiterate Literature*. Cambridge, UK: Cambridge University Press, 2011.

Corti, Maria. *Percorsi dell'invenzione: il linguaggio poetico e Dante*. Turin: Einaudi, 1993.

Cosentino, Augusto. *Animals in Greek and Roman Religion and Myth*. Newcastle-on-Tyne: Cambridge Scholars Press, 2016.

Costa, Iacopo. "The Will of the Emperor and Freedom in the Empire." In *Dante as Political Theorist: Reading Monarchia*, edited by Maria Luisa Ardizzone, 98–112. Cambridge, UK: Cambridge Scholars, 2018.

Coulson, Frank. "Ovid's *Metamorphoses* in the School Tradition of France, 1180–1400: Texts, Manuscript Traditions, Manuscript Settings." In *Ovid in the Middle Ages*, edited by J. Clark, F. T. Coulson, and K. McKinley, 48–82. Cambridge, UK: Cambridge University Press, 2011.

Coulson, Frank. "Ovid's Transformation in Medieval France, c. 1100–c.1350." In *Metamorphosis: The Changing Face of Ovid in Medieval and Early Modern Europe*, edited by Alison Keith and Stephen Rupp, 33–60. Toronto: University of Toronto Press, 2007.

Coulson, Frank. "The Vulgate Commentary on Ovid's *Metamorphoses*." *Mediaevalia* 13 (1987): 29–61.

Cox, Virginia, and John O. Ward, eds. *The Rhetoric of Cicero in Its Medieval and Early Renaissance Commentary Tradition*. Leiden: Brill, 2006.

Curtius, E. R. *European Literature and the Latin Middle Ages*. Translated by Willard R. Trask. Princeton: Princeton University Press, 1953.

Dameron, George. "Church and Orthodoxy." In *Dante in Context*, edited by Zygmunt G. Barański and Lino Pertile, 85–86. Cambridge, UK: Cambridge University Press, 2015.

Davis, C. T. "Dante and the Empire." In *The Cambridge Companion to Dante*, edited by Rachel Jacoff, 257–69. Cambridge, UK: Cambridge University Press, 2007.

Davis, Peter J. *Ovid and Augustus: A Political Reading of Ovid's Erotic Poems*. London: Duckworth, 2006.

d'Onofrio, Mario, ed. *I Normanni: popolo d'Europa 1030–1200*. Venice: Marsilio, 1994.

Dragonetti, Roger. "Dante and Frederick II: The Poetry of History." Translated by Judith P. Shoaf. *Exemplaria* 1 (1989): 1–15.

Dronke, Peter. "A Note on Pamphilius." *Journal of the Warburg and Courtauld Institutes* 42 (1979): 225–30.

Dubouloz, Julien, and Sylvie Pittia, eds. *La Sicile de Cicéron: Lectures des Verrines*. Besançon: Presses Universitaires de Franche-Comté, 2007.

Duc, Thierry. *Le* De raptu Proserpinae *de Claudien: Reflexions sur une actualisation de la mythologie*. Bern: Peter Lang, 1995.

Duffey, T. "The Proserpinean Metamyth: Claudian's *De raptu Proserpinae* and Alan of Lille's *Anticlaudianus*." *Florilegium* V (1983): 105–39.

Durling, Robert M. " 'Io son venuto': Seneca, Plato and the Microcosm." *Dante Studies* 93 (1975): 95–130. Reprinted in *Dante: The Critical Complex. Vol. 1. The Poet's Life and the Invention of Poetry*, edited by Richard Lansing, 349–83. New York & London: Routledge, 2003.

Edbury, Peter W., and John Gordon Rowe. *William of Tyre: Historian of the Latin East*. Cambridge, UK: Cambridge University Press, 1988.

Elliott, Kathleen O. and J. P. Elder. "A Critical Edition of the Vatican Mythographers." *Transactions of the American Philological Association* 78 (1947): 189–207.

Ellsworth, J. D. "Ovid's 'Odyssey': *Met.* 13.623–14.608." *Mnemosyne* 41 (1988): 333–40.

Engelbrecht, Wilken. "Fulco, Arnulf, and William: Twelfth-Century Views on Ovid in Orléans." *Journal of Medieval Latin* 18 (2008): 52–73.

Erdmann, Carl. *The Origin of the Idea of Crusade*. Translated by Marshall W. Baldwin and Walter Goffart. Princeton: Princeton University Press, 1977.

Farrell, Joseph. *Juno's* Aeneid: *A Battle for Heroic Identity*. Princeton: Princeton University Press, 2021.

Farrell, Joseph. *Latin Language and Latin Culture from Ancient to Modern Times*. Cambridge, UK: Cambridge University Press, 2001.

Feeney, Denis. *Beyond Greek: The Beginnings of Latin Literature*. Cambridge, MA: Harvard University Press, 2016.

Feeney, Denis. "*Tenui . . . latens discrimine*: Spotting the Difference in Statius' *Achilleid*." *Materiali e discussioni per l'analisi dei testi classici* 52 (2004): 85–105.

Feeney, Denis. *The Gods in Epic*. Oxford: Oxford University Press, 1991.

Feldherr, Andrew. "Ships of State: *Aeneid* 5 and Augustan Circus Spectacle." *Classical Antiquity* 14, no. 2 (1995): 245–65.

Feldherr, Andrew. *Playing Gods: Ovid's* Metamorphoses *and the Politics of Fiction*. Princeton: Princeton University Press, 2010.

Fenzi, Enrico. "Dante e Seneca." In *I classici di Dante*, edited by Paola Allegretti and Marcello Ciccuto, 177–213. Florence: Le Lettere, 2018.

Fenzi, Enrico. "Seneca e Dante: da Alessandro Magno a Ulisse." In *Studi sul canone letterario del Trecento: per Michelangelo Picone*, 67–78. Ravenna: Longo, 2003.

Ferrante, Joan M. *The Political Vision of the* Divine Comedy. Princeton: Princeton University Press, 1984; online 2014.

Fielding, Ian. *Transformations of Ovid in Late Antiquity*. Cambridge, UK: Cambridge University Press, 2017.

Finley, M. I. *Ancient Sicily*, rev. ed. New York: Rowman and Littlefield, 1979.

Fo, A. "Osservazioni su alcune questioni relative al *De raptu Proserpinae* di Claudiano," *Quaderni catanesi di studi classici e medievali* 1 (1979): 385–415.

Foley, Helene. *The Homeric Hymn to Demeter*. Princeton: Princeton University Press, 1994.

Forti, Carla. "Ulisse dal *nostos* al *folle volo*: fonti classiche e tradizione medievale in *Inf.* XXVI." *Nuova Rivista di Letteratura Italiana* 9 (2006): 9–24.

Fortuna, Sara, Manuele Gragnolati, and Jürgen Trabant. *Dante's Plurilingualism: Authority, Knowledge, Subjectivity*. London: Legenda, 2010; online 2017.

Franke, William. *Dante's Interpretive Journey*. Chicago: University of Chicago Press, 1996.

Fränkel, Hermann. *Ovid: A Poet Between Two Worlds*. Berkeley: University of California Press, 1945.

Fratantuono, Lee. "*Nondum Proserpina abstulerat*: Persephone in the *Aeneid*." *Revue des Etudes Anciennes* 114 (2012): 423–34.

Fratantuono, Lee. "*Tumulum antiquae Cereris*: Virgil's Ceres and the Harvest of Troy." *Bollettino di Studi Latini* 45 (2015): 456–72.

Frantantuono, Lee M. and R. Alden Smith. *Virgil, Aeneid 5: Text, Translation and Commentary*. Leiden: Brill, 2015.

Frazel, Thomas D. *The Rhetoric of Cicero's "In Verrem."* Göttingen: Vandenhoeck and Ruprecht, 2009.

Freccero, John. "Dante's Prologue Scene." In *Dante: The Critical Complex*, vol. 7, edited by Richard Lansing, 63–87. New York: Routledge, 2003.

Freccero, John. *Dante: The Poetics of Conversion*. Cambridge, MA: Harvard University Press, 1986.

Fubini, Mario. *Il peccato di Ulisse e altri scritti danteschi*. Milan-Naples: Riccardo Ricciardi, 1966.

Gambale, Giacomo. "La Dimensione morale del linguaggio: l'exemplum di Ulisse." In *La lingua di fuoco: Dante e la filosofia del linguaggio*, 83–132. Rome: Città Nuova, 2012.

Galinsky, G. Karl. *Aeneas, Sicily and Rome*. Princeton: Princeton University Press, 1969.

Gee, Emma. *Mapping the Afterlife: From Homer to Dante*. New York: Oxford University Press, 2019.

Geymonat, Mario. "Callimachus at the End of Aeneas' Narration." *Harvard Studies in Classical Philology* 95 (1993): 323–31.

Ghisalberti, Fausto. "Giovanni del Virgilio espositore delle *Metamorfosi*." *Giornale dantesco* 34 (1933): 1–110.

Gillespie, Vincent. "From the Twelfth Century to c. 1450." In *The Cambridge History of Literary Criticism*, vol. 2, edited by Alastair Minnis and Ian Johnson, 145–236. Cambridge, UK: Cambridge University Press, 2005.

Ginsberg, Warren. "Ovid's *Metamorphoses* and the Politics of Interpretation." *Classical Journal* 84.3 (1989): 222–31.

Giusti, Elena. *Carthage in Virgil's* Aeneid: *Staging the Enemy under Augustus*. Cambridge, UK: Cambridge University Press, 2018.

Gladhill, Bill. "Gods, Caesars and Fate in *Aeneid* 1 and *Metamorphoses* 15." *Dictynna* 9 (2012), n.p.

Glazewski, J. "The Function of Vergil's Funeral Games." *Classical World* 66 (1972): 85–96.

Gorman, Vanessa B. "Vergilian Models for Scylla in the *Ciris*." *Vergilius* 41 (1959): 35–48.
Gowers, Emily. "Dangerous Sailing: Valerius Maximus and the Suppression of Sextus Pompeius." *Classical Quarterly*, New Series 60 (2010): 446–49.
Gowers, Emily. "The Road to Sicily: Lucilius to Seneca." *Ramus* 40 (2011): 168–97.
Gowing, Alain M. *The Triumviral Narratives of Appian and Cassius Dio*. Ann Arbor: University of Michigan Press, 1992.
Graf, A. "Artu nell'Etna." In *Miti, leggende e superstizioni del Medio Evo*, 2 vols., edited by A. Graf, 301–35. Bologna: A. Forni, 1965.
Granara, William. *Ibn Hamis the Sicilian: Eulogist for a Falling Homeland*. London: OneWorld, 2021.
Granara, William. *Narrating Muslim Sicily: War and Peace in the Medieval Mediterranean World*. London: Tauris, 2019.
Gransden, K. W. *Aeneid 8*. Edited by K. W Gransden. Cambridge Greek and Latin Classics. Cambridge, UK: Cambridge University Press, 1976.
Grayson, Cecil, ed. *The World of Dante*. Oxford: Clarendon Press, 2004.
Guidoboni, Emanuela, Cecilia Ciuccarelli, Dante Mariotti, Alberto Comastri, and Maria Giovanna Bianchi, eds. *L'Etna nella storia : catalogo delle eruzioni dall'antichità alla fine del XVII secolo*. Bologna: Bononia University Press, 2014.
Gura, David. "A Critical Edition and Study of Arnulf of Orléans' Philological Commentary to Ovid's *Metamorphoses*." PhD diss, The Ohio University, 2010. http://rave.ohiolink.edu/etdc/view?acc_num=osu1274904386.
Habinek, Thomas N. *The Politics of Latin Literature: Writing, Identity, and Empire in Ancient Rome*. Princeton: Princeton University Press, 1998.
Hadas, Moses. *Sextus Pompey*. New York: AMS Press, 1966.
Hall, J. B., ed. *Claudian*, De Raptu Proserpinae. Cambridge, UK: Cambridge University Press, 1969.
Hardie, Philip, ed. and Gioachino Chiarini, trans. *Ovidio*, Metamorfosi, Volume VI: Libri XIII–XV. Milano: Fondazione Lorenzo Valla, 2015.
Hardie, Philip. "Ships and Ship-Names in the *Aeneid*." *Homo Viator: Classical Essays for John Bramble*, edited by Michael Whitby, Philip Hardie, and Mary Whitby, 163–71. Bristol: Bristol Classical Press and Bolchazy-Carducci, 1987.
Hardie, Philip. "Warring Words: Ovid's 'Contest for the Arms of Achilles' (*Met.* 13.1–398)." In *Contests and Rewards in the Homeric Epics: Proceedings of the 10th International Symposium on the Odyssey (15–19 September 2004)*, edited by M. Paizi-Apostolopoulou, M. Rengakos, and A. Tsagalis, 189–98. Ithaca, Greece: Kentro, 2007.
Hardie, Philip. *Virgil's Aeneid: Cosmos and Imperium*. Oxford: Clarendon Press, 1986.
Harris, W. V. *War and Imperialism in Republican Rome, 327–70 B.C.* Oxford: Clarendon Press, 1979.
Härter, Andreas. *Digressionen: Studien zum Verhältnis von Ordnung und Abweichung in Rhetorik und Poetik*. Munich: Fink, 2000.
Hawkes, Terence. *Shakespeare in the Present*. London: Routledge, 2002.
Hawkins, Peter S. "Watching Matelda." In *The Poetry of Allusion: Virgil and Ovid in Dante's Commedia*, edited by R. Jacoff and J. T. Schnapp, 181–201. Stanford: Stanford University Press, 1991.
Hays, Gregory. "Tales out of School: Grammatical Culture in Fulgentius the Mythographer." In *Latin Grammar and Rhetoric: From Classical Theory to Medieval Practice*, edited by C. D. Lanham, 22–47. New York: Continuum, 2002.

Hays, Gregory. "The Mythographic Tradition after Ovid." In *A Handbook to the Reception of Ovid*, edited by John F. Miller and Carole E. Newlands, 129–43. Chichester: Wiley & Sons, 2014.

Hexter, Ralph. "Imitating Troy: A Reading of *Aeneid* 3." In *Reading Vergil's* Aeneid*: An Interpretive Guide*, edited by Christine G. Perkell, 64–79. Norman: University of Oklahoma Press, 1999.

Hexter, Ralph. "Ovid in the Middle Ages: Exile, Mythographer, and Lover." In *Brill's Companion to Ovid*, edited by Barbara Weiden Boyd, 413–42. Leiden: Brill, 2002.

Hinds, Stephen. *Allusion and Intertext: Dynamics of Appropriation in Roman Poetry*. New York: Cambridge University Press, 1998.

Hinds, Stephen. "Claudianism in the *De Raptu Proserpinae*." In *Generic Interfaces in Latin Literature: Encounters, Interactions, and Transformations*, edited by Theodore D. Papanghelis, Stephen J. Harrison, and Stavros Frangoulidis, 169–92. Berlin: De Gruyter, 2013.

Hinds, Stephen. "Return to Enna: Ovid and Ovidianism in Claudian's *De raptu Proserpinae*." In *Repeat Performances: Ovidian Repetition and the* Metamorphoses, edited by Laurel Fulkerson and Tim Stover, 249–78. Madison: University of Wisconsin Press, 2016.

Hinds, Stephen. *The Metamorphosis of Persephone: Ovid and the Self-Conscious Muse*. Cambridge, UK: Cambridge University Press, 1987.

Hollander, Robert. "Le opere di Virgilio nella *Commedia* di Dante." In *Dante e la "Bella Scola" della poesia: autorità e sfida poetica*, edited by A. Iannucci, 247–343. Ravenna: Longo, 1993.

Hollander, Robert and Jean Hollander. *Purgatorio*. New York: Doubleday, 2003.

Holloway, R. Ross. *The Archaeology of Ancient Sicily*. London: Routledge, 1991.

Holmes, Olivia. "Dante's Choice and Romance Narratives of Two Beloveds." *Dante Studies* 121 (2003): 109–47.

Holmes, Olivia. *Dante's Two Beloveds: Ethics and Erotics in the* Divine Comedy. New Haven: Yale University Press, 2008.

Honess, Claire E. "Divided City, Slavish Italy, Universal Empire." In *Vertical Readings in Dante's* Comedy*: Volume 1*, edited by George Corbett and Heather Webb, 119–42. Cambridge, UK: Open Book Publishers, 2015.

Honess, Claire E. *From Florence to the Heavenly City: The Poetry of Citizenship in Dante*. London: Legenda, 2006.

Horden, Peregrine and Nicholas Purcell. *The Corrupting Sea*. Oxford: Blackwell, 2000.

Horsfall, Nicholas. "Aeneas the Colonist." *Vergilius* 35 (1989): 8–27.

Horsfall, Nicholas. *Virgil,* Aeneid *2: A Commentary*. Leiden: Brill, 2008.

Horsfall, Nicholas. *Virgil,* Aeneid *3: A Commentary*. Mnemosyne Supplement 273. Leiden: Brill, 2006.

Hult, David. "Ovide Moralisé: Anonymat et autorisé." In *Ovidius explanatus*, edited by Simone Biancardi, Prunelle Deleville, Francesco Montorsi, and Marylène Possamaï-Pérez, 141–53. Paris: Classiques Garnier, 2018.

Hyde, Walter Woodburn. "The Volcanic History of Etna." *Geographical Review* 1.6 (1916): 401–18.

Issa, Mireille. *La Version latine et l'adaption française de l'*Historia Rerum in Partibus Transmarinis Gestarum *de Guillaume de Tyr, Livres XI–XVIII: étude comparative fondée sur le recueil des historiens des croisades–historiens occidentaux*. The Medieval Translator 13. Turnhout: Brepols, 2010.

Jacoff, Rachel. "Intertextualities in Arcadia: *Purgatorio* 30.49–51." In *The Poetry of Allusion: Virgil and Ovid in Dante's* Commedia, edited by R. Jacoff and J. T. Schnapp, 131–44. Stanford: Stanford University Press, 1991.

Jakobi, R. "On the Early Influence of Claudian's *De Raptu Proserpinae*." *Hermes* 126 (1998): 507.

Johnson, Patricia J. "Constructions of Venus in Ovid's *Metamorphoses* V." *Arethusa* 29 (1996): 125–49.

Johnson, Patricia J. *Ovid before Exile: Art and Punishment in the* Metamorphoses. Madison: University of Wisconsin Press, 2008.

Jung, Marc-René. "Aspects de l'Ovide Moralisé." In *Ovidius redivivus: von Ovid zu Dante*, edited by M. Picone and B. Zimmermann, 149–72. Stuttgart: M & P, 1994.

Jung, Marc-René. "Ovide, texte, translateur et gloses dans les manuscrits de l'*Ovide moralisé*." In *The Medieval Opus: Imitation, Rewriting, and Transmission in the French Tradition*, edited by D. Kelly, 75–98. Amsterdam: Rodopi, 1996.

Kallendorf, Craig. "Virgil, Dante and Empire in Italian Thought, 1300–1500." *Vergilius* 34 (1988): 44–69.

Kantorowicz, Ernst H. *Frederick II: 1194–1250*. New York: Ungar, 1967.

Kassler-Taub, Elizabeth. "At the Threshold of the Mediterranean: Architecture, Urbanism, and Identity in Early Modern Sicily." PhD diss., Harvard University, 2017.

Kay, Tristan. *Dante's Lyric Redemption*. Oxford: Oxford University Press, 2016.

Kellum, Barbara A. "Sculptural Programs and Propaganda." In *Age of Augustus*, edited by Rolf Winkes, 169–76. Providence, RI: Brown University Press, 1985.

Kingsley, K. Scarlett and Richard Parry. "Empedocles." In *The Stanford Encyclopedia of Philosophy* (Summer 2020 Edition), edited by Edward N. Zalta. https://plato.stanford.edu/archives/sum2020/entries/empedocles/.

Kingsley, Peter. *Ancient Philosophy, Mystery, and Magic: Empedocles and Pythagorean Tradition*. Oxford: Clarendon Press, 1995.

Knox, Peter E, ed. "Commenting on Ovid." In *A Companion to Ovid*, edited by Peter E. Knox, 327–40. Oxford: Wiley-Blackwell, 2009.

Kupfer, Marcia A. *Art and Optics in the Hereford Map: An English Mappa Mundi, c. 1300*. New Haven: Yale University Press, 2016.

Langlois, Charles Victor. *La Connaissance de la nature et du monde au Moyen Âge*. Paris: Hachette, 1911.

Lansing, Richard, ed. *Dante Encyclopedia*. London: Routledge, 2010.

Lanzafame, Iolanda. "Linguistic Contaminations in Sicily: From the Roman Rule to the Present." In *Sicily and the Mediterranean: Migration, Exchange, Reinvention*, edited by Claudia Karagoz and Giovanna Summerfield, 111–23. New York: Palgrave Macmillan, 2015.

Lazzeretti, Alessandra *M. Tulli Ciceronis, In C. Verrem actionis secundae liber quartus (De signis): commento storico e archeologico*. Pisa: ETS, 2006.

Le Goff, Jacques. *La naissance du Purgatoire*. Paris: Gallimard, 1981.

Leigh, Matthew. "Early Roman Epic and the Maritime Moment." *Classical Philology* 105 (2010): 265–80.

Lerner, Robert E. *Ernst Kantorowicz: A Life*. Princeton: Princeton University Press, 2017.

Leroux, Virginie. "L'Etna dans les récits antiques du rapt de Proserpine." In *Mythologies de l'Etna*, edited by D. Bertrand, 33–55. Clermont-Ferrand: Presses Universitaires Blaise Pascal, 2004.

Levenstein, Jessica. "Resurrecting Ovid's Pierides: Dante's Invocation to Calliope in *Purgatorio* 1.7–2." *Dante Studies* 126 (2008): 1–19.
Lintott, A. W. *Imperium Romanum: Politics and Administration*. London: Routledge, 1993.
Lobur, J. "*Festinatio* (Haste), *Brevitas* (Concision), and the Generation of Imperial Ideology in Velleius Paterculus." *Transactions of the American Philological Association* 137 (2007): 211–30.
Lombardi, Elena. "26. The Poetics of Trespassing." In *Vertical Readings in Dante's Comedy*, vol. 3, edited by George Corbett and Heather Webb, 71–88. Cambridge, UK: Open Book Publishers, 2017.
Loud, Graham A., and Thomas Wiedemann, eds. *The History of the Tyrants of Sicily, by "Hugo Falcandus," 1154–69*. Manchester, UK: Manchester University Press, 1998; online 2013.
MacDonald, Fiona. "The Path through the Woods: An Alternative Interpretation of Dante's *selva oscura*." In *Percorsi Danteschi*, edited by Antonio Pagliaro, 53–61. Melbourne: The Italian Program, La Trobe University, 2005.
Mackay, Jamie. *The Invention of Sicily: A Mediterranean History*. London: Verso, 2021.
Mallette, Karla. *European Modernity and the Arab Mediterranean: Toward a New Philology and a Counter-Orientalism*. Philadelphia: University of Pennsylvania Press, 2010.
Mallette, Karla. *The Kingdom of Sicily, 1100–1250: A Literary History*. Philadelphia: University of Pennsylvania Press, 2005.
Marchesi, Simone. *Dante and Augustine: Linguistics, Poetics, Hermeneutics*. Toronto: University of Toronto Press, 2011.
Marks, Raymond, "Off the Beaten Path: Generic Conflict and Narrative Delay in *Punica* 14." *Classical Journal* 112 (2017): 461–93.
Martelli, Francesca. *Ovid's Revisions: The Editor as Author*. Cambridge, UK: Cambridge University Press, 2013.
Matthew, Donald. *The Norman Kingdom of Sicily*. Cambridge, UK: Cambridge University Press, 1992.
Mayer, Hans Eberhard. *The Crusades*. Translated by John Gillingham. New York: Oxford University Press, 1988.
Mayer, Roland. "Seneca Redivivus." In *The Cambridge Companion to Seneca*, edited by Shadi Bartsch and Alessandro Schiesaro, 277–88. Cambridge, UK: Cambridge University Press, 2015.
Mazzara, Federica. "Persephone: Her Mythical Return to Sicily." *Arco Journal* (2003): 1–55.
McKitterick, Rosamund. *History and Memory in the Carolingian World*. Cambridge, UK: Cambridge University Press, 2004.
Meek, Mary. *Historia Destructionis Troiae*. Bloomington: Indiana University Press, 1974.
Meeks, Wayne, and John Fitzgerald. *The Writings of St. Paul: Annotated Texts, Reception and Criticism*. New York: W. W. Norton, 2007.
Mendolia, Anna. "Servius, ad *Aen*. VI. 136." *Atti della Accademia Peloritana dei Pericolanti, Classe di Lettere, Filosofia e Belle Arti* 65 (1989): 253–66.
Mengaldo, Pier Vincenzo. *Linguistica e retorica di Dante*. Pisa: Nistri-Lischi, 1978.
Mercatanti, Leonardo. "Etna and the Perception of Volcanic Risk." *Geographical Review* 103 (2013): 486–97. https://doi.org/10.1111/j.1931-0846.2013.00016.x.
Mercuri, Roberto. "Ovidio e Dante: le *Metamorfosi* come ipotesto della *Commedia*." *Dante: Rivista internazionale di studi su Dante Alighieri* 6 (2009): 21–37.

Mezzadroli, Giuseppina. *Seneca in Dante*. Florence: Le Lettere, 1990.

Miles, Margaret. *Art as Plunder*. Cambridge, UK: Cambridge University Press, 2008.

Miller, John F. "Ovidian Allusion and the Vocabulary of Memory." *Materiali e discussioni per l'analisi dei testi classici* 30 (1993): 153–64.

Moreira, Isabel. *Heaven's Purge: Purgatory in Late Antiquity*. Oxford: Oxford University Press, 2010.

Morgan, Alison. *Dante and the Medieval Other World*. Cambridge, UK: Cambridge University Press, 1990

Moro, Costantino. "Il vulcano degli dei: geografia del mito, tradizione poetica e tecnica compositiva nel *De raptu Proserpinae* di Claudiano." In *Sicilia e Magna Grecia: spazio reale e spazio immaginario nella letteratura greca e latina*, edited by Guido Avezzù and Emilio Pianezzola, 171–226. Studi, testi, documenti 10. Padova: Imprimitur, 1999.

Morreale, Laura K. and Nicholas L. Paul, eds. *The French of Outremer: Communities and Communications in the Crusading Mediterranean*. Fordham Series in Medieval Studies. New York: Fordham University Press, 2018.

Moser, Marianne. "Ovide lecteur d'Empédocle: pour une nouvelle réinterprétation du fr. 6 DK." *Bulletin de l'Association Guillaume Budé* 1 (2017): 80–96.

Most, Glenn. "Dante's Greeks." *Arion* 13 (2006): 15–48.

Munro, Dana C. "The Speech of Pope Urban II at Clermont." *American Historical Review* 11 (1906): 231–42.

Munro, Dana C. *Urban and the Crusaders*. Philadelphia: Dept. of History of the University of Pennsylvania, 1910.

Murray, Alexander. "Counselling in Medieval Confession." In *Handling Sin: Confession in the Middle Ages*, edited by Peter Biller and A. J. Minnis, 63–77. Rochester, NY: Boydell & Brewer, 1998.

Nardi, Bruno. "La tragedia d'Ulisse." In *Dante e la cultura medievale*, edited by P. Mazzantini, 125–34. Bari: Laterza, 1983.

Neil, Bronwen, and Matthew dal Santo, eds. *A Companion to Gregory the Great*. Leiden: Brill, 2013.

Nelis, Damien. *Vergil's* Aeneid *and the* Argonautica *of Apollonius Rhodius*. ARCA 39. Leeds: Francis Cairns, 2001.

Nelis, Damien and Jocelyne Nelis-Clément, "Vergil, *Georgics* 1.1–42 and the *Pompa Circensis*." *Dictynna* 8 (2011): n.p.

Nicholson, Helen J., and Susan Edgington, eds. *Deeds Done beyond the Sea: Essays on William of Tyre, Cyprus and the Military Orders Presented to Peter Edbury*. Farnham, UK: Ashgate, 2014.

Norwich, John Julius. *The Middle Sea: A History of the Mediterranean*. London: Chatto & Windus, 2006.

Nugent, S. Georgia. "Vergil's Voice of the Women in *Aeneid* V." *Arethusa* 25 (1992): 255–92.

O'Hara, James J. "Callimachean Influences on Vergilian Etymological Wordplay." *Classical Journal* 96 (2001): 369–400.

O'Hara, James J. *Inconsistency in Roman Epic: Studies in Catullus, Lucretius, Vergil, Ovid and Lucan*. Cambridge, UK: Cambridge University Press, 2007.

O'Hara, James J. *True Names: Vergil and the Alexandrian Tradition of Etymological Wordplay*. Ann Arbor: University of Michigan Press, 1996.

Padoan, Giorgio. *Il pio Enea, l'empio Ulisse: tradizione classica e intendimento medievale in Dante.* Ravenna: Longo, 1977.

Pagliaro, Antonino. *Ulisse: Ricerche semantiche sulla Divina Commedia.* 2 vols. Messina and Florence: D'Anna, 2010.

Papaioannou, Sophia. *Epic Succession and Dissension.* Untersuchungen zur antiken Literatur und Geschichte 73. Berlin: De Gruyter, 2005.

Paris, Gaston. "La Sicile dans la littérature française du Moyen Age." *Romania* 5 (1876): 108–13.

Parodi, E. G. "I rifacimenti e le traduzioni italiane dell'*Eneide* di Virgilio prima del Rinascimento." *Studi di Filologia Romanzo* 2 (1887): 97–366.

Pasquini, Emilio. "Il canto XXVIII del *Purgatorio*." In *Gli ultimi canti del* Purgatorio, edited by Fabio Dainotti, 121–33. Roma: Bulzoni, 2010.

Pasquini, Emilio. "Presenze di Seneca in Dante." In *Seneca nella coscienza dell'Europa*, edited by Ivano Dionigi, 111–36. Milan: Mondadori, 1999.

Pavlock, Barbara. *The Image of the Poet in Ovid's Metamorphoses.* Madison: University of Wisconsin Press, 2009.

Pavlovskis, Z. "*Aeneid* V: The Old and the Young." *Classical Journal* 71.3 (1976): 193–205.

Peirano Garrison, Irene. *Persuasion, Rhetoric and Roman Poetry.* Cambridge, UK: Cambridge University Press, 2019.

Pellegrini, Giovan Battista. *Terminologia geografica araba in Sicilia.* Trieste: Universitá degli Studi di Trieste, 1961.

Pensabene, Giuseppe. *La Guerra tra Cesare Ottaviano e Sesto Pompeo (43–36 a.C.) e le corrispondenze attuali.* Rome: Gangemi, 1991.

Pepin, Ronald. *The Vatican Mythographers.* New York: Fordham University Press, 2008.

Peterson, W. "The MSS. of the *Verrines*." *Journal of Philology* 30 (1907): 161–207.

Peterson, W. "The Vatican Codex of Cicero's *Verrines*." *American Journal of Philology* 26 (1905): 409–36.

Petrocchi, Giorgio. *La Commedia secondo l'antica vulgata.* Milan: Mondadori, 1966–67. https://digitaldante.columbia.edu/.

Pfuntner, Laura. *Urbanism and Empire in Roman Sicily.* Austin: University of Texas Press, 2019.

Picone, Michelangelo. "Dante, Ovidio, e il mito di Ulisse." *Lettere italiane* 431(199): 500–516.

Picone, Michelangelo. "Giullari d'Italia: una lettura del 'Detto del gatto lupesco.' " *Versants* 28 (1995): 73.

Picot, Jean-Claude. "La brillance de Nestis (Empédocle, fr. 96)." *Revue de Philosophie Ancienne* 26 (2008): 75–100.

Pihas, Gabriel. "Dante's Ulysses: Stoic and Scholastic Models of the Literary Reader's Curiosity and *Inferno* 26." *Dante Studies* 121 (2003): 1–24.

Poddi, E. "L'invidia di Ibla: primavera e metaletteratura in Claudiano." In *Il dilettoso monte: raccolta di saggi di filologia e tradizione classica*, edited by Massimo Gioseffi, 113–37. Milan: LED, 2004.

Portale, Elisa Chiara. "Le 'nymphai' e l'acqua in Sicilia: contesti rituali e morfologia dei votivi." In *Cultura e religione delle acque: Atti del Convegno interdisciplinare "Qui fresca l'acqua mormora...",* edited by Anna Calderone, 169–91. Archaeologica 167. Rome: G. Bretschneider, 2012.

Possamaï-Pérez, M. *L'Ovide moralisé: Essai d'interprétation.* Paris: Champion, 2006.

Possamaï-Pérez, M. "L'Ovide moralisé du XIVe siècle: mort ou renaissance des *Métamorphoses* d'Ovide?" *Acta Universitatis Lodziensis. Folia Litteraria Romanica* 9 (2014): 7–15.

Powell, Anton. "'An Island Amid the Flames': The Strategy and Imagery of Sextus Pompeius, 43–36 BC." In *Sextus Pompeius,* edited by Anton Powell, Kathryn Welch, and Alain M. Gowing, 103–33. London: Classical Press of Wales, 2002.

Powell, Anton. "The Peopling of the Underworld (Aen. 6.608–27)." In *Vergil's Aeneid: Augustan Epic and Political Context,* edited by Hans-Peter Stahl, 85–100. Swansea: Classical Press of Wales, 1998.

Powell, Anton and Kathryn Welch, eds. *Sextus Pompeius.* Swansea: Classical Press of Wales, 2002.

Powell, James M. *The Crusades, the Kingdom of Sicily and the Mediterranean.* Aldershot, UK: Ashgate, 2007.

Prag, J. "Sicily and Sardinia-Corsica: The First Provinces." In *A Companion to Roman Imperialism,* edited by B. Dexter Hoyos, 53–65. History of Warfare 81. Leiden: Brill, 2013.

Prag, J. *Sicilia nutrix plebis Romanae: Rhetoric, Law, and Taxation in Cicero's Verrines.* Bulletin of the Institute of Classical Studies, Supplement 97. London: Institute of Classical Studies, 2007.

Prag, Jonathan. "Sicily and the Punic Wars." In *Sicily and the Sea,* edited by Diederik Burgersdijk, Richard Calis, Jorrit Kelder, Alexandra Sofroniew, Sebastiano Tusa, and René van Beek, 83–86. Zwolle: W-Books, 2015.

Putnam, Michael C. J. *The Poetry of the Aeneid.* Cambridge, MA: Harvard University Press, 1966.

Putnam, Michael C. J. *Virgil's Aeneid: Interpretation and Influence.* Chapel Hill: University of North Carolina Press, 1995.

Putnam, Michael C. J. *Virgil's Epic Designs: Ekphrasis in the Aeneid.* New Haven: Yale University Press, 1998.

Putnam, Michael C. J. "Virgil's Inferno." In *The Poetry of Allusion: Virgil and Ovid in Dante's Commedia,* eds. R. Jacoff and J. T. Schnapp, 94–112. Stanford: Stanford University Press, 1991.

Quacquarelli, Antonio. "La Sicilianità di Firmico Materno: i suoi Matheseos libri e la cultura Cristiana delle scienze nel IV secolo." *Cristianesimo in Sicilia dalle origini a Gregorio Magno.* Edited by Vincenzo Messana and Salvatore Pricoco. Caltinessetta: Edizioni del Seminario, 1987.

Quint, David. *Epic and Empire.* Princeton: Princeton University Press, 1993.

Quint, David. *Virgil's Double Cross: Design and Meaning in the Aeneid.* Princeton: Princeton University Press, 2018.

Rajna, Pio. *La materia e la forma della Divina Commedia: i mondi oltraterreni nelle letterature classiche e nelle medievali,* edited by Claudia Di Fonzo. Florence: Le Lettere, 1998 [1874].

Rauk, John Neil. "Macrobius, Cornutus, and the Cutting of Dido's Lock." *Classical Philology* 90 (1995): 345–54

Reeve, Michael D. "The Medieval Tradition of Cicero's Verrines." *Exemplaria Classica* 20 (2016): 19–90.

Regn, Gerhard. "Mythopoiesis, Cosmogony and Authorship in Dante's Commedia—Virgil's 'Perhaps' in *Inf.* XXXIV, 106–26." *Germanisch-Romanische Monatsschrift* 63 (2013): 313–28.

Reynolds, L. D. *Texts and Transmission: A Survey of the Latin Classics*. New York: Oxford University Press, 1983.

Reynolds, L. D. *The Medieval Tradition of Seneca's Letters*. London: Oxford University Press, 1965.

Ribémont, Bernard. "Le volcan médiéval: entre tradition 'scientifique' et imaginaire." In *Mythologies de l'Etna*, edited by Dominique Bertrand, 65–76. Clermont-Ferrand: Presses Universitaires Blaise Pascal, 2004.

Richardson, Lawrence. *A New Topographical Dictionary of Ancient Rome*. Baltimore: Johns Hopkins University Press, 1992.

Richardson, Nicholas. *The Homeric Hymn to Demeter*. Oxford: Clarendon Press, 1974.

Richmond, John. "Manuscript Traditions and the Transmission of Ovid's Works." In *Brill's Companion to Ovid*, edited by Barbara Weiden Boyd, 443–83. Leiden: Brill, 2002.

Riley-Smith, Jonathan. *The First Crusade and the Idea of Crusading*. Philadelphia: The University of Pennsylvania Press, 1986.

Rimell, Victoria. *The Closure of Space in Roman Poetics: Empire's Inward Turn*. Cambridge, UK: Cambridge University Press, 2015.

Rimell, Victoria and Marcus Asper, eds. *Imagining Empire*. Heidelberg: Universitätsverlag Winter, 2017.

Rodríguez Almeida, Emilio. *Forma Urbis Marmorea: Aggiornamento Generale 1980*. Rome: Quasar, 1981.

Romano, D. "Cicerone e il ratto di Proserpina." *Ciceroniana* 4 (1980): 191–201.

Rosati, Gianpiero, ed. *Ovidio, Metamorfosi, Volume III: Libri V–VI*. Rome: Mondadori, 2013.

Rosier-Catach, Irène (with Tuedi Imbach). "La tour de Babel dans la philosophie du langage de Dante." In *Zwischen Babel und Pfingsten / Entre Babel et Pentecôte*, edited by Peter Von Moos, 183–204. Zurich, 2008.

Rossi, Luca Carlo. "Dante in un commento trecentesco alle *Epistole* di Seneca." In *Il ritorno dei classici nell'Umanesimo: studi in memoria di Gianvito Resta*, edited by Gabriella Albanese, Claudio Ciociola, Mariarosa Cortesi, Claudia Villa, 513–30. Florence: Sismel, 2015.

Rubenstein, Jay. *Armies of Heaven: The First Crusade and the Quest for Apocalypse*. New York: Basic Books, 2011.

Runciman, Steven. *The First Crusade*. Abridged edition. Cambridge, UK: Cambridge University Press, 1980.

Salmeri, Giovanni. "The Emblematic Province: Sicily from the Roman Empire to the Kingdom of the Two Sicilies." In *Tributary Empires in Global History*, edited by Peter Fibiger Bang and Christopher Alan Bayly, 151–68. New York: Palgrave Macmillan, 2011.

Salvo García, I. "Les sources de l'*Ovide moralisé*, livre I: Types et traitement." *Le Moyen Age* 124 (2018): 307–36.

Sampieri, Teresa. "La cultura letteraria di Pietro da Eboli." In *Studi su Pietro da Eboli*, 67–88. Rome: Istituto Storico Italiano per il Medio Evo, 1978.

Sampson, Christopher. "Callimachean Tradition and the Muse's Hymn to Ceres (Ov. Met. 5.341–661)." *Transactions of the American Philological Association* 142 (2012): 83–103.

Sandys, J. E. "The Vatican Palimpsest of Cicero's Verrine Orations." *Classical Review* 17 (1903): 460–61.

Sasso, Gennaro. "Matelda nel suo contesto. Considerazioni e ipotesi." *La Cultura: Rivista di filosofia letteratura e storia* 50.3 (2012): 363–442.

Sasso, Gennaro. *Forti cose a pensar mettere in versi: studi su Dante* 2. Turin: Nino Aragno, 2017.

Sasso, Gennaro. *Ulisse e il desiderio: il canto XXVI dell'* Inferno. Rome: Viella, 2011.

Scott, John A. *Dante's Political Purgatory*. Philadelphia: University of Pennsylvania Press, 1996.

Segal, Charles. *Landscape in Ovid's* Metamorphoses: *A Study in the Transformations of a Literary Symbol*. Wiesbaden: Franz Steiner, 1969.

Senatore, F. "Sesto Pompeo tra Antonio e Ottaviano nella traditione storiografica antica." *Athenaeum* 79 (1991): 103–39.

Seriacopi, Massimo. *All'estremo della "Prudentia": l'Ulisse di Dante*. Rome: Zauli, 1994.

Shapiro, Marianne. De Vulgari Eloquentia: *Dante's Book of Exile*. Lincoln: University of Nebraska Press, 1990.

Sigursson, Haraldur. *Melting the Earth: The History of Ideas on Volcanic Eruptions*. New York: Oxford University Press, 1999.

Smith, Christopher, and John Serrati, eds. *Sicily from Aeneas to Augustus*. Edinburgh: Edinburgh University Press, 2000.

Solodow, Joseph B. *The World of Ovid's* Metamorphoses. Chapel Hill: University of North Carolina Press, 1988.

Spence, Sarah. "The Geography of the Vernacular in Dante." *Tenso* 28 (2013): 33–45.

Spence, Sarah. "Meta-Textuality: The Boat-Race as Turning Point in *Aeneid* 5." *New England Classical Journal* 29 (2002): 69–81.

Spence, Sarah. "Reading against the Grain: Hypercorrection in a Medieval Cicero." *Bollettino del centro di studi filologici e linguistici siciliani* 29 (2018): 5–19.

Spence, Sarah. *Rhetorics of Reason and Desire: Vergil, Augustine, and the Troubadours*. Ithaca, NY: Cornell University Press, 1988.

Spence, Sarah. "The Straits of Empire: Sicily in Vergil and Dante." In *Medieval Constructions in Gender and Identity: Essays in Honor of Joan M. Ferrante*, edited by Teodolinda Barolini, 133–50. Tempe: Arizona Center for Medieval and Renaissance Studies, 2005.

Steel, C.E.W. *Cicero, Rhetoric, and Empire*. Oxford: Oxford University Press, 2001.

Stone, Shelley C. "Sextus Pompey, Octavian and Sicily." *American Journal of Archaeology* 87 (1983): 11–22.

Sutherland, C.H.V., and R.A.G. Carson, eds. *RIC I / The Roman Imperial Coinage, vol. 1*. London: Spink & Son Ltd., 1984.

Syed, Yasmin. *Vergil's* Aeneid *and the Roman Self: Subject and Nation in Literary Discourse*. Ann Arbor: University of Michigan Press, 2005.

Syme, Ronald. *The Roman Revolution*. Oxford: Oxford University Press, 1960; online 2002.

Takayama, Hiroshi. *Sicily and the Mediterranean in the Middle Ages*. New York: Routledge, 2019.

Tanguy, Jean-Claude. "Les Éruptions historiques de l'Etna: Chronologie et localisation." *Bullétin Volcanologique* 44 (1981): 585–640.

Tanguy, Jean-Claude, Michel Condomines, Maxime Le Goff, Vito Chillemi, Santo La Delfa and Giuseppe Patanè. "Mount Etna Eruptions of the Last 2,750 Years: Revised Chronology and Location through Archeomagnetic and 226Ra-230Th Dating." *Bulletin of Volcanology* 70 (2007): 55–83. https://doi.org/10.1007/s00445-007-0121-x.

Tavoni, Mirko. *Qualche Idea su Dante*. Bologna: Il Mulino, 2015.

Thomaidis, Konstantinos, Valentin R. Troll, Frances M. Deegan, Carmela Freda, Rosa A. Corsaro, Boris Behncke, and Savvas Rafailidis. "A Message from the 'Underground Forge of the Gods': History and Current Eruptions at Mt. Etna." *Geology Today* 37 (2021): 141–49. https://doi.org/10.1111/gto.12362.

Tilliette, J. Y. "L'Écriture et sa métaphore: remarques sur l'*Ovide Moralisé*." In *Ensi firent li ancessor: Mélanges de philologie médiévale offerts à Marc-René Jung*, vol. 2, edited by L. Rossi, C. Jacob-Hugon, and U. Bähler, 543–58. Alessandria: Edizioni dell'Orso, 1996.

Todorov, Tzvetan. *The Conquest of America: The Question of the Other*. Translated by Richard Howard. Norman: University of Oklahoma Press, 1984.

Tronzo, William, ed. *Intellectual Life at the Court of Frederick II Hohenstaufen*. Studies in the History of Art 44. Washington, DC: National Gallery of Art, 1994.

Tribulato, Olga, ed. *Language and Linguistic Contact in Ancient Sicily*. Cambridge, UK: Cambridge University Press, 2012.

Tuzzo, Sabina. "Further Discussion on the 'Two Suns Theory' and the *Monarchia* of Dante." *History Research* 5 (2015): 98–108.

Ulrich, Jeffrey. "*Vox omnibus una*: A Reassessment of the Feminine Voice in *Aeneid* 5." *Vergilius* 67 (2021): 139–60.

Van Peteghem, Julie. "The Vernacular Roots of Dante's Reading of Ovid in the *Commedia*." *Italian Studies* 73 (2018): 223–39.

Van Peteghem, Julie. *Italian Readers of Ovid from the Origins to Petrarch: Responding to a Versatile Muse*. Leiden: Brill, 2020.

Vasaly, Ann. *Representations: Images of the World in Ciceronian Oratory*. Berkeley: University of California Press, 1993.

Vigo, Leonardo. *Dante e la Sicilia*. Palermo: Luigi Pedone Lauriel, 1870.

Volk, Katharina. *The Poetics of Latin Didactic: Lucretius, Vergil, Ovid, Manilius*. New York: Oxford University Press, 2002.

Wallace, David. *Europe: A Literary History*. Oxford: Oxford University Press, 2016.

Wallis, Faith, and Robert Wisnovsky, eds. *Medieval Textual Cultures: Agents of Transmission, Translation and Transformation*. Judaism, Christianity, and Islam: Tension, Transmission, Transformation 6. Berlin: De Gruyter, 2016.

Ward, J. O. "Reading and Interpretation: An Emerging Discourse of Poetics: Cicero and Quintilian." In *The Cambridge History of Literary Criticism: The Renaissance*, edited by Glyn P. Norton, 77–87. Cambridge, UK: Cambridge University Press, 1999.

Ware, Catherine. *Claudian and the Roman Epic Tradition*. Cambridge, UK: Cambridge University Press, 2012.

Wattenbach, Wilhelm. "Aus den Briefen des Guido von Bazoches." *Neues Archiv der Gesellschaft für Ältere Deutsche Geschichtskunde* 16 (1891): 69–113.

Welch, Kathryn. "Both Sides of the Coin: Sextus Pompeius and the So-Called *Pompeiani*." In *Sextus Pompeius*, edited by Anton Powell, Kathryn Welch, and Alain M. Gowing, 1–30. London: Classical Press of Wales, 2002.

Wells, Courtney Joseph. "Pensemus qualiter viri prehonorati a propria divertentur." *Mot so razo* 18 (2019): 23–40.

Wells, Courtney Joseph. "'In lingua est diversitas': Medieval Francophone and Occitanophone Literary Cultures in Catalonia and Italy." In *Medieval Francophone Literary Culture*

Outside France. Edited by Nicola Morato and Dirk Schoenaers, 473–505. Turnhout: Brepols, 2019.

Westrem, Scott D. *The Hereford Map*. Terrarum Orbis 1. Turnhout: Brepols, 2001.

Wetherbee, Winthrop. *The Ancient Flame*. South Bend: University of Notre Dame Press, 2008.

Whitbread, L. G. *Fulgentius the Mythographer*. Columbus: Ohio State University Press, 1971.

Wilkinson, L. P. *Ovid Recalled*. Cambridge, UK: Cambridge University Press, 1955.

Williams, Gareth. *Pietro Bembo on Etna: The Ascent of a Venetian Humanist*. New York: Oxford University Press, 2017.

Williams, John R. "The Cathedral School of Rheims in the Eleventh Century." *Speculum* 29 (1954): 661–77.

Williams, Mary. "King Arthur in History and Legend." *Folklore* 73 (1962): 73–88.

Williams, R. D. *Aeneid*. 2 vols. London: Macmillan, 1972.

Willoughby, James. "The Transmission and Circulation of Classical Literature: Libraries and Florilegia." In *The Oxford History of Classical Reception in English Literature*, edited by Norman Vance and Jennifer Wallace, 95–120. Oxford: Oxford University Press, 2015.

Wilson, R.J.A. *Sicily under the Roman Empire*. Warminster, England: Aris and Phillips, 1990.

Wolfson, Susan J. *Borderlines: The Shiftings of Gender in British Romanticism*. Stanford: Stanford University Press, 2006.

Woods, Marjorie Curry. "The Classics and After: What's Still to Be Revealed." Endowed Lecture on the Reception of the Classics in the Middle Ages, Fifty-Third International Congress on Medieval Studies, Western Michigan University, Kalamazoo, MI, 2018.

Woods, Marjorie Curry. *Weeping for Dido: The Classics in the Medieval Classroom*. Princeton: Princeton University Press, 2019.

Worman, Nancy. *Landscape and the Spaces of Metaphor in Ancient Literary Theory and Criticism*. Cambridge, UK: Cambridge University Press, 2015.

Wright, J. *Geographical Lore of the Time of the Crusades*. New York: American Geographical Society, 1925; second edition, New York: Dover, 1965.

Yolles, Julian. *Making the East Latin: The Latin Literature of the Levant in the Era of the Crusades*. Dumbarton Oaks Medieval Humanities. Cambridge, MA: Harvard University Press, 2022.

Zanker, Paul. *The Power of Images in the Age of Augustus*. Ann Arbor: University of Michigan Press, 1988.

Zarrow, E. M. "Sicily and the Coinage of Octavian and Sextus Pompey: Aeneas or the Catanean Brothers?" *Numismatic Chronicle* 163 (2003): 123–35.

Ziolkowski, Jan M., ed. *Dante and the Greeks*. Washington, DC: Dumbarton Oaks Publications, 2014.

Zissos, Andrew. "The Rape of Proserpina in Ovid *Met*. 5.341–661: Internal Audience and Narrative Distortion." *Phoenix* 53 (1999): 97–113.

Zorzetti, Nevio and Jacques Berlioz. *Le Premier mythographe du Vatican*. Paris: Les Belles Lettres (Collection des universités de France, Série latine 328), 1995.

INDEX

Actium, 23–28, 165n31
Aeneid (Vergil), 5, 8, 17–22, 29, 30; absence of Proserpina in, 33–37, 63; boat race in, 38–46; detailed description of Sicily in, 17–18; focus on Sicily in openings of, 17; on the four roots, 40–45; funeral games in, 37–38; games in, 47–50, 53; language of fourteenth-century Italian translation of, 124; narrative strategy in, 20–21; reminders of the past in, 31–32; set after abduction of Proserpina, 35–36; shifting of locations and permeability of Sicily in, 50–53; Sicily's geography in, 18–19; story of Sicily's origins in, 18; straits of Messina and, 67–70; Trojan War in, 127–128; Ulysses' travel in, 127–129. *See also* Vergil
Amores (Ovid), 58–62. *See also* Ovid
Anderson, William S., 65, 172n48
Appian, *Roman History*, 21–22
Arethusa, 65–66
Argonautica (Apollonius Rhodius), 45–46, 56
Arnulf of Orléans, 110, 112, 179n23
Augustine, 134, 156, 187n49, 187n50
Augustus. *See* Octavian/Augustus Caesar
Aulus Gellius. *See* Gellius, Aulus

Badian, Ernst, 11
Bailey, Cyril, 40–41
Barchiesi, Alessandro, 8, 165n31, 166n48, 170n53, 172n47, 172n53
Barolini, Teodolinda, 119, 134, 135, 156, 181n10, 184n46, 184n7, 185n24, 186n33, 187n51

Beatrice, 146–153, 156–157, 187n55
Biggs, Thomas, 163n9, 170n54

Caesar, Julius 23–24, 27, 57
Calliope, 65, 184n10
Casali, Sergio, 168n6
Ceres, 1, 34–36, 61–62, 65–67, 75, 78, 82, 94–96, 100, 147–148; medieval interpretations of, 104–107; in *Ovide Moralisé*, 110; redemption and, 112–114
Chance, Jane, 173n6, 174n18
Cheyfitz, Eric, 16–17
Chronicon (Richard of Devizes), 97
Cicero, 2–3, 7, 29, 57, 64; attack on Verres, 2, 11–12; Dante on, 151–152; notion of empire's potential, 16; Proserpina myth of, 3–5, 77; on Sicily and the Roman Empire, 10–17, 30, 51, 54, 160, 164n13. *See also Verrines* (Cicero)
Claudian, 2, 5, 6, 93–94, 115, 139, 177n59; Proserpina myth of, 76–78, 94–96
Clay, Diskin, 133
Cleopatra, 25–26, 28
Commedia (Dante), 2, 7–8, 115–116, 132–136
Commentary of Geoffrey of Vitry on Claudian, The (Geoffrey of Vitry), 174n16
Confessions (Augustine), 156
Conrad of Muri/Conradus de Mure, 88
Cornish, Alison, 182n20, 187n54
Cupid, 58–59, 61–62, 73–74

211

Dameron, George, 184n4
Dante, 2, 3, 7–8, 53, 113, 115; on language of Sicily, 146–147. See also *Commedia* (Dante); *De Monarchia* (Dante); *De vulgari eloquentia* (Dante); *Inferno* (Dante); *Purgatorio* (Dante); *Paradiso* (Dante)
De bello civili/Bellum civile (Lucan), 142–143, 167n62
De brevitate vitae (Seneca), 182n15
De doctrina Christiana (Augustine), 134, 156, 187n49
De inventione (Cicero), 12
De Monarchia (Dante), 116–117, 155–156
De natura rerum (Isidore), 86
De Raptu Proserpinae (Claudian), 76–78, 97, 139
De rerum natura (Lucretius), 40–41
De vulgari eloquentia (Dante), 133, 141, 143–147, 157; vernacular and, 151–152
Dialogues (Gregory the Great), 6, 84–85, 97
digressio, 13–15, 54
Dio Cassius, 24, 25–26

Eclogues (Vergil), 42, 56, 76, 163n9
egressio, 13–14, 168n14
elegy, 58–59
Empedocles, 40–42, 44, 46, 169n39, 169n40
empire, 7–8; as aggressive and destructive, 60; games in reorganization and limits of, 47–50; geography of, 23–29; imperialism and, 62–64; links between rhetoric and, 16–17; of poetry, 62–67; potential for cooperation and enrichment in, 62; redemption and, 109; relationship between poetry and, 54–55; Sicily in narrative of, 8, 29–30, 32–33, 53, 54, 74, 160–161, 167n62; spatial versus textual expansion of, 56; Ulysses' speech and, 135
Enna, 57, 60, 64, 72, 75, 78–88, 93, 116
Ennius, 11
epic, 58–60, 163–164n14
Epic and Empire (Quint), 8–9, 26, 163–164n14, 166n48
Epistola . . . de calamitate Sicilie (Hugo Falcandus), 91
Epistulae Morales (Seneca the Younger), 129–131, 142, 153, 174n22, 183n30
Etna, Mt., 5–6, 78–95; heavenly qualities of, 91–92; medieval stories of, 92–93; Noah's flood and, 92; purgatory qualities of, 89–91, 112–114, 131, 152–159
Expositio Virgilianae continentiae (Fulgentius), 96

Fabulae (Hyginus), 81–82, 92
Fabularius (Conrad of Muri), 88
Farrell, Joseph, 44, 169n37, 170n51
Fasti (Ovid), 57, 65, 68, 75, 78, 79, 112, 171n33
Feeney, Denis, 26, 163n12, 166n50, 169n24, 169n27
Feldherr, Andrew, 39, 55, 57–58, 168n17, 169n28, 170n47
Ferrante, Joan, 134, 141, 184n44, 185n22, 187n45, 187n47
First Crusade, the, 77, 96, 97, 101–108, 115; expanded notion of empire and, 109
Fourth Lateran Council, 96, 109, 115, 179n21
Frederick II, 6, 7, 76, 97, 117, 140–142, 146, 150, 185n16–19, 186n34, 186n40
Fulcher of Chartres, 103
Fulgentius, 96

Galinsky, Karl, 11
Gehenna, 86–87, 175n32
Gellius, Aulus, 122
Geoffrey Malaterra, 89, 97, 176n42
Geoffrey of Vitry, 174n16
geography: of empire, 23–29; of poetry, 142–150; politics of, 17–22; of rhetoric, 10–17
Georgics (Vergil), 2–3, 5, 33–34, 47, 97, 148, 167n4, 168n7. See also Vergil
Gervase of Tilbury, 92–93, 176–177n51, 177n52
Giovanni del Virgilio, 110
Goethe, Johann Wolfgang von, 1
Granara, William, 163n11, 173n1, 180n33

Gregory of Tours, 95
Gregory the Great, 6, 84–86, 97
Gruzelier, Clare, 173n4, 174n11
Guido delle Colonne, 125–126
Guido of Pisa/Guido da Pisa, 128, 182n25
Guy of Bazoches, 176n41

Hades, 1, 36, 44–47, 60–61, 64–65, 73
Hardie, Philip, 40, 42, 169n19
Härter, Andreas, 14
Hawkes, Terence, 29–30
Henry V (Shakespeare), 29–30
Hinds, Stephen, 3, 8–9, 56, 57, 81, 163–164n14, 172n42
Historia Destructionis Troiae (Guido delle Colonne), 125–126
Historia Iherosolimitana (Robert the Monk), 103
Hollander, Jean, 136, 139
Hollander, Robert, 136, 139, 181n9, 184n1–2
Holmes, Olivia, 157
Homeric Hymns, 2, 65, 94
Honess, Claire, 86
Horsfall, Nicholas, 168n6
Hyginus, 81–82, 92

Ibn Jubayr, 178n6
I fatti di Enea (Guido of Pisa) 128, 182n25
Il convivio (Dante), 140–141
Iliad (Homer), 38, 56
imperialism, 62–64
imperium, 116–117
Inferno (Dante), 7–8, 115, 117–135; account of Ulysses' final journey in, 123–124; debate over where Ulysses traveled in, 122–123, 127–129; distinction between *Purgatorio* and, 136; flame of false counselors in, 120–121; language of Ulysses' speech in, 125; mountain of Purgatory in, 118–120; Sicily depicted in, 126–127, 137
Institutio oratoria (Quintilian), 10, 12–15, 164n15, 164n17
Integumenta Ovidii, 110
Isidore of Seville, 86

Jerusalem, pilgrimages to, 102–106
Johnson, Patricia J., 57, 60, 63–64, 72
Josephus, 92, 176n50
Julius Caesar. *See* Caesar, Julius
Juno, 17, 30, 32, 44–45, 51–53
Jupiter, 32, 44–48, 51–52

Kassler-Taub, Elizabeth, 180n34
Kenney, E. J., 172n42
Kingdom of Sicily (Mallette), 163n11, 180n33, 184n5, 185n13, 185n16, 186n32, 186n34
Kulcsár, P., 174n18

La naissance du Purgatoire (Le Goff), 175n28
Lansing, Richard, 187n55
Le Goff, Jacques, 85–86, 163n10, 175n28
Liber ad Honorem Augusti (Peter of Eboli), 76, 97–98, 177n3
Liber Catonianus, 78, 173n2
Liber de regno Sicilie (Hugo Falcandus), 91, 99
Lombardi, Elena, 130
love: Dante on, 139–140, 152; Ovid on, 58–59, 61–62, 64–67; Vergil on, 73–74
Lucan, 76, 82, 152; geography of poetry and, 142–144, 167n62. See also *De bello civili/Bellum civile* (Lucan)
Lucretius, 40–41, 43–44, 51

Mallette, Karla, 163n11, 180n33, 184n5, 185n13, 185n16, 185n18, 186n32, 186n34
Mark Antony, 21, 23–29
Medieval Mythography (Chance), 173n6, 174n18
Messina, straits of, 67–71, 99, 127, 142–143, 178n5
Metamorphoses (Ovid), 3, 5, 54–55, 78, 108–109, 158–159; Cupid in, 59; imperial terms used in, 55–56; medieval treatments of, 111–112; Mt. Etna in, 79; on potential and limits of empire, 62–63; rape of Proserpina in, 64; Sicily in, 56–58, 137, 139–140; straits of Messina in, 67–71. *See also* Ovid

Metamorphosis of Persephone, The (Hinds), 8–9, 171n10, 171n14, 171n34, 172n42, 172n44, 172n60
Milton, John, 186n41
Mythographi Vaticani (Kulcsár), 174n18

Naulochus, 24, 27–28
Nelis, Damien, 38, 167n2, 167n5, 168n15, 169n18, 170n42
Noah's flood, 92

Octavian/Augustus Caesar, 23–29, 30, 54, 57, 166n51; addressed in *Georgics*, 33–34; criticized for imperialism, 62; *imperium* and, 117
Odyssey (Homer), 19, 56, 69, 71
Otia Imperialia (Gervase of Tilbury), 92–93, 176–177n51, 177n52
Ovid, 2–3, 7, 16, 53; criticism of imperialism by, 62; on love, 58–59, 61–62, 64–67; political role of literature and, 54–55, 57–58; Proserpina myth of, 5–6, 47, 60–61, 77, 78–79, 157–158; Vergil and, 55. See also *Metamorphoses* (Ovid)
Ovide Moralisé, 76, 110–112, 113, 136, 189n30

Paradise Lost (Milton), 186n41
Paradiso (Dante), 117, 125, 134, 136, 187n54
Peirano Garrison, Irene, 164n15, 164n17
Pensabene, Giuseppe, 165n35
Peter Damian, 89
Peter of Blois, 89–90
Peter of Eboli, 76, 97, 98, 177n3
Pietro Bembo on Etna (Williams), 175n23
Pliny the Elder, 15–16, 127
Political Vision of the Divine Comedy, The (Ferrante), 134, 141, 187n45
politics of geography, 17–22
Pompey, Sextus, 23–29, 166n58, 167n60
Pompey the Great, 14, 15, 23
Possamaï-Pérez, Marylène, 180n30
Powell, Anton, 24, 27, 166n52
Power of Images, The (Zanker), 27–28, 166n57–58

Proserpina myth, 30, 76–77; Cicero's version of, 3–5, 77; Claudian's version of, 76–78, 94–96; Dante's version of, 136–137; deal struck in, 46–47; location of abduction in, 78–94, 116; medieval use of, 6–7; narrative of Western empire shaped by, 1–2; negotiation, return, and redemption of, 97, 108–112; in *Ovide Moralisé*, 76, 110–112; Ovid's version of, 5–6, 47, 60–61, 78–79, 157–158; Proserpina's return to earth in, 74–75; rape of Proserpina in, 14, 63–64; as tale of loss, 94–96; Vergil and (see *Aeneid* (Vergil))
Purgatorio (Dante), 7–8, 113, 116–117, 132, 134–135; distinction between *Inferno* and, 136; geography of Sicily in, 142–143; invocation at beginning of, 137–138; languages encountered in, 150–151; mountain of Purgatory in, 118–119; poet-narrator of, 138–139; Sicily as model for purgatory in, 153–159
Purgatory, 85–86, 110–111, 112–114; mountain of, in *Inferno* XXVI, 118–120; Sicily as model for, 86, 153–159
Putnam, Michael, 38, 165n26, 168n16, 169n20, 169n22, 170n46, 170n50, 171n31, 171n32, 186n36

Quint, David, 8–9, 26, 163–164n14, 166n48
Quintilian, 10, 12–17, 30, 54–55, 164n15, 168n14

redemption: empire and, 109; Fourth Lateran Council on, 179n21; language of, 114; purgation and, 110, 112–114
rhetoric: geography of, 10–17; link between empire and, 16–17
Richard of Devizes, 97, 127
Riley-Smith, Jonathan, 102
Robert the Monk, 103, 104, 107
Romanitas, 6, 10, 78, 174n8
Rosier-Catach, Irène, 158–159, 188n59–60

Salmeri, Giovanni, 163n8
Seneca the Younger, 82–83, 129–132, 135, 137, 152–153, 182n15

Servius, 35, 47, 165n25, 168n6
sex auctores, 6, 76, 78
Sextus Pompeius (Powell and Welch), 23, 166n52
Sextus Pompey. *See* Pompey, Sextus
Shakespeare, William, 29–30
Shapiro, Marianne, 150
Sicily: changing role of language in, 77; Dante on, 132–133, 141, 142–150; empire and, 8, 29–30, 32–33, 53, 54, 74, 160–161, 167n62; as first overseas *provincia* of Rome, 11; four root elements of, 40–42; importance of, to Rome, 10–17, 32–33, 36–37, 160; language of, 146–147; literary representations of, 1–9, 29–30; as model for Purgatory, 86, 153–159; Norman conquest of, 97–99; Octavian and, 23–26, 28–29, 30, 54; in Ovid's *Metamorphoses* (see *Metamorphoses* (Ovid)); permeability of, 50–53; poetic rivalry in treatments of, 8–9, 54–55; relationship to empire, 8, 29–30, 32–33, 53, 54, 74; Sextus Pompey and, 23–29; straits of Messina near, 67–71, 99, 127, 142–143, 178n5; in Vergil's *Aeneid* (see *Aeneid* (Vergil))
Syed, Yasmin, 26, 170n46

Thomas, Richard, 167n4
Todorov, Tzvetan, 16
translatio, 16–17

Travels of Ibn Jubayr, The, 178n6
Trojan War, 26, 127–128
Tuzzo, Sabina, 116

Ugurgieri, Ciampolo di Meo degli, 124, 128
Urban II, Pope, 101–102, 106–107, 113

Van Peteghem, Julie, 76, 173n1, 179n25, 186n35
Velleius Paterculus, 24
Venus, 59–60, 62, 63–65, 73–74
Vergil, 2–3, 7–8, 129–134; Ovid and, 55; on poetry and politics as intertwined, 55. See also *Aeneid* (Vergil); *Eclogues* (Vergil); *Georgics* (Vergil)
Verres, 2, 11–12
Verrines (Cicero), 5–7, 12, 15, 51, 57, 60–61, 77; imperial structure outlined in, 114, 161; medieval treatment of, 100–108, 113
Vita Sancti Odilonis (Peter Damian), 89

Welch, Kathryn, 28, 166n52
Wells, Courtney, 182n27
William of Tyre, 103–104, 106–107, 113
Williams, Gareth, 175n23
Woods, Marjorie, 96
Worman, Nancy, 163n6

Zanker, Paul, 27–28, 57–58, 166n58
Ziolkowski, Jan, 184n42

A NOTE ON THE TYPE

This book has been composed in Arno, an Old-style serif typeface in the classic Venetian tradition, designed by Robert Slimbach at Adobe.

GPSR Authorized Representative: Easy Access System Europe - Mustamäe tee 50, 10621 Tallinn, Estonia, gpsr.requests@easproject.com

www.ingramcontent.com/pod-product-compliance
Lightning Source LLC
Chambersburg PA
CBHW032052300426
44116CB00007B/706